iDENTiTY

THE LIFE AND TIMES
OF A LOST SOUL

ADEKUNLE K IGE

The author has tried to recreate events, locales and conversations from their memories of them. In order to maintain their anonymity in some instances the author may have changed the names of individuals and places, the author may have changed some identifying characteristics and details such as physical properties, occupations and places of residence.

All rights reserved. No part of this publication may be reproduced, distributed, or transmitted in any form or by any means, including photocopying, recording, or other electronic or mechanical methods, without the prior written permission of the publisher, except in the case of brief quotations embodied in critical reviews and certain other noncommercial uses permitted by copyright law. For permission requests, write to the publisher, addressed "Attention: Permissions Coordinator," at the address below.

iDENTiTY: The Life and Times of a Lost Soul, ©2019
BY ADEKUNLE K IGE

INTRODUCTION

In "The Flyest," the tenth song on NaS's 2002 hip-hop classic album *Stillmatic*, legendary rapper AZ asked the lyrical icon, NaS, a question that I pondered for years. At the onset of the song, AZ asked, "If they wrote a book on your life, you think anybody would read it?" "No fuckin' doubt," NaS replied. For someone like me who is not famous, the answer isn't so certain.

Throughout the trials and tribulations of my life, I often wondered whether anyone would have the same curiosity about my story as they would for someone who is famous or wealthy. I mean, it's a fair question, one that is very logical to ask. I'm not famous, and I am damn sure not an emcee like NaS arguably considered by many to be the greatest hip-hop lyricist to ever live. Unlike the often boisterous nature of hip-hop, this book is about the real-life challenges I've faced with insecurity and learning about myself amid tragedies and triumphs.

PECKING ORDER

Let me tell you about the first time I realized that I was *different*. Growing up in a household as the middle child was confusing. If you are a middle child, then you understand what I am getting at. In case you don't, I'll explain. When you are the first-born child, you are the original and the center of your parents' world. You are the only child–their pride and joy. The world is your oyster. You get everything you want, you don't have to share, and your parents think that telling you no seems like a sin.

When you are the youngest child, you are the baby, the center of the world; all decisions are about you, and you benefit from everything your older siblings benefit from with less struggle. They get in trouble for their wrongdoings, but you don't. In fact, if you do something wrong, it's their fault for allowing it or not teaching you better. It's amazing! On the flipside, you don't get the privileges that they have such as watching R-rated movies or staying out late. That's a small price to pay when you consider all the benefits the youngest child receives. However, when you are the middle child, there is so much uncertainty. You are considered to be the older-young and left wondering what your role is. You are old enough to know better and too young to be able to.

In my case, my older brother was born five years ahead of me, and my younger brother was born three years after me. Without harping on my brother's five-year head start, let's just say he was the leader and the example I was supposed to obey and follow. I was supposed to be a leader to my younger brother but follow my older brother. I always wondered, "How can I practice my own leadership while following my older brother's leadership?" Isn't that technically just following HIS leadership? Where does my input come in? So much focus is put on what the oldest and youngest are doing that it's easy for the middle child to be an afterthought. It may make sense to you now, but can you see how confusing this is to a ten-year-old boy existing between fifteen-year-old and seven-year-old brothers?

I remember my mother telling her friend who playfully asked if she could have my younger brother because he was so adorable, "You can't have my baby, but you can take the middle one!" I think I was around seven or eight years old at the time. Can you imagine how unloved I felt? Instantly, I began pleading my case as to why I deserved to remain in the family with a sad voice, ugly crying face, and flowing tears. My mother later reassured me that she was just "playing around" and that she thought I was taking it too seriously. Perhaps, she was right, but I didn't think I was taking it too seriously; I mean she said it with conviction.

You ever heard of middle-child syndrome or MCS? If you haven't, I got you covered. Middle-child syndrome is a psychological condition where the middle child is often plagued by negative feelings of emptiness, unworthiness, and inadequacy and characterized by low self-esteem. The possible triggers are an identity crisis, no support system, and feelings of loneliness. Now, I'm not about to self-diagnose, but for all of you clinicians out there, have at it. Besides, MCS is the least of the topics we will cover in this book, believe me.

Being a middle child was one thing; but being an African kid in public school caused a whole different kind of confusion and insecurity. I often wondered what side I should be on. I was African in our home and a so-called black student at school. It wasn't like those school days welcomed me with open arms; in fact, it was the exact opposite. I was faced with all kinds of slander and ridiculed for being African, not by white people, but by my *own* people. At the time, my self-esteem was so low that I didn't even ask a girl to the prom in fear of being laughed at. Pathetic, I know, but we will talk about my experience in school to give context later.

You see, when you harbor self-hatred or insecurity as I did, you tend to care more about what other people think and less about what you know. That's a lesson that I had to learn throughout my life. Self-hatred and insecurity bleed into every aspect of a person's life, whether overtly or covertly, until the soul of that person dies. However, there are several opportunities and creative ways to rebuild your sense of self, and that process begins with being honest with yourself. That honesty will unlock your inner strength and potential.

Sometimes, your truest strength comes from the ability to be vulnerable by opening yourself to feedback and, unfortunately, to judgment. I don't like to use the phrase, "living your truth" because that sounds like the cliché fake woke rhetoric people use these days. What does that even mean anyway? It sounds like something a brotha wearing a fedora and some Ray Bans made up and everyone ran with. Instead, I'd rather live THE truth. Truth is not mine alone. It is a fact. It is consistent and reliable.

This book is an example of being open and honest about the events in my life. By the way, some names have been changed to protect people's privacy. Some of the content in this book may be disturbing for some readers. However, I cannot omit portions of my life or present falsehoods to gain favor. I have to keep it all-the-way real with you or else the purpose is defeated for all of us. This book is meant to reach people who feel unseen by demonstrating a willingness to own myself—the successes, failures, and all that comes with me. The goal is to help people rid themselves of judgment by recognizing the perfection in being imperfect.

> *"Honesty is but a blunt instrument, it bloodies more than it cuts."*
> —Robert Greene, *48 Laws of Power*

Writing this book is different from being a Facebook philosopher, a Twitter therapist, or an Instagram inspirator. You know, the people who always post some insightful message filled with wisdom and when you meet them in real life, they're a friggin mess. Unlike the facades and masks that people use on those platforms to present to us who they want us to *think* they are by covering up who they *actually* are, this book is about my *real* life experiences and lessons. Spoiler alert, this will not be a highlight reel of my shiniest moments. Instead, it will be an authentic depiction of my journey and destination in life.

By taking this journey with me, we will walk side-by-side through fun moments from childhood, the confusion of adolescence, and the maturation to adulthood. We will also sit in uncomfortable moments such as dealing with tragedies and other life-changing events. We will encounter social pressures, self-hatred, loneliness, and resilience. You will hear about my origin, including my father migrating from Nigeria, my parents and how their differing perspectives impacted my life in both positive and negative ways.

Throughout this book, you'll read about my greatest successes and my most crushing losses. You will read about the tragedies in my life that have shaped my worldview and impacted my relationships. This book will explore my love of basketball and women. You are going to learn about my family members, friends, and the environments that shaped my identity. You are going to hear about how making a bad mistake may actually be making the *right* mistake. So, get some popcorn, sit back, be ready to laugh, cry, experience anger, and happiness as you walk with me through many of my major life decisions as well as the positive and negative consequences of those decisions.

"Everyone is fighting their own battle to be free from their past, to live in the present, and create a meaningful future for themselves. Don't judge, have a heart."

—Unknown

Oprah Winfrey once said, "Everyone has a story. Tell your story." This… is my story.

—Adekunle K. Ige

May 1, 2019
California, USA

CHAPTER 1
THE FIFTH COMMANDMENT

"Honor thy father and thy mother, that thy days may be long upon the land which the LORD thy God giveth thee" (Exodus 20:12). For those of you that are not familiar with that scripture, it is one of the Ten Commandments in the King James Version of the Bible. This fifth commandment is the second most important commandment on the list. If you have read the Ten Commandments, you might've noticed that the first four are about God and how to respect the Lord. In order of importance, the next commandment is about respecting your parents, and that is exactly what I intend to do. For you to know who I am, you must first understand where I came from.

THE MOTHERLAND

Let's begin with Adegbola Ige, my father; his name means "The crown receives honor." My father was born in 1947 in Lagos, a large metropolitan city, which is the capital of Nigeria. My father is a devout Christian. His life growing up in Nigeria was very different from the life I knew growing up in the United States. For example, in Nigeria, my father went to elementary school for eight years; there was no middle school. My father played soccer and ran track while in elementary school. He was also a member of the Red Cross, where he learned how to provide emergency care for cases involving broken bones, heavy bleeding, and other first aid.

You may be familiar with that old story parents tell their children about how far they had to travel to school. Well, in my father's case, it was truly a long distance; he had to travel 25 miles away from his home to get to school. Fortunately for him, his school was one of the few that had a school bus for commuter students in 1962. In 1967, he graduated after completing the five years required for high school in Nigeria.

The educational system in Nigeria at that time was designed to limit the number of people who could attend high school and university. So, a large number of students attended elementary schools, but that number would be scaled down so that fewer students would be able to attend high school. To get into high school, students had to pass a standardized test, and those who did not pass the test were automatically sent to a trade school. The competition to go to high school was very fierce.

There were not as many high schools as there were elementary schools. So, according to my father, only the brightest of the brightest would be allowed to attend high school in Nigeria. Also, schools were privatized; therefore, parents had to pay for high school tuition, room and board, food, and clothing. That's right, for high school, they had to pay in a way that Americans associate with colleges and universities. Thus, the financial cost of education was another barrier that prevented people from obtaining advanced education. It was a system created by the British when they ruled in Nigeria.

HIS PARENTS

My grandfather, Emmanuel Adebanjo Ige, was a barber and a foreign trader, which means he bought items domestically for wholesale and sold them internationally. He also had a patient medicine store where he sold over-the-counter medicine. He sold everything except prescribed medications. So technically, my grandfather was a drug dealer—lame reach, I know.

My grandmother, Esther Ayodele Ige, made *fufu*, a signature Nigerian and West African dish. She sold her food to the public and supplied hotels, restaurants, and local taverns. She also sold traditional Nigerian clothing fabrics to the public and professional clothing designers. My grandmother also owned a patient medicine store of her own. My grandparents lived an upper-middle-class lifestyle in Nigeria. Together, they were able to provide all the essential things that my father needed to survive and most importantly, they were able to pay his school fees.

After high school, my father worked various jobs at a hotel, including receptionist, telephone switchboard control, cashiering, and hotel booking. He eventually worked as a tourism ambassador for the city of Lagos, a position which today would be called a tourist guide. My father also played soccer in Nigeria for the Bristol Hotel, his branch of Nigeria Hotels Limited; no doubt, I get my athletic ability from my father and his soccer prowess. Working at the hotel exposed my father to many foreigners and allowed him to learn about life in other countries around the world. He learned about foreign exchange and other forms of financial information; he enjoyed his life working at the hotel.

According to my father, everything in Nigeria was available for anyone who had a goal or dreams; he believed that people could accomplish anything they wanted if they worked hard. In his view, connections and networking were possible as long as one was respectful of others, which is an area of his life in which he excelled. Since he worked at a hotel, he connected with American tourists and people who traveled to Nigeria to work for oil companies.

Through those connections, my father also learned that American blacks thought Africans hated them. He believed this was a mentality established and propagandized ever since slavery. He was convinced that the psychological warfare perpetuated by the so-called "white devils" in slavery was still permeating the minds of victimized "black" people. He wanted to help disprove that propaganda and show that Africans are loving and compassionate.

My father was always curious about what life in the United States was like. He heard about the democratic society and freedom of speech and expression in America. Hotel visitors often told my father that in America, there was freedom to become whatever he wanted to be without any hindrance from the government. That's when he became interested in American colleges and universities as opposed to those in Nigeria at that time. Finally, my father decided to move to America to contradict the propaganda that Africans hated American "blacks."

My grandfather told my father that when he moved to the United States, he should live among the so-called black people to dispel the rumor that

Africans think they are better than them. On the other side of the coin, my father and other Africans heard that American blacks felt they were better than Africans. According to my father, he heard that American blacks did not want to associate with Africans because they had been taught that Africans live in trees, huts, and mud houses in the jungle.

Such a stereotype came from the way Americans saw Africans portrayed in *Tarzan* movies—you know, running with wild animals and throwing spears around. It was another example of how the horrific legacy of slavery caused division not only in America but around the world. Because of slavery and systemic racism, these tactics were a continuation of the plot to remove African people from our true culture as descendants of kings and queens. It was and is a divide-and-conquer strategy. As a result of that information, my father brought many pictures of advanced buildings, tourist attractions, and typical houses with him to show Americans who had never been to Nigeria.

COMING TO AMERICA

With a student visa, my father moved to the United States in 1970 at the age of 23. He attended Temple University in Philadelphia, Pennsylvania, where he studied business. Living in a new country without any local relatives, he needed to obtain employment to support himself while attending college. However, getting employment was difficult because he was in a new country and did not know where to begin. He quickly learned that if a person spoke with a heavy accent, people would shy away from them or assume they were unintelligent; this made finding employment even more challenging.

He was also paid less than his American counterparts because he was an immigrant. Africans who had come to America before my father informed him that he had to be ready to take any job that was available, and that included factory work, dishwashing, and other low-income jobs. Even when they found employment, foreigners like my father would be lucky to get a full-time position; most jobs were freelance, part-time, or temporary positions.

Fortunately, my father was able to adapt and find employment. As a foreigner, he was offered employment opportunities for which he was overqualified, so he held odd jobs as most foreigners do after coming to America. He's African and I said, "Coming to America," see what I did there? Anyway, he drove a taxi for many years and eventually began to work for a limousine service. Later, he worked for the Philadelphia Gas and Electric Company, and he also worked commercially and privately as a carpenter. Clearly, my dad was a hard worker.

Living in America wasn't easy for an African immigrant in the early '70s. When he first moved here, he realized that American culture was completely different from what he imagined. One of the biggest challenges my father faced was assimilating into American black society because he said, "The black folks in America had no knowledge of Africa or African people, and many resented Africans." It wasn't that he was expecting a warm welcome; however, being faced with that reality was a confirmation of the unpleasant remnants of slavery. Much like today with Trump and his hard-on for Mexicans, American blacks often accused Africans of coming to America to take their jobs and their women. They believed any immigrant coming from Africa must be an exchange student and that their parents were unable to pay for them to come to America. As a result, it was difficult making friends with so-called black people in America; they did not accept Africans as their equals.

SHOOT YOUR SHOT

My father was living at 91 E. Sharpnack Street where he rented a house with a guy from Ghana and another Nigerian. At the time, my father was working as a business tutor for high school students in the Philadelphia area. He also specialized in teaching business owners and assisting them with their homework. The goal was to keep the youth off the streets of Philadelphia and prevent them from selling drugs or turning to crime.

In 1975, my father was on his way to school at Temple University when he met a young woman who was walking past his home. My father liked her as soon as he saw her, so he decided to follow her. That's right my father was a stalker—I'm kidding, of course. He called to her, "Excuse me, miss, can I talk to you for a minute?" which is the old-head game or pick-up line back in the day. She said that she was going to her job at Simon Moore School on

Germantown and Allegheny Avenues. The school was designed for students who have mental health challenges, and she was a teacher's aide.

He offered her a ride to her job, but she declined; she was determined to take Septa, which is the public transportation in Philly. She was on her way to the trolley and, since my father knew that her job was only a few stops away from Temple, he decided to ride the trolley as well and continue talking to her. On the trolley, she gave him her name, Jewel. My father asked her for her last name. "Hudson," she replied; "Jewel Hudson." She told my father that she was a Jehovah's Witness. The conversation continued and, before she got off at her stop, my father asked if the two of them could take a ride in his car on the following day. She said, "No." She stated that she would be taking public transportation; "I guess I have to take it with you," my father replied. Slick.

My father waited for her to pass his home the next day, and he followed her again and rode with her on the trolley, both headed to the same destinations as the previous day. My father let her know that he lived at the place where she met him. She told him that she lived on the same street not too far from him and that she took the same route every morning to go to work. The two of them continued this pattern for about two weeks. Still, she did not confirm whether she was interested in him or give her phone number. After about two more weeks, my father got tired of riding the trolley and leaving his car behind. He told her that if she changed her mind and decided to give him her phone number, she should drop him a note in his mailbox.

Afterward, my father went to stay at his friend's place on campus for a few days. When she didn't hear from my father for a few days, she left a note. That's when he received a phone call from one of his housemates saying that some lady had left a message for him. My father returned home to receive the message, which was from Jewel, the woman from the trolley. The note said that she had been looking for him to take rides on the trolley, but she had not seen him in a while. She said she was ready to be friends with him and to see where it would go from there, and she left her phone number. My father called her and from then on, they rode together to work and school; they began dating from that time on.

That woman turned out to be my mother, Jewel Venus Hudson (later Jewel Venus Ige). My mother was born in 1953 in North Philadelphia. She began walking with God in her teens and was baptized in 1973; she was a dedicated Jehovah's Witness and was very active in the religious community. By active I mean studying the Bible, going on fellowships, knocking on doors, and the whole nine yards. She maintained her faithfulness to God no matter what trials and tribulations she encountered.

AFRICAN PRIDE

My father is a very proud man, and he wanted us to be proud as well. He would constantly remind us that we come from kings and queens in Africa. He often talked about our duties to our ancestors and how important it is to keep our culture alive. My father spoke to us in Yoruba, our tribe's language, to make sure that we learned as much as we could about our culture. He had no problem wearing his native Agbada outfit in America; my father's life work was to ensure that we carried the same pride in our history.

When it comes to being African and more specifically Nigerian, being proud cannot be overstated. My father always instilled in us that we are Nigerian first—before everything! As a young American-born African kid, I found this to be very confusing. I did not understand how I could be a blend of both parents' genes and favor one over the other. I was around seven or eight years old when I asked my father, "How does that make sense when we have yours and our mother's genes equally?" Side note: Whenever my father is asked an open-ended question, prepare for a story. The story he chooses to tell is usually heavy on analogies and metaphors.

In this case, he responded, "We come from Africa, and we are the original people. Life started in Africa, and that is why it is called the *Motherland*," he explained. He went on to describe how slavery impacted Africans and how some Africans were brought to America. He also talked about how Africans were already in so-called America before Columbus contrary to what has been taught in schools. I understood where he was coming from, but I still had questions.

I asked, "So, are we African-Americans?" In a thick Yoruba accent, he said, "What is this—this African-American nonsense? Is this what they are teaching you in school?" Then, he sucked his teeth with the long sound that is seemingly signature to Nigerians. He went on to correct us from what our teachers taught by boldly saying, "You are an African *in* America, **not** an African-American. And you are definitely not a *nigger*," he added.

I was waiting for a generation-bridging metaphor that always made his stories epic, but it never came. Instead, the conversation took a weirdly awkward turn for me, the eight-year-old listener. My father offered, "You came from my sperm, which came with me from Africa. That sperm was transferred to your mother's eggs." This conversation was getting pretty nasty to me. Who wants to hear about their father's sperm and their mother's eggs at seven or eight years old? "You came from me," he continued. "I even determined your gender."

It sounded like he did everything. "What did my mother do?" I asked. "She went through the hard work of holding you for nine months until you were fully developed," he responded. "She made sure that she ate the right things, so that you would be healthy. She lost her figure because she needed to gain weight to make sure that you were getting what you needed," he continued. "Then, she went through the painful process of birthing you. She nursed you, burped you, and changed you. She did all of that because she loves you." There it was, a crash course in the making of me.

My father was always a strong advocate of loving and respecting my mother. Even after the two of them had been separated for years, he would never stand for us disrespecting or disobeying her. He never wanted their separation to serve as a catalyst for us to rebel against either of them. He knew my mother's love for us and the sacrifices she made for us. Having three boys, especially us, would be a tall task for any single parent. Regardless of their separation, he continued to support my mother, and I suspect he still loves her.

AFRICAN PARENTING

My father thought that three things were most important: being African, respecting parents, and getting an education. He saw each of us becoming a lawyer, doctor, or an engineer. If you are African, specifically Nigerian, then you know that our parents think these are the only three professions worth pursuing; we must've heard these three job titles millions of times when we were lectured about education and making something of ourselves. Ever wonder why there are so many Africans in those roles? Just know that it was an intentional process leading to that outcome.

Except for his aforementioned non-negotiable items, my father was generally supportive of what we wanted to do with our lives as long as it made sense to him. He would often throw in his guidance and vision as he saw fit. When we wanted to play sports, he was excited because he played soccer or football as it is called around the world. Naturally, he wanted us to play soccer as well; he felt that it was in our genes to excel at soccer. However, our athletic talents were in other areas, which we will discuss later.

Growing up, I saw my father as very strict and authoritative. When he gave instructions, he expected them to be followed with precision. Unlike most parents, he was not the type of parent who lets events of the day make him forget that he had instructed us to complete a task. The tasks could be washing dishes, cooking dinner, cleaning the house, mowing the lawn, and many other things. If he saw something on the floor, instead of picking it up, he would allow it to remain there just to see how long it would take for us to notice it. When we were lectured or disciplined about something, then we would hear about it. "That piece of paper has been there for over a month!" he'd chastise.

That level of awareness never rang the same bells for me as it did for him. I would often wonder about the logic: "If you saw that a month ago and didn't pick it up, doesn't that make you part of the problem?" I remember thinking rebelliously. My father wanted to instill in us an eye for detail; he had expectations for us. He wanted to make sure that we knew our position in the hierarchy.

My father would often say, "I am your God. You get your instructions from me." As a kid growing up, I thought that he was either saying that *he* was God or comparing himself to the Lord. Either way, it was very intimidating and hard for me to understand. I didn't understand what he meant until I got older. If you read the Ten Commandments, then it's much easier to deduce. Since direct conversations cannot be had with the Lord with verbal responses, then second in command is the parents— the fifth commandment.

If my father learned that we were misbehaving or failing to meet his expectations, he had no problem disciplining us. My father's way of handing out discipline was not always typical. Soon the irony in the words "*handing out*" will become a clear pun. He was always creative about the way he disciplined us; it was as if he did not want us to get used to any of his methods. Therefore, his discipline would be different from time to time. Most times, his choice of discipline would be related to a the situation or circumstance.

For example, if we were caught stealing, then he'd tell us to hold our hands out in front of us with our palms facing the ceiling. "I'll beat the daylight out of you!" he would say angrily. Then, he would use his African leather belt and continuously beat our hands until he felt we had enough, which was usually about 10 hits per hand. See what I mean about "*handing out*" discipline? After he finished, we had to give a detailed apology acknowledging what we did and promising not to steal again.

My father has always been a forward thinker, and this held true when it came to discipline. He knew that if he kept performing the same discipline methods, we would get used to them, thus making them less effective. So, he would periodically have a new method almost like Jigsaw in the movie *Saw* but not as grim. When we were prepared for the belt, he would have us stand in the corner with both arms raised until he was satisfied. We stood in that pose for what felt like an eternity but was more like 30 minutes to an hour, depending on the offense.

Another type of discipline he used was having us stand facing a wall and holding our earlobes while we squatted up and down continuously. These forms of discipline do not sound very painful but try doing them for an hour or longer depending on when he felt we had learned our lesson. If we were caught cheating or being lazy during the punishment, then we would get the belt. By the time we finished those exercises, we were so tired that all we could do was go to sleep.

For all my father's worldviews and seemingly strict nature of parenting, he always loved us. He has always been unconditional with us, no matter what we did—even in the moments when we felt like he was going to hate us. Our reactions were usually an exaggeration of how things would turn out. He would be angry and punish us, and as time went on, he forgave us; to me, his response was Godly.

DEAR MOMMA

My mother was educated in the Philadelphia School District at Parkway High School, where she graduated in 1971. She furthered her education at Philadelphia Community College where she studied the special education curriculum. Her longterm goal was to finish college and become a full-time teacher, but she worked as a teacher's aide for the Philadelphia School District for 20 years. She spent those years being a strong advocate for the special needs of the mentally and physically challenged students that she served.

My mother was one of 10 siblings, and she had to navigate the cliques between them. Regardless, my mother remained close to all her siblings. She had a magnetic quality about her, and people loved to talk to her about any and everything, especially when they wanted advice or to discuss their problems. As I stated before, she loved to help people, and she was always there for her family.

My mother was a fun-loving person who made friends easily; she was friendly, outgoing, sensitive, and compassionate. She was also the kind of person who would stand up for the underdog. If she saw someone being disrespected or bullied, she showed up with a vengeance. Her integrity never allowed her to be ok with seeing someone mistreated.

My mother was also very fashionable and had a great eye for shopping. If there was a sale to be had, she made sure she got the absolute best price for whatever she bought. For her, it wasn't just about the sale; it's not like she was just into buying items for cheap. No, for her, quality always took priority. She wanted the best and most durable items made of good materials. She always bought the best items at the best prices; for her, shopping was like an art or a skill.

My mother faced a dilemma when she met my father. He was Christian but not a Jehovah's Witness, which was a big deal in both communities. Jehovah's Witnesses are not allowed to marry someone who is not a Jehovah's Witness. My mother had to choose between the religion that she held dear to her heart and her love for my father. In typical fashion, my mother chose to love.

In 1976, she joined my father in Holy Matrimony; she was pregnant with her first son at the time. From that union, my brothers and I were born.

My mother spent most of her life as a hardworking woman and a super mother; she took both jobs very seriously. There are many sides to her. She could be playful and silly unless we were misbehaving. Then, it would get real, real quick.

My mother respected education, and she made sure that we took it seriously, or else. She had no problem coming to our schools to prove her point. If we were doing well in school, she made sure we got the rewards we wanted which included bikes, trips, video games, and many other things. If she found out that we weren't taking school seriously, well, we got her hands, and she was accurate with them.

Her respect for education wasn't just something she pushed at home. It was also her profession. When she worked in special education classrooms, she tried to help her students reach their potential. She gave 110 percent of her energy and passion every day. She worked hard until she began to face challenges of her own that forced her into early retirement.

MY MOTHER'S INTERNAL STRUGGLE

My mother struggled with catatonic schizophrenia, which is a psychiatric disorder. Many people have heard of schizophrenia but may be unfamiliar with catatonia, which is a state of psychomotor immobility and behavioral abnormality manifested by a stupor. A stupor is the lack of critical mental function and a level of consciousness wherein a sufferer is almost entirely unresponsive and only responds to base stimuli, such as pain.

When my mother had catatonic episodes, we didn't understand what was happening. To me, it seemed like she was just ignoring us. It felt like we caused her so much stress that she was taking a mental vacation instead of giving us a beating. As an elementary school kid, I didn't know what to do in those moments. I just thought she wanted alone time and did not want to be disturbed.

I was eight years old the very first time I noticed there was a problem. One day, after watching Saturday morning cartoons with my little brother, which was routine, I went upstairs around 11:00 a.m. to ask my mother if we could go outside. There my mother sat on her bed facing a wall virtually motionless and expressionless. At first, I thought she was praying or meditating or simply thinking. I decided to leave her alone. I went outside to play with my friends in front of the house, so I would be able to hear if my mother called me. After a few hours, I went back to the house to see if she was making lunch. She was not in the kitchen or in the living room. I went back upstairs to her room, and she was still sitting in the same position. After calling her name a few times with no response, I became very alarmed. She had been sitting there for hours.

At that point, I called my father because the situation was scary, and I didn't know what else to do. Who was going to take care of us and most importantly in my mind, who was going to take care of her? My father called my Aunt Janet, and they came to my mother's house. My mother looked at them both as if she recognized them and wanted to respond to them but was incapable of doing so. It was like she had been possessed. When they both witnessed what my brother and I had seen, they called a local mental health treatment facility to have her admitted via code 302, which is the involuntary mental health admission code. I felt relieved that someone knew what to do for my mother and that she would be getting help, but then came the show.

TRAUMATIZED

There are pros and cons to everything. The con in this situation was that once the mental health professionals arrived and tried to move her, my mother became violent. She kicked, punched, and screamed, trying to get away from them. My mother is very strong, so if she opposed something physically or mentally, she fought with every fiber of her being. She kicked one of the mental health professionals so hard he flew across the room as if an invisible force had snatched him. Shout out to the mental health professionals because they were trying their best to be patient with her and admit her unharmed. Unfortunately, they had no choice but to have the police come in to restrain her.

When the police stepped in, it got worse. She was already pretty riled up and in her fighting stance. I remember wondering what she was seeing and what she thought was happening to her. I would like to believe that she was fighting because she thought they were trying to take her away from her children. I knew we meant everything to her, and she was fighting for her life. I mean she was throwing cops across the room with one arm as they were trying to restrain her by holding her other arm. It got so bad that they had to put handcuffs on her, which wasn't easy.

Watching the police officers wrestle my mother to the ground, put a knee in her back, and forcing her head to the ground is by far the most frightening thing I have ever seen in my life. It took about 10 or 12 officers to subdue her. Once they had the handcuffs on her wrists and ankles, they thought it was over. Nope, she was still fighting and trying to get out of the handcuffs at all costs. It was obvious that she was not going to leave the house of her own free will, so they had to lift her up and carry her while she was still fighting.

It was the middle of the day, and everyone was outside. When I say everyone was outside, I mean EVERYONE. Neighbors I hadn't seen in months were standing in the middle of the street around the police cars and ambulance. Store owners were standing in front of their businesses looking on. All the kids in the neighborhood were onlookers, standing there with their basketballs under their arms, girls holding jump ropes, and other kids holding water guns. I'm sure to everyone outside, it looked like she was being arrested for some horrible crime. My father and Aunt Janet tried to console us as my brother and I were standing on the porch crying. Indeed, it was one of the most frightening and embarrassing days of my life.

When they put her in the back of the police paddy wagon, they had to be very forceful. There was blood all over her arms and on her legs. She had serious lacerations on her wrists and ankles from struggling in the cuffs; she also had several other injuries including a fractured wrist and arm.

Over the course of my life, my mother going in and out of these catatonic states became routine as were the traumatizing involuntary admissions. As a result of my mother's mental health challenges and public battles with the police, I often got into arguments and fights when other kids teased us about it. In some places, the teasing is called "ranking" or "snapping"; some of you who are more old-school know it as "playing the dozens." In Philly, the teasing is called "bussing." The term predates me, but I assume the term derives from the phrase, "bursting your bubble," which turned into "busting your bubble" and eventually "bussing." It's what we had to do to survive, and I got really good at it.

MATERNAL MAGIC

As I said before, my mother stressed education and except for her children, nothing was more important to her. If we were good in school, she would take us out of school for the day to accompany her to her doctor's appointments. I often enjoyed the trips because I felt special, and afterward, we would get pizza or ice cream. Sometimes, she would buy me a new toy. I didn't know why she went to the doctor monthly or why she took medicine daily, but it's normal for young children not to understand what's happening with their parents. I always knew that something was going on for her, I just never knew what it was or what to make of it. I did not know what her diagnosis was until I was much older. That's when I realized that her doctor's appointments were with a psychiatrist for medication management.

During retirement, she spent her time taking care of us, taking walks, shopping, and sitting on her porch observing people in her neighborhood. She was a master at observation, and she always looked to keep us away from danger and dangerous people. Therefore, she was very particular about the people we were allowed to hang with.

I remember a guy from upper Rowan Street, adjacent to her house, who was playing basketball with us. He got into an argument with one of the other players. Now, to me basketball is a competitive sport and arguments happen. Apparently, my mother had been watching this guy for a long time and had better insight into him. She pulled me aside later and told me in a firm voice, "You are not allowed to hang with him. He is trouble." She called him trouble so much in that conversation that it became somewhat of an internal code name for him. From then on, he was referred to as *trouble*, in her house.

She didn't mind me hanging out with Esau because he lived around the corner from us on lower Dennie Street, and she knew his mother. Her only thing about him was that he was too silly. One summer, my mother saw Esau playing with a water gun in front of her house when he accidentally squirted a stranger who was passing by. There was a big fuss because the stranger was not happy to have been shot with the water gun. In Nicetown, that could have resulted in a much larger problems such as getting shot for real! She knew how connected we were to Esau as friends, and she didn't want to see us in the same predicament. That's when she decided that we were not going to get the newest water guns—the Super Soakers—that were scheduled to debut that summer. My mother told us that she had been planning to surprise us with those water guns until she saw what Esau did. She said, "Y'all were going to be the first kids in the neighborhood to have them, too." Thanks, Esau.

My mother spent most of her time saving us. That's the way my mother operated when we were young. She always saw *trouble*, no pun intended before it happened. Ok, pun intended. Lame, I know. She was always right about her assessments. Without her intervention, I could definitely see all three of us using the Super Soakers to completely drench a stranger. We probably would've run away laughing hysterically never thinking about the consequences.

My mother's goal was to avoid external consequences. Instead, she was more interested in giving us our consequences, and boy did she ever. As a kid, I learned fast what her warning signs were. Her eyes would get larger; then, she would tighten her lips and clench her fists. That's when I knew it was over. As a result, whatever rules she had, we tried to follow them. We didn't want any problems.

With my father, we knew we had some time for him to cool down because he would say, "You're gonna get it when we get home." As I stated before, my dad was more methodical. My mother, on the other hand, had no problem with giving an impromptu ass whupping. It didn't matter if we were walking down the street, in a supermarket, or at church. If we were acting out and embarrassing her, a slap could come out of nowhere, like a UFO or Kramer on *Seinfeld*. And she hit hard, really hard!

Over time, we learned to predict what she wanted from us. When the street lights came on, we would hear her yelling, "Kunle! Wale!" from the corner of Wayne Avenue and Dennie Street. The routine was repeated so often that we would already be running to her as she made her way to the corner, which was her plan all along. Smart.

DIFFERENT STROKES

My father was the saver, and my mother was the spender. If I asked my dad for five dollars, I'd have to tell *him* a story as to why I needed the money. Between them, I had to strategize when asking for things. If I needed to pay for a school trip that I knew about for weeks but forgot to tell my parents, I knew I should ask my mother. I knew that with her, all I needed was the permission slip and proof that I was doing well in school. The proof was easy because she was always stopping by my school randomly anyway. Except for one time in high school, which we will get into later, she always knew how I was doing.

With my father, I had to be more methodical and somewhat Nostradamus-like. He had to see the vision. My father has always been heavy on structure and planning. These are skills that he constantly drilled into our psyches since we were born. If my father was not aware of the financial need ahead of time, I knew I would be in for a long day. I learned over time to talk to my father for long-term needs.

After he and my mother separated, the differences in their two separate worlds became more pronounced. For my father, everything was a secret. We were not allowed to talk to anyone about family-related issues. He didn't want anyone to know his age, anything he was working on, where he got his car, or anything for that matter. As a result, I learned that anything that had to do with my life was to remain personal and private.

Most people have things that nag them about their parents. When it comes to my dad, I used to hate when he would call me from the third floor to the first floor to get something that was about 10 feet away from him. It was not like he was elderly or incapable of retrieving it himself. It felt like it was a game to him. Many times, he would send me up and down the stairs in succession to perform mundane tasks. I hated it. I later learned that it was his way of working us out. "Why not put us in sports?" I often thought. As I mentioned before, he is a private man, and no one was ever in on his plans.

Take when I got my driver's license, for example. Here I am driving my car home after taking my father to the store. There was enough space for about three to four cars in front of my father's house; it was an easy parking opportunity. So, I drove directly into the space perfectly and was ready to exit the car. My father got upset and started telling me to reverse the car. Then, he told me to turn the wheel to the left and then to the right. He told me to drive forward; I was so confused. I'm sure the people who were watching were just as puzzled as I was as they saw me make several unnecessary maneuvers. It was like watching the final scene of *The Sopranos* as Meadow is trying to park her car, only there were no other cars around.

When he was satisfied, we exited the car, but I was still puzzled. Later, he told me he was teaching me how to parallel park the car. I was even more confused. Number one, I had already gotten my driver's license weeks earlier. On the road test in Pennsylvania, the very first task to complete is parallel parking. If it is not done properly, the test is automatically failed. I passed my road test on the first try, and he knew that. Number two, the parking space he was so adamant about was about three to four car lengths, so naturally I just pulled in. I thought the whole exercise was a waste of time.

NEW RULE

The other thing I noticed as I grew older was that my brothers and I seemed to take on the roles that my mother vacated when they separated. Let me explain. My father would make us do all the food shopping, the cooking, the dishes, taking out the trash, and the laundry. If my father came home late and we hadn't cooked for him, he would wake us with the belt yelling and screaming. At age 11, it was terrifying. To this day, Deontay Wilder voice, I hate to be awakened from my sleep.

Funny story. I remember Wale and I were trying to prevent him from getting upset with us for forgetting to cook dinner. So, we cooked the food ahead of time in anticipation of his return home. We made rice, African stew with chicken, and spinach. We waited until we saw his car turning the corner on to our street and plated his meal. The meal was complete with hot tea and lemon, which he always drank. We wanted to surprise him by having everything ready for him. We did not have dining tables in our home, so we placed the food on his bed where he usually ate.

When my father came home, there was a short pause and then lots of yelling. "Kunle! Wale!" he yelled. We didn't understand why he was so angry with us. It was not the reaction that we expected to get from him. When we got downstairs, we immediately saw the problem. We noticed a big red tomato sauce stain on the back of his pants with grains of rice and pieces of chicken falling off. He was not thrilled. Apparently, he walked to his bed and sat directly on the plate of food we spent so much time preparing for him. We didn't get punished for it, but we had to wash his pants and make him a new plate. Of course, when Wale and I went back to our room we were dying laughing.

When it came to shopping, it wasn't like he drove us to the supermarket and helped us make decisions. Instead, Wale and I had to walk one and a half miles to and from the supermarket regardless of the weather. I feel cold right now just thinking about those Decembers in Philly. What took us over an hour each way could have been a six-minute drive with our father. The trip usually took longer on the way back because we were carrying about 10 bags each. With so many bags wrapped around my wrists trying to be efficient, I was just happy to have blood circulation in my arms when I got home. Being efficient was the name of the game for us because if we forgot something, he would send us back for a second or third trip.

At this point in my life, I understand what he was trying to do and why, but I did not understand while I was completing those tasks. I saw him as a dictator who did not want to take any part in the tasks for which we common folk were responsible—the common folk being my brother Wale and I. As I got older and began to use the skills my father was teaching us, I learned that he was trying to teach us to be independent. He wanted us to have responsibility because life isn't all about playing sports and video games with our friends.

My father wanted us to be able to take care of ourselves, so he made sure that the chores we had were building life skills. He did not want us to rely on any woman. My father would say, "Women are liars and manipulative," especially when it came to American women. Those words became a soundtrack in my psyche for years. He often told me not to settle down and to date as many women as I could, and he said, "Don't marry an American woman, especially a white woman." He often drilled into my head that I must marry a Nigerian woman.

FATHERLY ADVICE

One of my father's classic metaphors was his comparison of American women and Nigerian women. He often compared American women to American chicken and African women to African chicken. Let me explain. When you go into a Superfresh or whatever your local supermarket is called and you buy chicken, you'll notice there is a lot of fat on the meat and that the meat falls off the bone when cooked. The meat is usually full of GMOs and other unnatural steroids. African chicken is very fit and tough, so when cooked in a stew, the meat doesn't fall off the bone. If you are having trouble with the imagery, think of organic chicken, it's the closest comparison to African chicken.

My father's point was that American women are fat and out of shape. When you look at their arms, the meat or fat appears to be falling off the bone. He often blamed it on the diet and American culture. He saw African women as hard workers and physically fit.

My father had a problem with the attitude of the so-called black woman in America. He saw them as confrontational and challenging in relationships. He described African women as people who saw themselves and their family as an institution, women who understood submitting to their husband. Naturally, he taught me from this perspective.

In my opinion, some of what my father taught us about women appeared to be bitterness and resentment caused by his separation from my mother. My father seemed to express regret for marrying my mother by always comparing American black women to Nigerian women. It seemed like he was throwing "subliminals" at her. My father is a very opinionated man, but to him, his perspectives are normal. For me, some of his perspectives made my brain boil. After hearing his perspectives on women over the years, I deduced that relationships were temporary and that I could not count on them lasting.

"Normal is an illusion. What is normal for the spider is chaos for the fly."

—Morticia Addams of the Addams Family

CHAPTER 2
BROTHERLY LOVE

BIG BRUH

Adetokunbo Oluwafemi Ige is my elder brother. His first name means "The crown from across the seas." We, his family, call him Femi, which is exactly half of his middle name. His friends and non-family acquaintances call him Tok, short for Adetokunbo. Femi was born in December, and his astrological sign is Sagittarius. I can describe him in a few words: *a talented disaster*. Let me explain. Tests showed that Femi was born with a genius level IQ; he could do anything he wanted—and I mean anything! You ever hear the saying, "You can do anything if you put your mind to it?" That was Femi, literally.

My mother told this story about Femi. She said, "I remember driving in the car with your father when Femi was three years old. He would look out the window and be able to name every car on the road accurately." The story was later confirmed when I asked my father about it. Femi had an amazing memory and along with his memory, attention to detail, and curiosity came incredible creativity.

Growing up, I didn't really like Femi most of the time; that was primarily because he would beat me up often. Every time he felt I was not listening to him or he found me annoying, he would punch me. Then, he would pressure me not to tell my mother or father about what he had done. Femi is five years older than I am, and he was always much bigger and stronger than I was, so I felt bullied by him. The irony is that Femi always—and I mean always—protected us from anyone who was trying to bully us. I appreciated that about him; it gave me a sense of security, especially with people who were too old to be bothering Wale and me.

One day while we were living in my mother's studio apartment, Femi hauled off and punched me in the face. BAM! The blow was so loud and hit me so hard that I felt that my eyes were going to explode out of my head. To this day, I am unsure why he hit me. All I know is that I had enough of him hitting me, and I refused to be bullied. I wanted it all to end. With tears running down my face like geysers and fists balled like my life depended on it, I was ready to take him on. I remember following him around the house and challenging him to a fight. But Femi was not interested in continuing the physical altercation. I guess he felt that he made his point by punching me in the face. He knew that I was not a challenge nor was I an immediate threat to him, so he just ignored me. Having him ignore my challenges bothered me more than the punch itself. It made me feel helpless.

MENTALLY GIFTED

As I said before, Femi was extremely talented at anything that he put effort into. That's another thing that always bothered me—and also something I admired about him. Things that most people like me had to work at came so easy to him. I remember in the summer of 1993, Femi, who was 15 at the time, drew a detailed picture of Michael Jordan wearing his Chicago Bulls uniform kneeling down to tie his shoes. The picture featured a close-up of the new black and red Air Jordan 6 sneakers. You know, the ones with the holes in the tongue, those suede and nubuck things of beauty. The Air Jordan 6 sneakers were the obsession of every 11- or 12-year-old that I knew. I remember all my friends watching him draw this picture from memory.

Once he completed the picture, we all marveled and talked about how realistic it looked. We could see the stitching on the shoes, the jersey, and the sweat on Michael's hands. You could even see the texture of the suede for crying out loud! Just the thought of that picture had me full of adrenaline. Not Femi though. For some reason, the picture was not good enough for Femi's liking; we were astonished. Ten seconds later, he took the picture, balled it up, and threw it away like trash. We were all puzzled. My friend,

Dre, reached in the trash and smoothed the paper, trying to iron it to make it straight again. Dre eventually hung the picture up in his room. That's how good the picture was.

Another example of Femi's impromptu talents also happened in 1993. We were too poor to go to the barbershop to get haircuts regularly. My father, whom we lived with at the time, was against the *Americanized way* as he called it of constantly cutting our hair off. "Cutting our hair off," that's literally how he saw it. According to my father, as Nigerian people, we should have been more into growing our hair as a representation of strength and culture.

My father told stories from the Bible about Samson and Delilah. In the Bible, Samson was the most powerful person in the world, and his strength came from his hair. And, of course, Delilah is the reason Samson's hair was cut, and that's when he lost all his strength. It's interesting when you think about it because we cut our hair to impress women. I would argue that most of the self-improving things men do are done both consciously and unconsciously to gain the favor of women, but I digress. My father, as usual, was on to something. Femi was 17, I was 12, and Wale was 9; we were not trying to hear that message.

In school, we would constantly be teased about having African names, nappy hair, and hand-me-down clothing. Naturally, we all opposed my father's perspective because we wanted to avoid being teased and at the same time impress the girls. My father knew how to cut hair, but he was not willing to cut our hair every two weeks like the cool kids in school. When he cut our hair, he would give us a haircut that was suited for someone who was 50 years old. You know, the haircut you get when you are middleaged and do not have to worry about middle schoolers teasing? Yeah, that haircut. It was fine for us before we left the house because at least we weren't *wolfing*. That's what we called a person without a haircut who just lets their hair grow uncontrollably, wolfing. *Urban Dictionary* defines it as "A motherfucker who BADLY needs a damn haircut!!!" Close enough. I don't know where the term originated, but I know it's not a characteristic that we wanted to have as our physical representation.

In the summer of 1993, Femi decided that he would begin cutting our hair. And what do you know? He was amazing at it. He started cutting our hair almost every two weeks, and we would come outside looking fresh! You couldn't tell us nothing— we literally came out of the house with the WWF Vince McMahon's, now famous, "Mr. McMahon" walk. Google it for a quick laugh. When our friends and peers at school saw our haircuts, they all changed their tune for at least two weeks. Then, we were back to being dirty-nappy-headed African booty scratchers. I didn't mind it too much because after my next haircut, just like DMX said in the movie *Belly,* "I bet you be back on my dick." That was my attitude towards those who teased us.

Femi cut hair so well that we became walking advertisements, models if you will, of his skill. People took notice and soon after, he started to get clients. When the barbershops were closed, people would come to Femi to get their hair cut. That's when Femi saw big business. The next thing you know, everybody on my block was getting their hair cut on our front porch while Onyx's song *"Slam"* played in the background. Femi charged five dollars for shape-ups and 10 dollars for haircuts. I'm talking about not just any haircuts; we're talking Caesar fades, the Gumby, the Jeff hairstyle named after DJ Jazzy Jeff, and several designs he was able to do because his talent was limitless. Just like that, everyone had a mean haircut to rock with their Easter gear, which for the guys consisted of airbrushed jean outfits with their nicknames on them and some new sneakers.

Speaking of airbrushing outfits, Femi was also talented at designing clothing and later began making tattoos for people. I remember him making money as a teenager by mowing lawns in the fall and shoveling snow in the winter to earn money to buy his supplies. He worked at Burger King part-time and would bring food home for us to eat while we played *Tecmo Bowl* on Sega Genesis.

NIGERIAN NIGHTMARE

One time, Femi got into an argument with a guy named James who lived up the street from my mother's house in Nicetown, Philadelphia. One thing led to another and next thing I knew my mother was taking all of us to James's mother's house to help resolve the issue. Apparently, Femi had uppercut James so hard that his top teeth bit completely through his bottom lip. James had so many stitches on his mouth that he looked like Jack Skellington from the *Nightmare before Christmas* movie. Shout out to Tim Burton. I guess James didn't know that Femi used to box at the Happy Hollow Gym in Germantown. Happy Hollow is famous for many things in Philly, particularly training boxing champions such as Ivan "Mighty Mouse" Robinson and former cruiserweight champion Nate Miller.

I was proud of him being my older brother for so many reasons. Being Femi's younger brother, of course, I would do things to purposely get on his nerves, and I was great at it. Mostly because I was the middle child trying to find my own identity. However, I did not want to become him even though he was somewhat of a hero. As a result, everything Femi liked, I had to like the opposite just to be different even though I liked most of the things he liked. If he knew that I liked similar things as he did, he would get angry and say, "Stop copying me" in that big brother tone of voice. In order to avoid that, if he said he liked Michael Jackson, I'd say Prince was better. When Femi was a Mike Tyson fan and he was undefeated, I'd tell him that Evander Holyfield would beat Tyson, and we would debate. Ironically, when they fought in real life, Holyfield beat him twice. Maybe I'm a prophet, nah.

SIBLING RIVALRY

Femi and I would debate about everything. When discussing hip-hop, which he introduced me to, we had our most epic debates. For example, when I was younger, MC Hammer was the most popular rapper at the time; he had sold 10 million records and was everywhere. Hammer was on *The Simpsons* cartoon, he had his own cartoon, he was on T-shirts, and he had everyone saying, "You can't touch this," which was one of Hammer's most successful records at the time. I used to tell Femi that Hammer was the best rapper, and he would be pissed. He would go off on rants about how commercial he felt Hammer was and begin detailing why Ice Cube was the better rapper.

Ice Cube was Femi's favorite rapper. In many ways, Femi reminded me of Ice Cube, especially back in those days. Ice Cube's character named Doughboy, in the movie *Boyz N the Hood* was a good comparison to Femi's energy in the late '80s and early '90s. Doughboy was very aggressive and confrontational. He was hyper-masculine with strong street savvy, but he still managed to come off as sensitive when he felt the situation warranted it. The difference between Doughboy and Femi is that Femi was eons smarter and more gifted than Doughboy while carrying the same demeanor.

I was more like Doughboy's brother Ricky minus the shotgun blast to his back. If you haven't seen the movie even though it was released nearly 30 years ago, just know that I forgot to say spoiler alert, sue me. I was the intelligent athlete that dreamed of making it out of the hood. The difference between Ricky and me is that I was more hood and less nerd. I was also more mischievous and less preppy.

I used to tease Femi for liking Ice Cube and make fun of his songs, even though I secretly liked them. Femi got so mad once, he hit me. It was shocking when it happened, but over time it became a normal outcome from our debates. I continued to make fun of Ice Cube until Femi let me hear *No Vaseline*, a diss record he made aimed at his former group NWA. In that record, he methodically used his lyrics to destroy his former group mates based on what he perceived as their wrongdoings. Once I heard that record, I could no longer hide my secret: I loved Ice Cube.

Speaking of Ice Cube. He had a song on an Ep (extended play) from his hip-hop classic album appropriately titled, *Amerikkka's Most Wanted* in which he talks about male groupies. The Ep was called "Kill at Will." The song was called "Get Off My Dick and Tell Yo Bitch To Come Here." The purpose of the song was to address how Ice Cube felt about male groupies or people who act too familiar with him. Ice Cube talked about wanting men to act like men when they see him and not like teenage school girls; I connected with that. Femi wanted to make sure that I understood the message clearly. That's when Femi pulled me to the side at an early age and lectured me against dickriding celebrities.

He used Ice Cube's bars to illustrate how I would be perceived by the celebrity if I acted overzealous. That message stuck with me for the rest of my life. To this day, I cannot bring myself to get too excited about celebrities that I have met in my life. Femi taught me not to ever treat anyone famous or otherwise as if they were better than I am. I respected that about him. Therefore, I tend to use hip-hop lyrics to learn and illustrate perspectives to people. I learned these communication and illustration tactics from my father and his many metaphors.

IT'S MY LIFE

At this point, you may be wondering why I described Femi as a talented disaster. Having shared about his IQ and some of his talents, it's time to satisfy your curiosity about Femi's *disaster* side. I'll start off by saying this: Femi has always been about individualism. He never wanted to copy or be copied by anyone. He is a trailblazer who never liked to be told what to do. I mean, he knows how smart he is and that he has more native intelligence than most. I think for him, this is where all the challenges began.

One thing about Femi is that while his entrepreneurial spirit was admirable, he was also very stubborn. Femi is not the type of person to take advice at face value. He challenged everything—and I mean everything. According to my father, Femi was just too hardheaded, pause. My mother used to call him "Nucki," short for knucklehead. As you can see, both of my parents agreed on this.

As I mentioned before, my mother and father separated due to many things, one of which was the early conflict my father had with my mother's side of the family. According to my father, his mother-in-law, my grandmother, was always trying to counterparent Femi. My father took offense that whatever he was trying to accomplish with Femi and establish in him was being undermined, in his opinion.

My father took a greater offense that my mother would often side with her mother, which on some level was understandable. The rift between my father, my grandmother, and ultimately my parents created a highly stressful environment for Femi. Femi always identified more with our maternal side of the family since extended family on our paternal side resided in Nigeria. The pressure of trying to figure out who and what he was supposed to be caused him to rebel at a young age. Femi was also present when my mother had her very first episode. They were riding the subway when it happened, he was about five years old; I cannot imagine how traumatizing that must've been for him.

My mother once told Wale and me a story about what it was like parenting Femi. She talked about giving Femi instructions when he was about three or four years old. Femi was getting annoyed and irritable about being told what to do. And here comes Femi's memory, attention to detail, and creativity again. He began to sing his response to my mother, and it was classic! "I don't care what you say anymore, this is my life. Dah, dah, dahdah, dah. Go ahead with your own life, leave me alone!" My brother sang Billy Joel to my mother to get his point across. I guess using lyrics to express ourselves runs in the family.

When I heard this story, I was screaming laughing! I mean tears flowing, stomach hurts, could barely breath laughing! Side note: I am listening to that song while I am writing this. Just thought you ought to know.

When I think about the Billy Joel song "My Life," it is a perfect soundtrack for Femi's life and ultimately mine, which we will explore later. As for Femi, rebelling happened slowly and progressed rapidly. In elementary school, Femi's intelligence was on full display. However, so was his rebellion. Femi began hanging out with what my mother called less-than-desirable kids. Eventually, he went from misbehaving in class and fights in school to cutting class and school entirely. Over the course of his educational career, Femi was kicked out of two middle schools and a few high schools.

THE HUSTLE

He then went to Job Corps in Pittsburgh where he earned his GED; then, he began attending the Art Institute of Philadelphia where he drew and painted amazing portraits. Somewhere around the time he was in the Job Corps and the Art Institute of Philadelphia, Femi discovered marijuana. How he was introduced to weed is unclear to me because I was very young at the time. We lived in the Nicetown section of Philadelphia, so I am sure it was not hard to find.

Even with his newfound interest in weed, which he sold out of my mother's house, he was still ahead of everybody. Once again, Femi found a big business opportunity. Femi not only sold weed, he had to take it up a notch because everybody sold weed. It is not like Femi to be ordinary. Instead, he started package deals, like McDonald's with the extra-value meals. If a customer bought a $5 bag of weed, they would get a free Phillies Blunt cigar to roll it with. How innovative and forward thinking was that? Customers came pouring in as expected, so Femi moved his operation to the corner of Wayne

Avenue and Dennie Street. Once again, Femi's intelligence and creativity brought him success.

However, in Nicetown, success in the drug game comes with a hefty price. As soon as customers took notice of Femi, so did his competitors. Have you seen the HBO show *The Wire*? The scene in which Bodie takes the other drug dealer's corner? Femi's former friends, who had also become drug dealers, began to turn on him. Some of them began to rob and jump him. As I stated before, Femi knew how to box, so he would get the best of some of them during the fights.

One day, a guy confronted Femi on the corner of Wayne and Dennie Streets and tried to strong-arm rob him solo. Very bad move. Femi beat this guy like Nick Cannon did the drums in the movie *Drumline* while everyone watched. Femi felt vindicated after standing up for himself; he returned to his post to finish his sales. A few moments later, the same guy returned to the corner to confront Femi. This time, he had a gun, and he began to threaten Femi. Realizing the situation, Femi punched him in the face and ran up Dennie Street. The cowardly gunman chased Femi and shot his gun wildly. Femi was hit three times in the back and eventually fainted.

I remember coming home from a high school summer league basketball game and hearing the news. I immediately went to the hospital to see him. He was full of tubes and could barely talk. With my basketball in hand and my jersey still sweaty, I could not let him see me cry. Femi did not want Wale and me to be seen as weak. Femi didn't want to focus the conversation around what happened to him. Instead, he gave me instructions about what to do when I got home to my mother.

OLD HABITS DIE HARD

One would think that the shooting, which nearly cost him his life, would deter Femi from his business venture. Unfortunately, it did not. Like so many others before him, Femi continued selling weed and hanging out with undesirables, and it eventually got him arrested. He was arrested for possession of drugs and possession of a firearm. Femi had several stints in jail—some lasting three years and upwards of 10 years.

During his time in jail, Femi and my father clashed. Femi had rage and resentment toward our father because he felt like my father put too much pressure on him. He also felt that my father was too strict. On the other hand, my father saw that Femi was becoming unruly, and he tried to correct his behavior while also fighting against feeling undermined by his in-laws. My father had told Femi that if he went to jail, he would not bail him out and that he would not send him money or write him. Femi would write letters home to my father accusing him of abandoning him.

If you think about your own parents or if you are a parent, then you know that it is very difficult to keep the promises that my father made. He did not bail Femi out because he couldn't, and he wanted him to learn a lesson. However, my father did give Femi money, and he wrote Femi because he loved him.

Femi could have been anything that he wanted; he was so gifted that I often wondered what my true talent was. Unfortunately, the positive version of his intellectual and creative promise has yet to happen for him, and it's everybody's fault. From the bickering between my parents to the conflict with my father and my grandmother to Femi's own stubbornness: All these factors played a part in Femi's rebellion. Ultimately, he chose the wrong direction and being in the in-crowd, which cost him a spleen, several felonies, imprisonment, and estranged family relationships—leaving us all to wonder what could have been.

MOMMA'S BABY

Adewale Olayinka Ige is my younger brother. His name means "The crown came home." Everyone calls him Wale. Wale was born in July, and his astrological sign is Cancer. I think he fits that sign perfectly. He has a huge heart, is hyper-vigilant, is easily offended, and expects everyone to see the world the way he does. Wale will give you the shirt off his back and suffer for weeks if it means helping someone that he cares about, and he will just as easily give you a piece of his mind when he feels violated or underappreciated.

Wale is my mother's baby. Honestly, he was probably the most handsome baby I've ever seen. I have only one picture of myself as a baby, and I've never seen Femi's baby pictures, so Wale gets the nod. Wale and I always had the closest relationship growing up as we spent the most time together.

Wale and I went to the same schools since our time at the ABC Daycare. Because he and I are three years apart, it made for a weird blend of total connectivity and awkward separations as we aged. Naturally, we had some of the same teachers over the years. As we grew older, Wale and I would walk to and from school together; most of the time, we picked a meeting place after school, so we could walk home safely. Sometimes, we had to defend ourselves from bullies, or I had to go chump somebody for picking on Wale. Wale and I were practically joined at the hip for most of our lives. My idiotic self didn't understand the importance of that in real time. Let me explain.

I know what it's like to be a little brother, but Wale sure does walk around with a Mount Everest sized chip on his shoulder. When Wale was about three years old, Femi and I used to make him run across the room in my mother's studio apartment. "Let's see how fast you can run, Wale," we challenged. Willing to prove himself, he would take off running as fast as he could. While he was running, one of us would throw a pillow at his legs and watch him fall. Boom! As he hit the floor, we would be crying laughing! Pretty mean I know, but that's what big brothers did in my household.

THE BOND

When we were younger, I used to call Wale "Ickis" after a character in the Nickelodeon cartoon, "Real Monsters" back in the day. As kids, he and I watched that show. Ickis was very small compared to the other characters in the show; he was very silly and playful. He would laugh at just about anything; I mean he would laugh very hard. Ickis had a superpower that separated him from the other monsters: When he got upset, his eyes turned red, he grew taller, and he grew fanged teeth. Clearly, his appearance and energy changed drastically. That was Wale; he could transform just like Ickis, mostly because of Femi's and my antics.

Wale and I were not always on opposite sides, however. Some of our most fun times together were spent in the "heat hole" at my mother's house. See, the heat hole was a space between my mother's couch and the faux fireplace in the living room. We called it the "heat hole" because that was where the heat vent was located.

On Saturday mornings, we would wake up around 7:00 a.m., take our covers downstairs, and get cereal while we waited for Nickelodeon to air our favorite cartoons. The Saturday morning lineup went as follows: at 8:00 a.m., *Doug* came on followed by *RugRats* and *Ren & Stimpy*. After those cartoons, we often watched shows such as *Salute Your Shorts*, *Pete & Pete*, and sometimes *Hey Dude*. By the time all the shows went off, it would be about noon, and we knew our friends would be coming outside soon, and so were we. That's what our Saturdays typically looked like.

We had a similar routine when we came in for the night. Once the street lights came on and we heard our mother's voice, we came in. My mother would already have dinner ready for us, and we were more than happy to devour whatever tasty delight she had waiting for us. After dinner, Wale and I would regroup at the heat hole to watch our favorite evening shows. On Saturdays, we watched *SNICK*, which stood for Saturday Night Nickelodeon.

Our favorite shows were *All That* featuring Keenan Thompson, who is now a *Saturday Night Live* mainstay and *Are You Afraid of the Dark?* which was Nickelodeon's attempt at a horror show that catered to little kids. It sounds counterintuitive, but it worked for us. Believe me, it had some scary episodes. Sometimes, we stayed up watching *Mary Tyler Moore* on *Nick-At-Nite* to forget about the scary stories. I even had to turn the night light on for Wale; that's what he needed to feel safe back then.

DON'T TRY THIS AT HOME

When we weren't outside or watching Nickelodeon, we were either fighting or wrestling. I grew up a huge WWF, now WWE fan. My favorite wrestler was Macho Man Randy Savage back then. Yep, the guy with the funny cowboy hat, iconic shades, and tassels hanging from his colorful outfits. He was also the spokesperson for the old Slim Jim commercials.

When we lived at my mother's studio apartment, Femi and I shared a bunk bed, and Wale slept on the couch with my mother. I was six years old, and Wale was three years old at the time. One day, Wale and I were play wrestling. It was the end of our epic matchup, and it was time for my finishing move. Naturally, I copied my finishing move from Macho Man. I climbed to the top of the bunk bed, which in my mind was the top rope of a wrestling ring, and I jumped off and landed a flying elbow to Wale's head. That was when I learned why they say, "Do not try this at home." I injured both of us. I ended up with a high ankle sprain, a bandaged leg, and a pair of uncomfortable crutches. Wale ended up with migraine headaches over the course of the next several years.

My mother was pissed. Unfortunately, I earned another one of her famous ass-whuppings. Do you think that stopped us from wrestling each other? Nope. As we got older, our wrestling matches got more sophisticated. I used to take cardboard boxes and cut them into the shape of a wrestling belt and then use my mother's aluminum foil to cover the "belt" as if it were championship metal. Then, we put on tube socks as if they were our wrestling boots and tied another pair of tube socks to our elbows and knees to mimic the pads our favorite wrestlers wore.

We even went as far as using a T-shirt on our heads to mimic the hair grabbing that took place in matches. Wrestling was real to us—so real that I was about 15 years old when I realized The Undertaker wasn't dead.

"A sibling may be the keeper of one's identity, the only person with the keys to one's unfettered, more fundamental self."

—Marian Sandmaier

BROTHERLY BULLYING

We were so into wrestling that we had the toys. My prized possession was a Bret "Hitman" Hart action figure that my mother bought me for Christmas; Wale got The Undertaker. When Femi would get angry with me, he would threaten to take my toys to his school and give them away. It was either that, or he would threaten to throw them onto a roof. "Keep playing with me; I'm a roof that fucking toy," he would threaten. One day, I apparently got on his nerves so he took my Bret Hart toy from me, and I never saw it again. He did the same with my Captain Power toy that I bought at the Value Plus discount store on Germantown Avenue. I always wondered: Did he break the toys, throw them on the roof, or sell them? If he sold them, did they go to a good home? All I know is that I cried for months!

Another story that shows my relationship with Femi was on my 12th birthday. My father gave me a card that was addressed to Dr. Adekunle K. Ige. He titled it that way because, as a child, I wanted to be a medical doctor. As I said earlier, Nigerian and African kids were conditioned to think that medicine was one of the few relevant professions in the world. Inside the card was a generic message by Hallmark, a few words from my father, and most importantly a twenty-dollar bill. My father said he gave me

$12 because I was turning 12 years old, and he gave me an extra $8 because I would be 20 years old in eight years, and my birthday is on the 20th of August (8/20). Creative, right? Now, you know how my father thinks.

When Femi learned that my father had given me $20 for my birthday, his wheels started spinning. Then, I watched him get his idea: He wanted some of the cash. He told me that he needed the money to buy something for school; I cannot remember what he said he needed to buy because it was so long ago, but that isn't the point. It was my birthday money! I didn't believe his story about needing money for school. However, being the brother that I am and being scared of him at the time, I felt compelled to give it to him. I was very reluctant, but he said that he would pay me back, which I also knew would not happen. So, there I was sad and crying on my 12th birthday because my gift had been swindled from me. I know this sounds like a victim stance, but if you had seen Femi fight in those days, you would thoroughly understand. On top of that, Femi was a master con artist. Twenty-five years later, he still owes me $20 and a Bret "Hitman" Hart action figure.

When we weren't wrestling or fighting, Wale and I were always into some scheme. Like the time my mother bought us a PlayStation for Christmas. She hid the Christmas gifts in the house, so we couldn't find them, but we were kids with too much time on our hands, so we found them every time. Wale and I had the PlayStation for about three weeks prior to Christmas. We would stay up late at night waiting for her to go to sleep and then, I would hook up the PlayStation to play Mortal Kombat Trilogy. That's just the kind of things we did as kids.

"Our siblings push buttons that cast us in roles we felt sure we had let go of long ago — the baby, the peacekeeper, the caretaker, the avoider… It doesn't seem to matter how much time has elapsed or how far we've traveled."

—Jane Mersky Leder

A FAMILY IN NEED

I love my brothers, but what I didn't love was sleeping in the same room and bed with both of them when we were younger. We lived with my father in a three-story, five bedroom house. The other rooms were often taken by my father's friends whom he had helped by renting rooms to them. Therefore, the three of us stayed in the same room and slept in the same bed. That meant we never had privacy, ever. It also meant that if any one of us peed in the bed, we all got wet, which happened often. It's not fun be peed on; it made me very angry.

Even when the extra rooms were not occupied by people, they were occupied by things. My father would hoard all kinds of things in the house, from construction supplies to obsolete computers he bought in bulk at auction. Anytime my mother came over to the house to see us, she would say my father's house was a fire hazard. One of the things I did when I got very angry was clean up the house. My goal was to make space for us to move around and have the house be presentable, so I could bring my friends over. But when I cleaned and organized the house, my father took it as a green light to add more items to the house. It was as if my cleaning up was saying, "Look, Daddy, look at how much space you missed," which frustrated me. After a while, I just stopped cleaning the house.

One of the things that really kept us together was having to fend for ourselves. When my mother went in and out of the hospital, Femi would have to take care of us. He was responsible for connecting with other family members to get assistance as well as going shopping. Oftentimes, it was just the three of us. When Femi was in jail, I was immediately thrust into that role. At the age of 12, it was very scary to think that I was now the man of the house. At that age, I could barely take care of myself let alone take care of my 9-year-old little brother. It was scary being forced into the role of a parent before I even really got to know puberty.

My mother kept a pantry full of ramen noodles and canned goods, so that's what I would make. Dinner would be SpaghettiOs and water. Because Femi was older, he would make more sophisticated meals. Creating something out of nothing was Femi's specialty and one of his many talents. I remember he once found some freezer-burned pork chops in the back of the freezer and turned them into a Worcestershire sauce-marinated dinner full of deliciousness.

In case you are wondering where my father was in all of this, he would do his best to provide groceries for us and try to settle our sibling disputes when my mother was hospitalized. Depending on how long my mother would be in the mental health hospital, we would either stay at her home until she returned or move into my father's house. Most times, she would be gone for several months, and we'd end up moving to my father's house.

I remember one Christmas when I was about 10 years old, she was hospitalized violently by police officers. Wale and I were traumatized. My Uncle Morris, Aunt Joan, and my cousins came through with Christmas presents for all three of us. I remember exactly what I got for Christmas, *Battleship* the board game. I was more than grateful. My cousin Peach, whom I call my Aunt because she's much older than I am, took Femi shopping for groceries so that we could eat. At the time, we had no food in the house. Shout out to my cousins Barbara, Lisa, Debbie, and little Morris. I never forgot what you all did for us that Christmas.

> "To the outside world we all grow old. But not to brothers and sisters. We know each other as we always were. We know each other's hearts. We share private family jokes. We remember family feuds and secrets, family griefs and joys. We live outside the touch of time."
>
> —Clara Ortega

CHAPTER 3
IDENTITY CRISIS

"I wanna know who am I, and what is my purpose? Should I live, or should I die? I'm not sure which is worth it." Those are the opening lines I rapped over the instrumental of Juelz Santana's song called "Who Am I?" Those bars derive from the ongoing journey I traveled as I tried to navigate life. There are many trials and tribulations throughout life, and the struggles we face often build character.

Adekunle Kayode Ige was born on August 20, 1981, in Philadelphia. My name means "The crown filled the house." If you are astrologically savvy, you probably noticed that I am a Leo, but I am on the cusp of being a Virgo, which begins three days after my birthday. Over the years, I've noticed that

I have strong traits of both signs and, depending on the situation, one sign's traits may be more dominant.

FITTING IN

As early as I can remember, I've always felt like an outsider— in my home and in school. Being a middle child always gave me a sense of uncertainty about where I fit not only in my family, but also in the world. My parents were separated most of my life, so I was constantly moving back and forth between my parents' homes. Even though I was not in foster care, it often felt like it. I had to make new friends, leave them, rejoin them, and then repeat. Even though it was not as rapid as it sounds, the impact left me with a constant desire for social stability.

Let's take elementary school for example. I attended John B. Kelly Elementary in the Germantown section of Philadelphia for kindergarten and first grade. I attended Kelly because it was within the school district nearest my father's home although we lived with my mother in a studio apartment on Seymour Street. I still remember my last teacher at John B. Kelly, Ms. Ballard. I remember her because she had a game in which she'd throw a bag of bite-sized Twizzlers in the air, and whoever caught the bag got to keep the candy. I remember having an epic jump elevating higher than my classmates and snagging the bag. It was one of the most satisfying feelings in my life. Other than doing front flips and backflips on the school's front lawn, I really cannot remember too much from my time at Kelly.

By my second-grade year, my mother retired early from teaching in the Philadelphia school district. With help from my father, she bought a new home, and we moved to the Nicetown section of Philadelphia. Although my father's house was in walking distance, Germantown and Nicetown were two different worlds entirely. Given that I spent the next several years in Nicetown, that is where my identity began to form.

I was transferred from John B. Kelly to Edward T. Steel Elementary, which happened to be one block to the left of my mother's home—a very short walk to school. When I entered the school, I was seven years old and in the second grade. I remember the teacher calling roll for the first time. Back then, they called roll alphabetically by the last name: "I cannot even pronounce this. Odukunkle Idge!" she called out. Immediately, all the other students started laughing hysterically. They had not heard an African name before. Obviously, I was embarrassed. "Adekunle Ige," I corrected. I was the new kid at the school, and from then on, I was the butt of every joke—what a great start.

Students laughing at my name became a daily occurrence over the next few months. It escalated when we were shown the movie *Roots* during so-called black history month. To this day, I cannot understand why they would show that movie during black history month. I was taught by my father that our history does not start with slavery—that we were kings and queens with gold and a rich culture. Those images became harder and harder to imagine the more I attended school. It was as if the whole world knew a big secret that I didn't.

Once *Roots* progressed to the Kunta Kinte part, my first nickname was born. The bullies of the school or the guys everyone saw as the "tough guys" started calling me "AntaKunta" as a way to further make fun of my name. Eventually, they just started calling me Kunta. You see, nowadays, Kendrick Lamar has a song called "King Kunta," which makes the name sound kind of cool. However, Kendrick Lamar did not exist back then nor did this current "woke" movement. Whether AntaKunta or Kunta, I never liked either name because it was a mockery of not only my name but my culture.

There I was seven years old living in a new section of the city, in a new school, and being laughed at daily. They began to talk about my hand-me-down clothes and my run-down sneakers. I didn't know what to do. I told Femi what was happening in school, and he gave me advice. "You gon have to punch one of them kids in the mouth. Trust me; they gon start respecting you," he said. Femi never told me whether he had faced this problem when he was my age, but I suspected he had because he knew exactly how to handle the problem. I wasn't sure whether taking his advice would be the best move because it could land me my first suspension.

One day during recess, I was on the playground when a boy called me Kunta. I didn't respond to him. I thought that if I did not respond, he would stop trying to get my attention. I was wrong. He ran over to me and said, "You's an African booty scratcher." At that point, I had enough. Blam! Out of nowhere, I punched him in the eye. I didn't hit him in the mouth as Femi suggested, but either way, he caught these knuckles. I grabbed him by the back of his head to pull him into the uppercuts he was about to receive. He got his head loose from my arm and started swinging wildly with his head down. I kept throwing uppercuts with both hands one after another, landing each one. Eventually, the fight was broken up by school staff. My heart was pounding like an African drum. All I could think about was getting in trouble when I got home.

The school suspended us both. They didn't care that I was being harassed and teased daily. Their policy was that when there was a fight, both parties were sent home no matter who started it. I got a three-day suspension, and the other boy got a five-day suspension. The good news was that I was not punished when I got home. I told my mother what happened, and she double-checked with the school, as she was known to do. Therefore, serving my suspension was not nearly as bad as it could've been. I spent it doing worksheets that my mother got from the school when she picked me up from the principal's office. My mother always kept her eye on education.

When I returned to school, I expected people to start calling me by my real name. Instead, some of them kept calling me Kunta. The boy I beat up was not seen as one of the tough guys or bullies, I guess. However, I noticed the way they called me Kunta changed in tone. It almost sounded like they were just joking around or treating it like an actual nickname. Nevertheless, the African jokes and name butchery continued.

That lasted until I was in the fourth grade and a boy named Khalil joined our class. Khalil never treated me like an outcast. He was not afraid of any of the so-called tough guys at the school. In fact, the reason I remember him most is that he was the first person to call me by my last name, Ige. After he started calling me Ige, everyone wanted to call me by my last name. It became the cool thing to do.

Although people started calling by my last name, it did not stop teachers from mispronouncing my name and students from laughing. It also didn't stop the students from laughing at my "peazy ass head" or my out-of-style clothing. That's when I realized that fighting wasn't the way to solve the issue. I would have to fight daily, which would get me nowhere fast. Instead, it would make me look like a problem child. The torment was inescapable especially when my name had to be called in assembly, which gave the entire school a chance to laugh at my name and my clothes as I walked toward the stage. It was a very hopeless experience.

> *"A truly strong person does not need the approval of others any more than a lion needs the approval of sheep."*
>
> —Vernon Howard

WHO DO YOU BELIEVE?

The contrast of being taught at home that I am from royalty versus facing harsh rejection in school vastly distorted my self-perception. The self-doubt began to make me hate school. I felt as if I was less than the other students. At lunch, I often sat alone though I badly wanted to be accepted in the larger group and feel connected.

I remember brushing my hair constantly so that it wouldn't be called peazy or nappy. I tried to get waves in my hair like the cool kids in school and the drug dealers they looked up to in the neighborhood. I was unsuccessful. In my mind, it was because I am African, and African hair was not able to get waves because it was like a Brillo pad. I believed that, which says a lot about how deep into my psyche all the teasing and bullying had gotten.

With so much African pride in my household, it may be hard to believe that I experienced self-hate. The self-hatred and feelings of unworthiness caused me to argue with my father about my culture. I was angry. My school experience armed me with all kinds of rhetoric to prove my point that what he had been teaching us was an outdated fairy tale. The arguments always infuriated my father because he knew better; I didn't. My so-called perspective hurt his feelings. Over the years, he would say things like, "You don't want to be African." I would deny his claims, but he was right. The idea that being African was a negative thing was being drilled into my head daily, but it never penetrated my soul.

Over time, I had a problem with everything. After hearing what other kids at school had for dinner, which they would come to school bragging about, I got tired of eating the same food every day. I thought we ate the same stewed soup with rice and meat daily because we were poor. I would often ask my father for variety in our meals. His version of variety was to add chopped spinach into the soup or substitute mackerel for the usual oxtail. It angered me. I wanted macaroni and cheese, mashed potatoes, burgers, fries, and pizza. Those were the foods that the "normal" kids ate. According to my father, these were junk foods. I don't know how many times I broke my father's heart this way.

> *"Be careful how you talk to yourself because you are listening."*
>
> —Lisa M. Hayes

CULTURAL CLEANSING

The irony is that I loved eating our native foods, just not every day for breakfast, lunch, and dinner. When we went to Nigerian parties at our family's houses, all I could think about was all the great food I would eat once we got there. The part that angered my father was that I didn't want to go to the parties in the first place. That was partly because I didn't want to wear my Nigerian attire in my neighborhood and get teased. The other part was that my father would say that we would be gone for about two hours, which usually meant we were not coming home until around 2:00 a.m. I was not trying to miss all that playtime with my friends.

Once I got to the parties with my father, I loved being accepted by my family and other Nigerians. I felt comfortable wearing native clothing and eating native food. I loved when they spoke Yoruba to me to make sure I could understand what they asked. Suddenly, being African felt normal and organic. It felt like being a part of a secret society. We had our own language, customs, clothing, music, and food. We had a strong bond and support for each other. That's when I realized how far away from my identity I had gotten.

I remember overhearing a conversation in Yoruba that my uncles were having. One of my uncles talked about how he was facing discrimination and overt hatred at work. He mentioned that because he has an accent when he talks, people automatically assume that he is unintelligent. He talked about being stereotyped and micromanaged. I observed as many of my family members related to his experiences. The ignorance never ends, I remember thinking. At least, I knew I wasn't alone in the social struggle. After hearing what they all had to say and watching how they remained positive, I was inspired. Through conversations and experience, the parties served as confirmation that I come from great people; more importantly, they confirmed my father's teachings.

The only thing I felt embarrassed about was when my aunt kept asking me if I had a girlfriend yet. She would tell me how handsome and intelligent I was. That's when I learned that I lived in one world with two realities, the awoken and the ignorant. From then on, the parties were like cleansing myself from the world of ignorance, the way the church does for believers. I always left the parties thinking about how great the experience was and all the funny things that Wale and I saw. We took note of everything.

I noticed that my Uncle Niyi was always in a great mood. I figured one of the reasons was that he always brought a bad chick to the parties. Often Wale and I would wait for his arrival because we knew he would have something nice on his arm. We looked at him as a celebrity; seeing him was like an event for us. He never disappointed. "Where is your girlfriend, Kunle?" he would ask. Before I could answer, he would add, "Too many to count, ah?" Then, we would laugh, and off he went to tour the party with his Beyoncé of the week.

My Uncle Femi, not to be confused with my brother, was the direct opposite. He seemed to always be in an angry mood. It was like he couldn't wait to show everybody, especially us kids. As soon as he felt that we did something wrong or out of line, he was ready. "Ah-Ahh, what are you doing?" he'd ask in a thick Yoruba accent. Then, he'd hit us with his favorite line, "I'll smack your face!" Wale and I always found him comical because even when he wasn't talking, he looked angry. We never found out why, but to silly kids like us, it was hilarious.

"The best way to fight an alien and oppressive culture, is to embrace your own."

—African Proverb

THE JOKER

Around the middle of my fourth-grade year, I started listening to Richard Pryor's comedy records. I could not believe how funny he was and how much people loved him. That's when I decided to become a class clown in school. It was my way of taking the pressure off being publicly embarrassed daily. I learned that I had the ability to make people laugh impromptu. I had good timing, and it felt natural. Whether I was making a funny noise at the right time or telling an inappropriate joke, I could make the class erupt with laughter. The teachers were not happy, but I couldn't care less. It got me in trouble, but it also got me a positive reaction from my peers. That's right my peers.

By fifth grade, I was getting two dollars per day as an allowance from my mother. I used my daily allowance to buy one hundred pieces of penny candy, which was usually fruit-flavored Tootsie Rolls and a box of Cry Baby Tears Candy. Hyped on sugar, I had Ms. Vaughn's class lit with jokes every day. Making the class laugh became like an event for me. People would wait for the moment that I did something silly or funny. In those moments when I was making farting sounds as an overweight teacher bent over or passing notes that made fun of other students, I felt accepted. Unfortunately, my talking in class got me in trouble, which prevented me from going on the senior class trip to New York.

When Ms. Vaughn took the class on a trip to a Philadelphia 76ers game, she told me that she had a surprise for me at halftime, and I was excited. At half-time, they were giving away a bike for a random person in the crowd. I was sure that the bike was going to be for me. I was hoping and praying, but it turned out that another kid's name was called. After the game, Ms. Vaughn told me that she had submitted my name to receive the bike and was assured by the team that my name would be called, but for whatever reason, they didn't call my name. I could imagine the announcer trying to pronounce my name in a stadium full of kids, I'll pass. She apologized. I am not sure if what she told me was true or if she just felt sorry for me because of what I went through in school. Either way, I knew that she cared.

Even though I was able to carve out a niche with my classmates, it only temporarily stopped people from teasing me. One thing I couldn't understand was how teachers who saw my name on the roll, graded my papers, and often spoke to my mother over four years constantly misspelled my name. There were exceptions, but the majority continued mispronouncing and misspelling my name. To this day, my name is misspelled in my fifth-grade yearbook from Edward T. Steel School.

THE POPULAR STRANGER

When I got to middle school, it was somewhat of a fresh start. Most of the students who graduated from Edward T. Steel School eventually went to Elizabeth D. Gillespie Middle School because it was a Nicetown neighborhood school. However, many other students from various sections of North Philly also attended Gillespie Middle School; I wasn't just going to school with kids from my neighborhood anymore. I was determined to make the most of my middle school experience.

I remember preparing for the first day of middle school. My mother took us shopping on Germantown and Chelten Avenues as well as Germantown and Erie Avenues. This time, I was picking my clothes although we were on a tight budget. I had lived in Nicetown for almost five years, and I knew what was cool. At the time, Polo shirts and Guess jeans were must-haves.

Jordache jeans were not considered cool.

There was no way that I was going to get Polo Shirts, so that was out of the question. Instead, my mother bought me Hugo Boss shirts, which were semi-cool. My mother held up a pair of Jordache jeans asking me to try them on, and I was not having it. I was able to get Guess jeans. They were not the most up-to-date versions, but I was excited because they were Guess Jeans. Then it was time to get the most important part of an outfit, the sneakers or "sneaks" we called them.

I went shopping with my mother to get new sneakers. I wanted a new pair of Jordans, but there was no way that she was going to pay the $50 they cost. Paying $50 for sneakers for an 11-year-old was not something we could afford. Instead, she took me to Payless on Chelten Avenue. I was not thrilled.

Here I am pouting ungratefully around the store. I eventually see from a distance in the back of the store a pair of sneakers that looked like Jordans. As I approached them, I noticed that they were not actually Jordans, but they bore a roundabout resemblance to them. They looked like the Jordan 7 sneaks, but they were called XJ-900s. I remember them clearly. They were white and cardinal red, and I figured that if I was kind of fooled by those sneaks, then kids in school would be also. I begged my mother to buy them; they cost $30.

Wearing those XJ-900s on the first day of school was the worst mistake I could've possibly made. The first day of school is when everybody is inspecting each other's gear to identify people's status so to speak. It was the day when everybody paid close attention to everyone's wardrobe. I got attention all right, unwanted attention. As soon as they noticed that I was wearing fake Jordans, the laughter and pointing began.

NEW TEACHER

In sixth grade, I got paired with a teacher who helped to change my school experience, Ms. Price. Everyone loved Ms. Price; she was very personable and hip. She never allowed people in the class to make fun of me or anyone for that matter. Her teaching methods were very modern, and she understood how everyone learned. Not many people misbehaved in Ms. Price's class, including me.

One day, while off work, Ms. Price got into an accident and suffered a broken leg and other injuries. I was very sad because I felt the most accepted and normal in her classroom. Another teacher had to take over for most of the school year; her name was Ms. Sawyer. I didn't like Ms. Sawyer right away because I felt she was too strict. Most of the class thought she was strict with us because she was jealous of our love for Ms. Price. We always talked about Ms. Price.

Once I knew that Ms. Sawyer was going to be our teacher for most of the school year, I rebelled. The return of the class clown. I was throwing paper balls at other students, getting out of my seat without permission, and making jokes nonstop in class. The more I behaved like that the more the other kids accepted me. Poor Ms. Sawyer. She was just trying to do her job, and I was one of the many kids in her class who made it extremely difficult for her.

I remember that my mother came to school randomly just to check on me. She would do that if she was in the neighborhood. I saw her outside my classroom door, but I pretended not to see her. I continued doing my work. Once I finished, I began moving around the classroom and playing with my friends as she spoke to Ms. Sawyer. I was trying to keep the same energy that I had when my mother wasn't at school, but not enough to get myself embarrassed. Do you know how kids try to be cool in front of their friends? Yeah, I took that risk. I heard Ms. Sawyer say, "See like right now." I was shook. I just knew that I was about to get my ass beat in class, but for whatever reason, Ms. Sawyer must have been telling my mom something good because my mother didn't embarrass me for misbehaving. My class clown reputation remained intact.

Several months passed and we heard a commotion in the hallway. There were many excited students and teachers making lots of noise. I sat in the back of the classroom. My seat was close to the door, so I had the best vantage point. I peeked out into the hallway to see what the commotion was. That's when I saw Ms. Price coming down the hallway. I jumped out of my seat yelling, "Ms. Price is here!

Ms. Price is here!" I ran out of the classroom immediately to give her a big hug. The entire class ran after me to greet her. She had come in to visit and see how we all were doing. We were all thrilled, everyone except Ms. Sawyer.

Ms. Sawyer was not excited in the least bit. We knew she was not happy with the entire class emptying out to go see the beloved Ms. Price, the teacher none of us could stop talking about. When Ms. Price left, Ms. Sawyer let us have it. She talked about how disrespectful and ungrateful we were. She gave us long writing assignments and told us we were not going to get recess at lunchtime. That was significant to me because it meant no basketball for the day. We were wrong for leaving the class without permission. I was wrong for starting the riot. I understood why she was upset, but I also believed that she was jealous of the love we showed Ms. Price.

Ms. Sawyer was a great teacher, but she just wasn't Ms. Price. I remember her telling us a story about when her parents were going to school—how they had to pass a brown paper bag test. The brown paper bag test was used in those days to determine whether a student would be accepted into the school. The idea was that if the student was darker than the brown paper bag, that student would be refused admission. She used the story to express to us the importance of education and the sacrifices people had to make for it to be accessible. It was a very valuable lesson and lent credence to what my father had taught me about America.

After hearing that story, I had more respect for Ms. Sawyer. I was still being a class clown and getting myself into trouble, but I was trying to have more compassion for her. In my mind, there was no better way to keep my classmates distracted from laughing at me than to keep them laughing with me. None of that was Ms. Sawyer's fault; it was my own insecurity. When it came time to be considered for the class trip, I was denied and for good reason. Once again, being a class clown gained me favor with my peers but prevented me from going on the sixth-grade class trip to Atlanta.

EIGHTH GRADE

Fast forward to eighth grade. By this time, I had a reputation in school. I had been separated from the kids I went to elementary school with based on the way the school enrollment was designed. We were all sent to different floors of the school based on what they called "houses." Each floor was assigned and identified by a color. In sixth and seventh grade, I was in Peach House, which was on the second floor. Blue House was on the third floor, and Yellow House on the fourth floor. By the time, I got to eighth grade, they had added a new house, Green House. I was in Green House, which was on the first floor.

TRUTH OR DARE

One of the most memorable moments in eighth grade was when we had a substitute teacher in the class. When we had substitute teachers, the classroom was full of defiant kids doing whatever we wanted; it was pure chaos. This time, we were playing the truth or dare game, which required the player to either tell the truth about a secret, answer a personal question, or accept a dare. Most times, people just answered whatever question they were asked. I don't know what they asked this girl in my class, but she was unwilling to answer, so by rule she had to accept the challenge of the dare.

Let's call the girl Nia; she was the baddest girl in our classroom. When I say bad, I mean good-looking. I'm hip-hop and from the hood, what do you want from me? Anyway, she was one of those fully developed girls in middle school that looked like she was older than she was. She had two huge and perfectly shaped breasts; I mean these were grown woman breasts. They were so beautiful that it was all us horny eighth-grade boys would talk about. I made sure that I got my daily view of them, especially when she wore V-neck shirts. Little did I know that I would be getting closer to those beautiful breasts than I ever imagined.

Remember that dare she had to accept? Yep, you guessed it. The dare that she had to accept was to allow me to put my hand in her shirt and grab her breasts for 30 seconds. Because she was involved in the game, she knew it was her turn to accept a dare, and she was willing. I don't know why the other kid chose me to be the one she had to allow to feel those titties, but that man is the MVP. At this point in my life, I was usually shy when it came to girls and kept my crushes to myself. But not that day! I went in, all the way in, as the other kids in the class counted the seconds. It was everything I dreamed of. Man, I enjoyed every single second. So much so that I didn't wash my hand for like three days. I think this was the birth of my love for breasts.

HEALTH FAIR

Later that year, we had a health fair at school, discussing the human body and sexuality. At the fair, they discussed safe sex and STDs. I knew I wanted to have sex, but after seeing the outcome of getting an STD in those graphic pictures, I wasn't sure anymore. At the end of the fair, they gave out pamphlets and condoms. I took the condoms; it was the one message that got across loud and clear that day.

About a month or so later, my mother and her boyfriend Mr. Leonard woke me up from my sleep and called me downstairs to the living room. Getting called to the living by my mother was always a bad sign. It felt like I was in the mob, and I was being called to a private location to be whacked. I wondered what the problem was this time and why it couldn't wait. She asked, "You out here having sex?" I was puzzled. She pulled out a brown paper bag full of condoms and held it up. "I found this in your bag!" she yelled. I was more puzzled, but this time about why she went through my book bag.

At first, I had no idea how a bag of condoms had gotten into my bookbag. It took me a while to remember because she woke me from my sleep. "I got those from the health fair at school," I recalled. "I forgot they were in there," I told her. My mother checked with the school the next day, and it was confirmed. Realizing that I was reaching pubescent milestones, my mother decided that I would be moving back to my father's house on Apsley Street in Germantown. I was not eager because my father was exponentially stricter than my mother. That also meant, that my walking commute to school got longer.

FRIEND OR FOE

Eighth grade was also when I met Stewart, a loud, brash, silly kid from 22nd Street and Lehigh Avenue in Philly. Stewart came to our eighth-grade class around midyear. He had been kicked out of his previous school. When he first got to our class, most of us didn't really accept him right away. I mean, for the first time I felt like I was on the inside of the cool group. Stewart would constantly make loud noises and yell mostly loud curse words in class. His antics made us laugh hard. Most people referred to him as "fat ass Stewart" or simply, "his fat ass."

One day, Stewart began making fun of a very feminine boy in our class named Sean. We all assumed the kid was gay because he wore soft-toe Reebok hi-top sneakers, the style that all the girls wore. He also switched his hips when he walked and had a very feminine drawl when he talked. Stewart was constantly making jokes about him. He was calling him a faggot or referenced him as "gay ass Sean." I felt bad for the kid. I know what it's like to be teased and feel like an outcast. It was also an opportunity for me to present myself as a tough guy in school. So, I told Stewart to leave him alone. Stewart didn't like me taking up for Sean. He responded, "Or what?" "Or I'll fuck you up," I responded. We couldn't fight in class because the teacher broke up the madness before we got anywhere. I told Stewart to meet me after school at 3:00 p.m.

Once the final bell rang, I waited in front of the school for about an hour and a half for him. I never saw him. I came to school the next day ready to talk my shit. When I saw him, he said, "I thought you wanted to meet me after school yesterday." I responded, "I waited for your bitch ass yesterday." Stewart didn't believe me. He had a few kids from our class as witnesses that he had been outside waiting for me, but I never showed. I had a few witnesses of my own to confirm that I had been outside waiting for him. None of these kids had any reason to lie because they all wanted to see the fight. It turned out that Stewart and I were waiting for each other at different exits at the school.

After solving the mystery of why we never saw each other, we gained respect for each other. We were both ready and willing to fight. Things smoothed over between us, and we became friends. Eventually, Mrs. Parks had to deal with two class clowns, and we were too much! I don't remember what Stewart did, but he managed to get himself sent to in-house suspension for the rest of the school year.

In-house suspension in our school was like jail. He was put on the top floor of the building where there were no other classes; he was isolated. Because we had developed a bond with each other, I would often ask for hall passes to the bathroom. Once I got the hall pass, I would run up to his floor and make loud funny noises to make him laugh. That was my way of visiting my best friend. Somehow, both Stewart and I graduated from the eighth grade. At the end of the year, he and I exchanged phone numbers and kept in touch all summer.

JUST ANOTHER LOST NIGGA

Over the summer, my mother took me school shopping for clothes. I made sure that I would not be made fun of in high school for having no-name gear. I wanted to make a good impression and establish myself early. The night before high school began, I remember laying my clothes out on the bed. I had a red, white, and blue Tommy Hilfiger shirt, which in those days were second best to Polo shirts. I had a pair of dark blue Guess jeans and a black belt with fake gold plate inserts on it; they were popping back then. I also had a pair of white Hanes socks and my Nike Air Go LWP aka the *Penny Hardaway* sneakers; they were black, white, and royal blue. The Pennys were second to Air Jordans when it came to status back then. I was so anxious to finally get to wear this outfit that I couldn't sleep the night before. Eventually, I went to sleep right next to my outfit on the bed. That's what we did back then.

Stewart and I met in front of Simon Gratz High on the first day of school. Simon Gratz High School is literally next door to Gillespie, my middle school. So, it was easy to find Stewart, unlike the time were supposed to fight in middle school. This was the first time we saw each other in a few months, so we checked out each other's outfits and then went to get our schedule. That's when we learned that we were not in the same advisory or classes. So, we found ways to maintain our connection, which included cutting into each other's classrooms for a period or two.

Since I was entering high school, my mother did not want another repeat of middle school. When she took her walks for exercise or went shopping, she would stop by my school periodically to see how I was doing. It was always at random; I never knew when she was coming. I would just be alerted by the office that she was in the school. Sometimes, my friends would say, "Yo, Ige, your mom is here!" Oftentimes, she would bring me lunch or check in with my teachers to see how I was doing. Sometimes, she even took me out of school to go shopping with her because my grades were good.

After a few months of school, I began to get bored. In my world history class, for example, we would get the test questions and answers the day before we were supposed to take the test. I always did well on the tests, mainly because it was about memorizing the cheat sheet. The class wasn't very interesting to me because I wasn't learning anything. That along with the fact that I was starting to get teased in school for wearing patent leather reeboks with the bubblegum soles while everyone else wore the patent leather Jordan 11s. That was all I needed to decide to not only begin cutting classes but cutting school entirely.

At first, I was cutting classes on Fridays. Then, I wasn't going to school at all. Stewart and I would meet in front of the school and then walk to Germantown and Erie Avenues to hang out. We would go holla at girls and play Mortal Kombat in Temple Pizza, a store located right off the Temple University campus. Soon, it escalated to me using the allowance money that my mother gave me to ride the subway all day or the Market Frankford El, which is the elevated train in Philly. We often went to Franklin Mills, a large mall on Knights Road. Since we both came from families that did not have a lot of money, we began stealing clothes from the mall. I stole clothes from Polo, Tommy Hilfiger, and Eddie Bauer; I was just tired of not having the clothes all the "cool kids" had. The outfit that I wore on the first day of school was the only socially cool outfit I had according to my peers. It was one outfit, and I could only wear it so many times in a school year. Back then, I was too stupid to be thankful that I had clothes at all. I always felt cheated in life.

During those rides on the subway and El, we had debates about who was better Biggie or Tupac and what girls we were interested in at the school. We also had more mature conversations about our lives. We talked about our struggles and dreams. I talked about wanting to play basketball in the NBA and make money for my family. I often dreamed about leaving my neighborhood and moving to California. During those conversations, I tried to talk Stewart into returning to school to take tests and pass his classes, but he was never interested. I don't think he really liked school.

One thing I learned about Stewart was that his older brother had been in jail, just like mine. We had that in common. Stewart had a strained relationship with his brother because he was gay, flamboyantly gay. According to him, his brother became gay after he was in jail. After learning this, I instantly thought about when Stewart was mean to the gay kid in our eighth-grade class.

I wondered if that was the source of his ire. Gradually, those days of cutting class turned into weeks of missed classes; I would often show up to classes only on test days. Stewart never went to his classes; he would just wait for me in the back halls or outside of school as I took the tests. I would pass the tests, and then cut school until there was another test. The class I cut most often was gym. Even though gym was the most fun of all the classes, it wasn't important enough for me to attend. I was having too much fun outside school.

Occasionally, we would sneak into Gillespie Middle school to mess with our old teachers. One day, we snuck into Gillespie to visit Wale because he attended there. Our goal was to not be seen by the school police while we trespassed in the school. It worked for a while, but in true Stewart fashion, things got loud and escalated quickly.

I was looking in the window of the classroom door while making faces at Wale to make him laugh. Stewart was a little too quiet, which was not like him. Suddenly, I hear Stewart getting a running start. "FUCK IT!" he yelled. As I turned around to see what Stewart was up to, I saw a huge steel trash can fly past my face barely missing me as it slammed into the door. BANG! It was so loud! Everybody including the teacher got scared, and we ran off laughing uncontrollably. We ran to the back hallways as the school police chased us. We ran into the fire escape and exited the school immediately. Once I caught my breath, I lost it again because I was laughing so hard.

That wasn't the first or last time Stewart did something like that. I remember one time, while he and I were cutting classes, we stayed inside the school. As we walked by the math teacher's classroom, Stewart got an idea. He took off his cult-famous splitpea colored jacket and placed it over the door window of Mr. Horan's classroom so he could not be seen for what he was about to do. He then began kicking the door as hard as he could. BANG, BANG, BANG! "It's the Green Caper!" he yelled. We both ran down the hallway, chased by the non-teaching assistants and school police. Man, I was laughing so hard I threw up. Stewart was classic for moments like that.

A MEANS TO AN END

After a fun day at Franklin Mills, I went home as was the routine. When I got home, Mom was standing at the door and asked, "How was school today?" I nonchalantly answered, "It was cool." She sent Wale upstairs. Instead of going to his room as instructed, Wale hid at the top of the stairs to witness the upcoming drama. She asked again, and I responded the same. She asked a third time, and I became suspicious about her insistence on asking this question.

I started backing up as my mother started walking towards me. She told me to stop moving. "I went to your school today, and you wasn't there!" she yelled angrily. "Where was you?" she asked. I got quiet. I knew there was no way out of this one. "I was in school," I responded. She immediately punched me in the chest, and I flew onto the couch. I couldn't breathe. It was like she knocked the wind out me and my ancestors. She said, "I was at your school, don't ever lie to me!"

My mother began cursing me out. I could not get a word in because she was yelling continuously and rightfully so. She said that I had been doing it for so long that when she went to my homeroom, they didn't even know who I was. Then, she called Wale downstairs and beat him too, just so he wouldn't be like me. Afterward, she dropped her famous line. She said, "Let me find out this again and you going to be living back on Apsley Street with your father."

My mother had gone to my school and found out that I had been cutting school for so long that I had been dropped off the roll for my gym class. She was pissed. That day, I got that ass-whupping of my life. "I went up there thinking that you were doing what you were supposed to do," she added angrily. "And you want to embarrass me?" she continued. "I'm taking yo' ass to school on Monday, and you better go to every class or I'm gonna beat yo' ass in front of everybody. And then I'm gonna sit in all your classes with you. We gonna see who gets embarrassed now," she added. After getting my ass beat for what seemed to be an eternity, my mother sent me to my room. She called my father to tell him what happened. She sent me to my father, where I got my ass beaten again, African style.

When my mother took me to school, she found out that I was cutting classes with Stewart. She knew Stewart from my eighth-grade class. She was not happy. From then on, I was not allowed to hang out with Stewart. But that didn't stop me from hanging out with him or talking to him. Back in those days, we did not have caller ID readily available like everyone does today. So, when Stew would call, he would use the name, James. Sneaky, I know, but he was my best friend, and I couldn't just drop him from my life like that.

The day my mother found out I was cutting school and delivered that epic ass-whupping changed my life forever. The path that I was on was not a good one. Even though the time I spent cutting class eating chicken wings and French fries with salt, pepper, and ketchup were fun memories, it was a one-way ticket to becoming a high school dropout. I had already been dropped from the roll in several classes. It was only a matter of time before I was dropped from the school altogether. Back then, I never thought through the long game. I never considered myself a high school dropout, but in hindsight, that's exactly what I was about to do. God and my mother saved my life for sure.

Afterward, Stewart stopped coming to school to attend his classes. He still would show up just to chill with me. He would let me know he was in school by walking through the hallways yelling or making loud noises. His voice was distinct and unmistakable. Or he would come to my classroom and yell something crazy in the room and slam the door super hard! I would be screaming laughing. It got so bad that he was expelled from the school and was no longer allowed to enter. If he did, I would hear on the radio, "Code red! Code red! Stewart is in the building!" That was always hilarious to me.

Stewart was not all bad; in fact, he was a good guy who, like myself, was dealing with pain of his own. He introduced me to a program in which the school was partnering with an outside agency that would provide a stipend for students enrolled. That program was called Environmental Education Development Program; it was technically my first job. We attended the program with students from other schools around the city. The meetings took place on the Temple University campus after school and in the summer. In those meetings, we talked about all sorts of topics like teen pregnancy, drugs, and other social issues. As usual, Stewart found a way to get himself kicked out of the program. I graduated from the program on my birthday in 1996.

LOOKING BACK

I never went to my junior or senior prom because I didn't believe that any of the girls at school would want to go with the most teased kid in school. I had a crush on a few, but none more beautiful than this chocolate colored sista named Farrah. I knew she liked this kid Jeff from Erie Avenue, so I never asked. Even if I had, I wouldn't have been able to afford a tux or a ride to the venue. In fact, aside from making her laugh, I didn't have much to offer her. As a result, in June 1999, I graduated from high school without that memory.

"80% of success is psychology and only 20% mechanics."
—Tony Robbins

I wanna know who am I and what is my purpose
should I live or should I die
I'm not sure which is worth it
this rap game, am I a legend in the making?
or is it just therapy while precious time is wasting?
I know where I've been but where should I go?
all this time I spent trying yet I've got nothing to show
for the blood, sweat, and tears headaches and depression
I'm still the favorite student for life's cruel lessons
Do I love? or do I hate? or have compassion for others?
Will I help? or will I laugh when I see other's struggle
Am I just a kid from the ghetto with dreams of getting out?
or will I leave this apartment and move into a house?
should I believe when teachers say that I can succeed?
or are they politicians that get paid for the speech?
My identity it seems it's so hard to find
So I wrote out a diary, it just so happened to rhyme
Who am I?

Song: *IDENTITY,* **Artist:** *Me,* **Album:** *IDENTITY, VOL 1.* **Year:** *2004*

CHAPTER 4

COME HOME WITH ME

PHILLY, PHILLY

Where are my manners? I didn't mean to leave you standing at the city limits. After all that talk about my family, I almost forgot to welcome you to my neighborhood. Welcome to Philadelphia, Pennsylvania, a city with so much history and rich with soul. Now, most out-of-towners know us for a few things such as cheesesteaks or the Liberty Bell, which was called the State House Bell until the mid-1800s when it was renamed in coordination with the abolitionist movement. Other things people commonly associate with Philly include the old *Rocky* films and the subsequent Rocky statue standing at the Art Museum located off Ben Franklin Parkway.

Philadelphia is much more than classic sandwiches, cracked bells, and fictional boxing movies. We have REAL boxers like Joe Frazier; Tim Witherspoon; Meldrick Taylor; Danny "Swift" Garcia; newly crowned IBF and WBA Super Welterweight champ at 154 pounds, Julian "J-Rock" Williams; and "The Executioner," Bernard Hopkins who is arguably the greatest middleweight ever. There is even a fighting style that just about every modern boxer copied from B-Hop, the Philly Shell Defense.

There's a ton of talent in Philadelphia; you name the genre, and we have major participants in it. Comedy fans are familiar with Kevin Hart who happens to be from my neighborhood. Michael Blackson is also a popping comedian from Philly, not to mention that he is Nigerian. Do you want hip-hop? Cool, Philly's got you. How do Beanie Sigel, State Property, Cassidy, Eve, and Meek Mill sound? Not into hardcore hip-hop? How about The Roots? Like R&B with some soul? Try Jill Scott, Musiq Soulchild, Jazmine Sullivan, and Vivian Green. What about sports? Philly's lineup includes Rasual Butler (R.I.P.), Wilt Chamberlain, Kobe "Bean" Bryant, Flip Murray, and Rasheed Wallace who graduated from my high school. And, of course, Will Smith was born and raised in West Philadelphia. There is so much talent from Philadelphia that I often wonder what my gifts are.

Here's something out-of-towners might not know. Benjamin Franklin founded the nation's first library, The Library Company of Philadelphia, which was built in 1731. It served as the Library of Congress from the Revolutionary War until 1800. Philadelphia also has the second largest Irish and Italian populations in the US, after only New York. Philly has a huge art presence in the city as well. With over 2,000 outdoor murals, we are sometimes called the Mural Capital of the US.

Here are a few other fun facts about Philly. The *Philadelphia Inquirer* is the third oldest daily newspaper still being published in the US. Philly is also the site of the first organized protest against slavery when the *1688 Germantown Quaker Petition Against Slavery* was drafted. Philadelphia has many nicknames including The Birthplace of America, The City that Loves You Back, The City of Neighborhoods, The Quaker City, and The Cradle of Liberty. Out-of-towners know it as The City of Brotherly Love.

If you are as superstitious as Philadelphians are, then you will appreciate the story of "The Curse of Billy Penn." It was commonly believed that building anything in the city taller than Philly's statue of William Penn would put a curse on the city. So, when the One Liberty Place skyscraper was built in 1987, exceeding the height of William Penn's statue, the curse was born. The curse held until a Penn Statuette was placed atop the new Comcast Center in 2007, restoring Penn as the highest point in the city. Wouldn't you know it, the Phillies won the World Series in 2008. The Eagles won their first-ever Superbowl in 2017 after a 52-year drought. Many other historical people, facts, and events originated in Philly, but I'll leave those for you to discover if you care to do some research.

As Philadelphians, we are prideful, brash, and we give it to you straight with no chaser. We are also a very rough city that gives zero fucks and has absolutely no chill. Let's take the Philadelphia Eagles and Sixers fans, for example. These are **the** most passionate Philly fans. Sixers fans booed Beyoncé and Destiny's Child during the 2001 NBA Finals when they faced Kobe Bryant and the Lakers. The reason they booed Beyoncé was because she was wearing an outfit that had the Lakers logo on it. Do you think they cared that her outfit was a combination of half Sixers and half Lakers jerseys? Nope. Regardless, you gonna get these boos, was the fans' attitude. They even booed hometown product Kobe Bryant because he said he would not take it easy on his home team in the Finals. The guy plays for the Lakers for crying out loud. Was he really expected to let the Sixers win? Philly fans were not to be reasoned with. Catch these boos, Kobe.

Philadelphia Eagles fans threw snowballs at Santa Claus in 1968 and cheered when Dallas Cowboys wide receiver Michael Irvin was carted off the field with a spinal cord injury in 1999. Like I said, no chill. In 1997, St. Louis Cardinals outfielder J.D. Drew had D-batteries thrown at him by fans who were angry that he didn't sign with the Phillies when they drafted him. Still, no fucks given. I was all for Phillies fans booing Jay-Z and Alicia Keys when they were allowed to perform *Empire State of Mind* during the 2009 World Series against the Yankees; that was just disrespectful.

AIN'T NOTHING NICE

I'm from North Philly, specifically the Nicetown section. Please do not be fooled by the name. As Jay-Z famously rapped in his 1997 Marcy Projects anthem *Where I'm from*, "ain't nothing nice." That is especially true of Nicetown. My mother lived in Nicetown, and my father lived in Germantown. I was born in Germantown, another ghetto neighborhood full of gangsters, crackheads, trap niggas, and killers. However, I was raised in Nicetown, which is where my identity began. Growing up, I moved back and forth between both neighborhoods.

"Sitting on my block, all I see is gutters, pipes, and crackheads. Drug dealers, four-wheelers, blunts, and bad kids." Those bars came from the first solo rap song I ever recorded. I wrote this while sitting on my porch observing. A song by Rain 910 may help to explain the environment I lived in, at least on an introductory level. Rain is a member of the battle rap stable NWX, which is a play off the WWF wrestling stable DGeneration-X while merging it with the World Championship Wrestling (WCW) stable NWO. You might not be good at remembering all these acronyms unless you are a wrestling fan or a social worker.

The battle rap mainstay Maybach Music Group artist has a song titled "Who Wants to Die" on his album *A Perfect Day to Die*. I know he was not thinking of me when he made this album; however, both those titles accurately describe the reality and mantra we had to live with in order to survive in Nicetown. I mean, there was never a guarantee that once I left the house, I would make it home safely. The opening lyric of the song promptly yells, "Who wants to die?" followed by a loud scream. Every time I set foot in my neighborhood or on to the porch, I knew the risk that I was taking. See, I grew up around the DDKARNs. That's my acronym for Drug Dealers, Killers, and *Real* Niggas.

One time, Wale and I were on our way to break into the Happy Hollow basketball gym to practice and wait for the old heads to arrive, so we could play full-court with them. That day, the gym had already been opened, and the old heads were already running a game. We opened the gym's front door after hearing the sound of sneakers rubbing against the newly waxed gym floor and the melodic sounds of a basketball hitting the floor. Before we could enter, a guy burst through the door and ran off yelling angrily. What he said was inaudible to me, but I knew he was pissed.

As we entered the gym, I saw that the game had stopped, and everyone was surrounding one of our favorite old heads, Dave. Dave looked like Keenan Ivory Wayans to me; they even had the same shaped head, pause. Dave was a cool guy, and all of us young bulls, which is what young guys are called in Philly, really looked up to him. He was a mainstay at the Hollow and in the community; Dave supported our summer leagues and even gave us spending money from time to time.

When we noticed why people were surrounding him, all I could say was, "Oh shit." Dave was sitting in the paint on the gym floor under the basket clutching his leg, which had a huge hole in it. Apparently, there had been an argument during the game, and one of the DDKARNs had gone for his bag and grabbed his gun—the weapon of choice for basketball players in the hood. "He shot him! Go get some tissues, lil man," an old head yelled. Yep, you heard that correctly—not call the police or the ambulance, go get some tissues. All I remember is hearing Dave scream, but nobody seemed too shocked. There were a few gasps, but for the most part, it seemed like a normal day. That was the scary part. To my knowledge, the guy was never caught; Dave eventually went to the hospital, and the game resumed.

On another occasion, I was walking through the mini-park in Nicetown on my way home from school. I was taking a detour home after walking my friends Vincent and Latifah home as I often did in the sixth grade when I smelled a weird odor. "What the fuck is that?" I wondered. No sooner than I could locate where it was coming from, I tripped over a shoe and found the source of the odor. It was a dead body. This was the first time I saw a dead body; I was 11 years old at the time. The body was that of a boy who looked like he was not that much older than I was at the time. He had been shot in the head.

I never told anyone about finding the dead body because honestly, I was scared. Eventually, someone must have told the police because later that day, there were caution tape, cops, and lights flashing everywhere. On the news, they said it was a random act of violence, but if you are from the hood you know better. I never found out who the boy was; I just knew that I didn't want to share his fate. From that day on, I avoided the mini-park as much as I could.

That's just the way it was growing up. I hate to say it, but it became numbing and at times comical. Like the time I had just bought a brand-new basketball—you know, the $30 leather joint. It was a hot summer day, and I knew everyone would be at the Hollow. I couldn't wait to show off my new basketball. I took it to the playground to get some 5-on-5 going. Out of nowhere, bang, bang, bang, boom, boom! In the middle of the game, a guy from the back section of the park, which we called the mountains, started shooting at someone on the basketball courts. The gunman gave zero fucks that there were kids playing on the court. He wanted to kill whomever he was shooting at.

When those shots rang out, everybody scattered like roaches when you turn the lights on in the middle of the night. If you are from the hood, then you've likely seen incidents like this. Instead of haul-assing away from the gunfire, what did my dumb ass do? I turned around realizing that I had left my brand-new basketball on the court. I ran back towards the courts while ducking gunfire just to get my ball. It was probably the stupidest thing I could've done, risking my life for a $30 basketball. I didn't care back then; getting my ball was that serious to me.

When my friends and I got back to the porch, you think we were traumatized? Nope! Man, we burst out laughing and I mean hard! "Yooo, dude came through bucking shots!" as we continued to imitate the gun sounds that nearly took our lives. We continued to recall the scared reactions that other people had while laughing at their fright. "He was scared as shit! He almost shit on himself! He better check his draws!" I added. Then, I would point at my friend while laughing, "You a bitch," I teased. "No, you a bitch," he teasingly rebutted. If you had walked by us at that moment, you would've thought we were recalling an action flick we had seen recently. That's how "young, dumb, and out of control" we were, to quote the great Melvin in the movie *Babyboy*.

Finally, there was the time I was walking up the block with my young bull, Phil. We were just shooting the shit as we walked up the middle of the street. That's what people in the hood did at nighttime. During our conversation, I vaguely saw sparks flashing around me—one from a van on my right and the other flew from cars on my left. I kept hearing zip sounds near my ears. Not realizing what was happening, we continued to walk and talk.

Do you remember that scene in *The Sopranos* in which Silvio was dining with Gerry Torciano? If not, YouTube it. In that scene, they are eating dinner and talking when Silvio suddenly gets blood on his face. Silvio was unaware of what just happened and didn't hear the gunshot even though it was happening less than three feet away from him. Right before the blood splashes on Silvio's face, there is a deafening sound before Gerry is whacked.

That sound or lack thereof was exactly how it happened as Phil and I were walking in the street. Turns out that prior to us walking up the block, there had been an argument, and a fight that was taking place. The fight was between a few guys from my block and some unknown guys from another neighborhood. Apparently, one of the unknown guys didn't like the ass whupping he was receiving, so he called for reinforcements. That's when a black car with tinted windows showed up on our block. One of the guys in the car hopped out with a gun and started firing; that's where the zip sounds and sparks were coming from.

By the time Phil and I realized what was going on, the guy was letting off more and more shots. Thoroughly aware of the situation, Phil and I began ducking bullets as we ran towards my father's house. When we got there, we began running up the steps, when just like in the movies, someone always trips and falls. Take a wild guess who that was—yours truly. Phil lifted me to my feet as the gunshots continued.

We made it into my father's house relatively safely. I say relatively because once we were inside, we realized how close we had come to being killed. Suddenly, Phil unzipped and opened his pants. My father and I were puzzled about his random display of exhibitionism. That's when we realized that Phil had been grazed by a bullet that passed through my pant leg and into his.

Miraculously, I was untouched, and Phil merely had a minor cut on his leg. Aside from the cut burning him, he was fine after some first-aid. That's just the way shit was in the hood. It was like life lottery; you never knew when your number would be called.

THE PORCH

When I wasn't dodging bullets or finding dead bodies, you could catch me with my friends Brian and Dre chilling on the porch. The porch served as a place for us to avoid getting into trouble, which was debatable. Most of the time, it was where we dreamed up our craziest ideas.

Like the time I got the bright idea to ride our bikes over to Andorra Mall. A month before, I had stolen a black and red NWO Wolfpack shirt from Kohl's. It had been easy. I just grabbed the shirt and put it in my pants and left with no resistance. This time, the goal was to steal some *And 1* basketball shorts. For you millennials, *And 1* basketball shorts were popping back then. They were expensive and something I could not afford, nor would my parents buy them. They would never understand why a 16-year-old boy needed $30 shorts.

The plan was for the three of us to go into the store and separate as we located what we wanted to steal. Dre was down for the plan, but Brian was skeptical. "You sure you want to do this? What if we get caught?" he asked. "Nah, trust me. I did it before. It's sweet," I assured. Brian didn't want any part of stealing from the store, but he rode with us anyway.

When we arrived at the mall, we went into Kohl's, and I began looking for the shorts. Once I located them, I casually grabbed them and stuffed them in my pants. As I made my way to the door, I noticed that I didn't see Dre. Not wanting to make myself obvious, I continued towards the exit. "Excuse me," a voice said. I was not in the mood to stay and have a conversation, so I started to walk faster. I saw a security guard in front of me heading towards the store entrance. That's when it hit me; I was caught. The voice that said, "Excuse me" was a loss prevention worker.

The reason I didn't see Dre was because they had already caught him and Brian earlier. They took me up to the security office where I could see that they had been watching me. That's also where they had placed Dre. They released Brian because he had not attempted to steal anything; he was just there with us. Later, I learned they gave him a warning.

"You two are going to jail!" the security guard said. "We already called the police," he continued. When he said that, my body got cold instantly. I was shook. But I wasn't shook about of the prospect of going to jail. I knew too many people from my neighborhood that were in jail. I was shook because of what my father was going to do once he caught wind of my not-so master plan.

Shortly after that thought, the police came in and put those cold handcuffs on us and took us to the car. I remember thinking that I never thought I would be wearing handcuffs and sitting in the back of a police cruiser. I thought of Femi and all the times he had been arrested and wondered what it was like for him. I never wanted to follow in his footsteps to jail, but I did.

"If you lie, you will cheat. If you cheat, you will steal. If you steal you will go to jail."

—Adegbola Ige

Once we arrived at the police station, Dre and I were placed in a holding cell. We were fed a cheese sandwich with no mustard or mayo and iced-tea with no ice. "I see they want us to suffer," I thought. Dre and I weren't alone in the cell. We were in there with this dirty Puerto Rican kid who wouldn't stop telling us what a gangster he was. In fact, he wouldn't shut up at all. He continued to give us his gangsta resume even though neither of us called him in for an interview. I knew he was a scared little bitch trying to hype himself up to hide his fear. I'm from Nicetown; I know the difference.

After a few hours, I had enough of his talking, and I knew he wasn't a threat to me, so I decided to lie down on the cold metal bench and take a nap. I was awaken from my nap by an officer. When I opened my eyes, I learned that both Dre and the dirty Puerto Rican kid were gone. Dre's mother came to pick me up from the precinct. She said, "They told me they called your father and he said he wasn't going to pick you up, so they said I could take you." Ever-so fittingly, I was the last one to be released. After all, it was my dumbass scheme that got us there. To be frank, I did not want to be released because the real jail was going to be when I got home to my father's house. It was a long ride home.

When I got home, it was around 3:00 a.m. I was prepared for the ass-whupping of the millennium. Instead, my father didn't say a single word; he wasn't even waiting for me when I returned home. He was in his room sleeping. I was on pins and needles, scared to go to sleep. My father was known for waking me up out of my sleep when he was angry. I sat up all night like I was in Shawshank Prison on death row and it was the night before my execution. My father's disappointment was obvious, and the silence was deafening.

The next day, my father told me my fate; he had decided that I would be grounded for a month, which was a far better outcome than I imagined. During my punishment, I felt ashamed. I actually felt ashamed that my father didn't think I was worth the effort of an ass-whupping. Had my father given up on me? Did he no longer care about me? I knew that I had deeply disappointed him because my getting arrested for stealing came out of left field. I wondered whether he would ever be proud of me again. After several days passed, I decided the best thing that I could do was write him a detailed letter apologizing for what I had done and promising never to do it again. To my surprise, he accepted my letter and eventually forgave me. It was all that I longed for.

About a month or two later, I had to go to court for shoplifting and trespassing. I went to court alone because my father decided that he would no longer be involved in any criminal processes for us. It was something that he would not support. Who could blame him? I told the judge that I made a poor choice out of financial desperation and that I have learned my lesson. I promised the judge that if he was lenient on me, he would never hear from me again.

Fortunately, the judge showed leniency. Since it was my first offense, the judge ordered that I could have my record expunged if I attended an anti-crime class and paid a fine of $80. After completing both tasks, I decided that I was never going to be in that situation again. That first offense was going to be my last offense. Shout out to that judge for giving me another shot at life.

VIDEO GAMES

When I wasn't cooking up schemes that could risk my freedom and shame my family or playing basketball, I was playing video games. Video games have always been a big part of my life. It was the safest way for me to be creative and use my imagination. Like most kids born in the 1980s, I started out with Nintendo and *Mario Brothers*. I eventually moved on to Atari, Sega, and eventually PlayStation. What really connected me to video games was the ability to be creative and dream.

I started to live in my dreams once I started playing basketball video games. It was a way for me to play basketball long after my parents called me in for the night. The game that inspired me the most was *NBA Live '96*. What was so important about that game was the addition of the "create-a-player" feature; it was the first time that I could remember being able to play in the NBA as myself. I got to see what my last name, Ige, and my favorite number, 21, would look like on an NBA Jersey. *Live '96* allowed me to live out my every athletic fantasy.

Being a kid with a crazy imagination, I didn't just create a player, I created backstories and mantras. The character I created was from Philadelphia and had attended college at UNC Chapel Hill where he had to fight to earn a spot on the team as a walk-on. He idolized Michael Jordan's basketball prowess and wanted to break all his records. I gave my player a backstory of not feeling accepted by his community and having fractured family relationships. The rage he carried translated into a competitive nature, and he became the greatest player of all time. The character was inducted into the Hall of Fame and was finally accepted by his peers. If you haven't guessed yet, I literally made me and the person I dreamed of becoming.

I felt seriously empowered when I played. I got to create my own narrative, and I wanted to share it. After messing around with an old VCR or video cassette recorder for you millennials, I figured out a way to record my games. Previously, I had to bring my PlayStation and TV to the porch to create moments in real time. Then, I was able to show my friends some of the most epic moments, dunks, and crossovers that I handed opponents in the game. They were just as excited about the plays they saw and even more excited about the ability to record the game we all loved. It was thrilling. It felt real—so real, that I felt it needed to be a part of the game.

Though *NBA Live '96* was an excellent video game, I saw potential for even more greatness that could be added. One day, I decided to expedite the evolution of the game by sending some ideas to the developers. In 1997, when I was about 16 years old, I wrote a six-page letter to EA Sports about all the things that would take the game to the next level.

The letter talked about adding features to record gameplay and the ability to rewind moments from the game. I talked about adding a story mode to the game because that's what I always did in my mind when I was playing it. I also talked about adding Air Jordan's and other popular sneakers to the game because I spent so much time imagining my created player wearing them in-game. Fast forward to 2018, all the things I was doing back then and wrote to the developers about are now intrinsic in gaming, including video capture. I was ahead of my time. Though I got no money from my suggestions, I like to believe that I had a part in the changes.

Now, an overly optimistic person would have just been satisfied with how great a game *NBA Live '96* was. They would have enjoyed the experience for what it was without a second thought. They would've thought of me as a pessimistic person for seeing "what's wrong" with the game. However, I am a realistic person, and I dare to question. I acknowledged that the game was great, but I also had a vision for more and, as it turned out, so did EA Sports. I learned from that experience, that I am someone who has good ideas and vision, and I also learned that if I put my mind into something, I can create change.

BACK TO THE BULLSHIT

During the time I played video games on the porch with Dre and Brian, there was always a bunch of things going on in the background. If there wasn't a fight, a loud argument, or gunshots on the block, there were more subtle events happening.

Take the Jehovah's Witness who frequented our block, for example. Now, before I get into this story, keep in my mind that my mother is a Jehovah's Witness. This particular guy was a short light-skinned black guy with glasses and a mustache like Ned Flanders from the *Simpsons*. At the age of 15 and 16 and being as silly as we were, just seeing him caused us to erupt in laughter.

I can't recall the guy's name for the life of me, so let's call him Joshua. Joshua is a biblical name, so I think that's fitting. The thing that always bothered me about Joshua was his relentless approach to seek me out. I mean, this guy would walk right past the houses where people were selling drugs, prostituting, and smoking weed to tell me that I needed God. I never doubted that I needed God, but in my mind, I didn't need God more than the crack dealers, pimps, and prostitutes on my block.

Joshua made it his mission to save me from going to hell. He would show up regularly no matter how many times I politely declined his evangelism and offers to attend his church. He wouldn't accept no for an answer. After a while, it became very disturbing, and I felt like he was stalking me. It got to the point that Dre, Brian, and I kept an ongoing lookout for him, so we could avoid him because *no* was clearly a word that he was not interested in understanding.

In true juvenile fashion, we turned it into a game that lasted all summer long. We decided that as soon as we spotted him, we had to find a hiding place and whoever got discovered by him had to sit and talk to him. Many times, we hid in my backyard or in the vestibule of my father's house as we peeked out of the mailbox waiting for him to leave. He would knock on the door, and we would be laughing so hard nearly peeing on ourselves trying not to be heard. It was pure hilarity to us until he became bolder.

He started coming to my backyard while we were playing basketball. That's right, he caught us slipping one day. I asked him angrily, "What the fuck you doing in my backyard?" I never liked being interrupted during competitive moments. "Get out of here, dude," I continued while holding the basketball in my left hand with Brian guarding me. It wasn't until I threatened to call the police on him for trespassing and harassment that he stopped coming around. I felt bad for threatening to call the police on him, but I had been telling him that I was not interested in becoming Jehovah's Witness all summer.

THOSE GUYS

By now, you can tell that the porch served as a social hub for my friends and me. Most of the time spent on the porch was split between playing video games, bitching about our parents, telling inside jokes, or, one of our favorite activities, observing the crackheads in our neighborhood. It was where we'd have serious conversations about what was going on in the world or laughing about the time we got arrested. That's right, it was funny to us. Even though we know how serious it could've gotten for us, we still laugh about it to this day. Back in those days, I felt somewhat invincible, and I suspect my friends did as well. Even though I was a naïve and silly kid, I still had my limits.

Although I was a silly knucklehead often finding my way into trouble, I knew I never wanted to be one of *those guys*. By *those guys*, I mean the drug dealers, killers, and drug users around my way. There were always things about them that repulsed me, even at an early age. According to them, wearing dusty Timberlands, riding around in their wack ass Pontiac Bonneville with audio systems that sounded terrible, and having rims that cost more than the car was balling. They thought smashing overweight prostitutes was getting bitches. We would always laugh at them and make constant inside jokes at their expense. Even as an 11-year-old kid, I knew those guys were playing themselves. Thanks to my parents, I knew those guys were the exact opposite of what I wanted to be in life.

Don't get me wrong, we had some very big-time drug dealers moving weight in the neighborhood. Most of them wore expensive jewelry, owned small hood stores, and drove expensive foreign cars like Range Rovers, Benzes, and even Porsches. When they weren't wrecking our community by selling drugs that destroyed families and homes, they gave back to the neighborhood in other ways. Many of them sponsored and coached the youth basketball teams in the neighborhood. If you saw the movie *American Gangster* in which Bumpy Johnson gave out turkeys and food for Thanksgiving, it was similar to that.

I was cool with some of the big-time drug dealers even though I had enough common sense not to get too close. I knew anything could happen at any time, like the time Brian and I were chilling on the steps at Dre's house. Out of nowhere, a black car with dark tinted windows came speeding through the block. A window was rolled down halfway, and we saw a gun poke out the window. Before we could get away, the driver started firing at us. I got hit three times in the back and Dre got a couple of shots in the arm. Once we were hit, we realized they were shooting bee-bee guns at us. Brian was so shocked and scared that he did not know which way to run. Instead, he stayed in place and kept turning his body left and right trying to figure out where to go. It was hilarious. I never saw anyone freeze like that before.

The driver was one of the big-timers around the way that we were cool with; let's call him Sticky. Moments like those were funny and very much worthy of conversation on the porch, but they could have been real moments in which a rival drug block came to shoot up the competition. If those bee-bees had been real bullets, all three of us would've been dead. I never wanted to be like the dealers in the hood because I knew that their lifestyle was going to end with them either in jail or dead. I couldn't see myself living with the paranoia of a rival block wanting to rob or kill me and having to avoid the police at the same time.

TIME ON OUR HANDS

About 1997, I came up with another crazy idea on the porch when I convinced my friends to start rapping. Dre used to fantasize about rapping over dope beats, and Brian always wanted to be in the background. Now, for three 15- and 16-yearolds, such aspirations were normal in the hood. What was not normal was why we were rapping. We decided that we would sneak diss these girls on our block that we felt spent too much time around the bum-ass nickel and diming weed pitchers in the neighborhood, like I said, we had too much time on our hands

We needed a reason to write raps; it wasn't like we were getting money or selling drugs. They became the perfect excuse. What really birthed the idea to focus on the girls was the fact that Dre used to date one of girls' cousin. Dre and the girl broke up because she ended up letting another dude that we know beat them guts, that means to have sex if you are not from the hood. Naturally, Dre was salty. I didn't mind doing the song, because I really didn't like them. I thought one of them dressed like a fake ass Foxy Brown, and the other tried to imitate everything Lil' Kim did. I called them Foxy Clown and

Lil' Him. Corny, I know, but I was 16 years old; it was the best I had at the time.

We managed to save our allowances to buy blank cassette tapes and a tape recorder. Dre already had a record player with tons of records that he got from his father. We bought instrumentals from a store called Sounds of Germantown, which no longer exists, so that we could rhyme over our favorite rapper's beats. There you have it; we had a makeshift studio.

Before we began recording, we chose our rap aliases. My name was Jonny Storm after my favorite *Fantastic Four* character. I identified with him; his superpower was to burst into flames. I connected that with my ability to turn my game to another level when I got focused on anything. Brian chose Professor X from the *X-Men*, as he was the musical guy behind the scenes. And Dre chose to use the whack name Drama, which was an accurate depiction of his saltiness towards his ex-girlfriend. To be honest, all of our names were whack.

We recorded in Dre's room. The recording process was fun. I went to my porch to write my verse for our first song that we performed over The Roots song "Respond/React" from their *Illadelph Halflife* album. I wrote my verse pretty quickly. It was tailored to Dre's complaints about his ex-girlfriend, and I was taking the role of his friend backing him up. Dre took hours to write a 12-bar verse. It took him so long because he was focused on finding an opening punchline. Ironically, once he had finished his verse, it had absolutely nothing to do with his ex-girlfriend. It was a bunch of random bars and lines with punchlines about nothing but guns and machetes. Instead of redirecting him to stick to the topic he presented, we were just happy that we could start recording. Immature, I know, but we **were** very immature. We were petty gang before it became popping.

Brian was not able to come up with a verse and didn't see himself as a rapper. So, I decided to write the hook and have him say it, which was pure comedy.

The chorus went: *"We retaliate, we bomb first. You fucking with the worst. We just the best, don't get stressed. The real shit, Apsley. Don't even fuck with us, our attitude is straight fucking nasty. But fuck the bullshit. You don't know who you fucking with. All that peace talk shit could suck my big fucking dick."* That chorus is terrible—nothing but a bunch of F-bombs and phrases that make no sense. None of it had anything to do with Dre's ex-girlfriend either, I might add. But hey, we were teenagers. It made sense to us.

What people don't know about Brian is that he has a very explosive temper. I mean, Incredible Hulk-like. What made the chorus so funny was Brian's delivery. During rehearsal, we all recited our parts. Brian consistently sounded so robotic as he pronounced every syllable. Dre and I would be laughing at him as he recited the chorus. We kept correcting him until he was able to stay on beat. The more we corrected him, the angrier he got.

When we started recording, we knew that we had to complete it all in one take. We didn't have a sophisticated studio. We just had a blank cassette tape, a radio, and a tape recorder. The radio played The Roots instrumental while we held the tape recorder close so we could rap in real time. The problem was it took more than one take to complete the song because we were amateurs. Recording the song was a long process, even after we were comfortable with our verses, mainly because of Brian. The closer he got to the end of the hook, the angrier and louder he got.

Brian said, "*We retaliate, we bomb first. You fucking with the worst. We just the best, don't get stressed.*" He said those lines perfectly. Then he instantly got angry, probably because he knew we were laughing. His voice gradually escalated. *The REAL SHIT! APSSSLEEYY!!* He continued. *Don't even fuck with us our attitude is STRAIGHT FUCKING NASTY!!* At this point, I was holding my stomach and covering my mouth because I was laughing so hard. *Fuck the Bullshit!* He said with a high-pitched voice.

It was one of those epic moments that you had to be there for. Listening to him say the hook had us laughing so hard we started crying. So much so, we had to hide in the closet while he performed it. It was really that funny. Luckily the tape recorder had a pause button, so we could finish laughing and regroup between takes.

After making a few corny records like that one, we mustered up the courage to play them outside. We would bring the tape recorder outside waiting for the girls to walk past us. As soon as they did, we would play the song as loud as we could. After realizing what we were doing, they began to avoid walking past us.

Once people on my block caught wind of us making raps about those girls, there were rumors that they would be making a record about us. We were preparing for an epic battle of songs. In our immature teenage minds, this was the moment we hoped for. Unfortunately, what happened was not what we planned for.

One day, they saw my father coming out of the house he had been renovating and began talking to him. It turned out that they were not going to make a record about us and participate in our immaturity. "You think they are bitches?" my father asked in his Yoruba accent. "You think they are dick-eaters or like to eat dicks all day?" he confronted. "No, Dad," I responded. Apparently, they heard the lyrics clearly, which means they told him exactly what I said. My father demanded that we apologize to the girls. What we were doing in good fun was hurting their feelings, who would've thought? We were too self-indulgent and self-centered to consider that possibility.

I was not happy that one of the girls told my father; I felt that she snitched on me. I was still sorry for hurting their feelings though. However, that didn't stop the three of us from getting some good laughs at the questions my father asked when he confronted us. We spent the rest of the week laughing at him asking if we thought those girls wanted to eat dicks all day. It's just not the sort of thing my father would say. It was hilarious to us. We were 15- and 16-year-old kids with too much time on our hands, what can I tell you?

After the fallout from the diss songs, we continued to dabble in music. We would take some of Dre's old records and speed them up or slow them down to rap to. Our favorite record to speed up was Average White Band's "A Love of Your Own." That record was complete FIRE. We never got around to recording a song to it, but we would listen to it daily. Hip-Hop wise, it had so much potential.

AROUND THE WAY GIRL

In times of boredom, we would sit on the porch and fantasize about the best-looking girls in our neighborhood. We would name certain girls and rank them. "Would you fuck so and so?" I would ask Dre. Most of the time, the answers were unanimous yes. So, we decided to make the game more interesting and choose the girls we thought were not so attractive and ask the same questions. We knew the answer would be no, so I decided to spice it up a bit just for fun.

"What about if she was the last girl on earth and a deranged guy had a Rambo knife to your nuts?" I'd ask. Depending on the girl, the answer could still be no. That would tell us all we needed to know about the girl. You don't have to tell me; I know we were mean misogynistic scumbags. Like I said earlier, we were bored and horny teenage boys. Sadly, it was normal behavior at the time.

There was this one girl who lived at the end of our block, who at the time, we thought was the baddest girl on the planet. She was beautiful and voluptuous. We all had a crush on her—I know I did. We knew she was out of our league though. We used to wait all day until she would come outside and head to the store for her mother. When she came strolling up the block, we all watched in amazement. It was like the sun always hit her just right.

Remember that scene in the movie *Friday*, when we first saw Ms. Parker, and everybody stopped in their tracks to stare at her? That's what it was like for us. No chaser, we were all thirsty for her. We would sit on the porch for hours trying to figure out how to get her number. The thing is, we were all afraid to just ask her. We were all afraid that she would shut us down in the most embarrassing way. We were three broke and dirty little boys from around the way; what did we have to offer? Therefore, we were reduced to talking about what we would do to her and what we would sacrifice for her.

One day, I decided to say, "Fuck it," I'm going to shoot my shot in the best way I knew how. So, I drew her nickname in graffiti letters and filled them in with pretty colors. I waited for hours to see her walk up the block. When she finally started walking up the block, my heart started pounding like the biggest earthquake ever recorded was happening in my chest. I couldn't even swallow spit. I was shook. But fuck it; I promised my boys that I would hand deliver the picture to her.

So, I got on my bike and met her about halfway up the block. She looked shocked that I was approaching her. What a coincidence because I was also shocked that I was approaching her. I greeted her as I would usually do but up close this time. I was mesmerized, but I couldn't walk away like a sucka, or I would get clowned by Dre and Brian forever. After all the tough guys shit I was talking to my boys, I had to make a move.

I handed her the picture I made for her. She smiled and said thank you as she accepted the drawing. I would love to tell you that I asked her for her phone number and that she gave it to me. I would love to say that we got together and lived happily ever after, but that is definitely not what happened. After she accepted the drawing, she continued her mission to the corner store. I was so stunned that I had completed my task and that she accepted it, that I forgot to ask for her phone number. It's not like she would've given it to me. Like I said, I had nothing to offer her. However, just giving the picture to her was a win for me. I felt like a legend instead of a failure because I was the only one with the balls to approach her.

Fellas, you know how the hot chick in your teenage years tends to let themselves go later on in life? Nope, not her. She is still just as fine as she was back then, even after having a child and gaining a few pounds. Today, she is a God-fearing woman with a promising career. Salute to her for taking great care of herself over the last 21 years. Today, we are Facebook friends, and she probably doesn't remember any of this, but I do.

MY CITY

I love my city and I would not want be from anywhere else in the world, other than Nigeria where my ancestors originated. Even though I am passionate about my city and love the memories, I always knew that my growth would be limited if I stayed. I always had a hunger for new places, new experiences, and new challenges. If I was going to grow into the man that I wanted to be I needed a way out.

CHAPTER 5

MY FIRST LOVE

The one place where I felt like I belonged was on the basketball court. It was the only place where I felt completely and utterly at peace. It was like all the noise of the world stopped for 90 minutes at a time. I wasn't worried about what I was going to eat for dinner or whether I was going to be shot on the way home or whether my mother was going to be admitted to the hospital that day. The basketball court was the one place where I felt totally focused and had my strongest ambitions to improve. It was also the place where I felt that I had the most control in my life. If something went wrong on the court, I always had a chance to change the course of the game if I made the right move or play. If I made too many mistakes, I'd reflect while sitting on the bench watching my opponents' tendencies to figure out what I could do better the next time.

DIGGING IN THE CRATES

I was eight years old when I was introduced to the game of basketball. I saw a group of guys playing on the bottom side of Dennie Street, around the corner from my mother's house. They were playing a pick-up game, using a basketball rim that they had stolen from a local playground. They had taken the rim and brought it back to the block to nail or screw it into a tree—an example of hood ingenuity. The game was intense and competitive, and I knew I wanted in.

Even though I wanted to play, I was nervous about going into a game that I had never played against a group of older kids who had probably played their whole lives. For whatever reason, I was able to put that fear aside and enter the game. If this were the movies, this would be the point where out of nowhere, I would realize I was a child prodigy. The scene would be in slow-motion as I caught the ball, squared up my opponent, and took him to the basket for a score, while some corny music played in the background.

Since this isn't the movies, I'll tell you what really happened. The guys were hesitant to let me play because I was so much smaller and younger than they were. These guys had to be about 13 years old. I was only able to enter the game because one guy quit after a bad call, yelling, "Y'all fucking cheating, that wasn't no foul." When the other guys didn't agree, he just left the game. Fortunately for me, I was the only other person around. I was happy to be picked to play with them even though they didn't have another option. "Youngbul, you got him," one guy instructed. Your job is to make sure he doesn't get the ball or score. He continued, "Ok?" I agreed.

Once the game started, I was excited, but I wasn't nervous. For most of the game, I was ignored on offense and defense. The guy I was guarding never scored and when he got the ball, he would just pass it to a teammate. It wasn't because of my stellar defense; I think it was because they thought it would be unfair to take advantage of me.

I was able to make one basket, but it didn't feel like luck, though it very well could have been. Making that shot was exhilarating. Although it wasn't a defining or game-winning shot, it was a confirmation that I should dedicate more time to get better at this game. My team ended up losing the game, but I won something much more valuable, confidence.

I wanted to duplicate the feeling that I had while playing in that game. When I got home, I found the closest thing to a basketball in my mother's basement. It was a green ball made of semi-hard plastic and did not bounce. I am not sure what game that ball belonged to, but it was now a basketball for me.

Using a saw that I found in the basement, I cut out the bottom of a milk crate to create a basket to shoot the ball into. There was no tree or post for me to hang the crate, so I used the laundry rope I found in the basement to tie the crate to the front door of the basement. There it was, my very first basketball hoop. I shot the green ball into the crate for hours that night and every day after.

Eventually, I convinced my mother to allow me to nail the crate to the tree in front of her house. I used a loose sheet of wood for the backboard and attached the crate to the tree. In no time, I was playing basketball in front of my mother's house with my friend Esau. Esau was a Hakeem Olajuwon fan. Olajuwon was great no doubt, but I preferred Michael Jordan. I figured if I was going to get better at this game, then I needed to study the absolute best player available.

When I wasn't practicing or playing with my friends, I went to the local library to get VCR tapes of Michael Jordan in college and in the NBA. I was interested in learning everything I could possibly learn about basketball. I also borrowed a book that taught the fundamentals of basketball, and I was more than happy to soak up all that juicy knowledge.

NEW KID ON THE BLOCK

As I mentioned before, I was too busy being a knucklehead and class clown to go out for my middle school's basketball team. However, every day after school I was studying and playing the game. I would play basketball until my mother called me in for the night. Once I was in the house, I continued reading the book about the fundamentals and shooting in the basement.

Basketball became such an obsession for me that my mother took notice.

She used to say, "My son is going to be a Sixer." I loved that she took notice and believed in me enough to plant the seed of basketball as a career goal. Little did she know that my goal was to train myself to become Michael Jordan's replacement on the Chicago Bulls. Not that I would've turned my nose up at a chance to play for the Sixers, but I wanted to outdo Jordan in his own house. Also, I spent so much time watching him and the Bulls that they became my team.

After one of my mother's visits to the hospital, I moved to my father's house when I was in the sixth grade. My father picked Wale and me up in his dark grey Peugeot. As we arrived on Apsley street, I noticed a group of kids playing basketball with a crate. I was amazed to see that someone else thought about using a crate for a basketball hoop and that there were kids that loved the game as well.

After quickly moving my items into my father's house, I begged him to let me go outside to play with the other kids. My father was very reluctant because he knew the kids and their families. If my father had his way, I would stay in the house all day reading books except for going to school or the library. Not that anything is wrong with learning, but I was 11 years old, and it was not about that. For me, it was all about basketball.

My father finally relented, and I got into the next game. This time, I was ready to play and had acquired some skills. I had come a long way from being an eight-year-old novice, and I was playing with kids in my age group this time. I immediately identified the alpha player on the court, which was a tall skinny kid named Kyle. Coincidentally, I ended up on the opposite team from him, and I took the challenge very seriously.

That basketball game is also where I first met Dre. When I entered the game, I was picked to be on his team. "My name is Kunle," I said while reaching for a handshake. "Kool-Aid?!" Kyle responded as his teammates laughed. When I looked at him, my eyes must've felt like laser beams. "Kunle," I corrected. "Yo, I'm just playing with you," he responded. This guy doesn't even know me and is trying to make fun of my name, I thought. That's when I made up my mind that I was not only going to take this challenge seriously, but I was going to kill him in this game.

The crate was low enough that he and I were both able to dunk the ball. That seemed to be all he wanted to do. He was very frustrated playing against me because I was his size and had many ways to attack him. I also guarded him better than he was used to. One thing that stood out about me versus the other players was my ability to shoot the ball. When I didn't get to the basket, I was able to make shots from most places on the court. I could tell that none of them put in the amount of work that I did to practice shooting. I dominated that game, and the other three games afterward.

THE CONFRONTATION

After the game, I made my first enemy, which was none other than Kyle. He did not like that he had been shown up in front of his friends and the drug dealers who had been watching the game. For some reason, he thought it was a good idea to challenge me in a different way. He started talking shit about my name, calling me a fake Jordan, and he threw a ball at Wale. The ball barely missed Wale.

When I saw him throw that ball at Wale, I lost it. I ran up on him pushed him hard enough to knock him back for what seemed to be about 10 feet. "I'm from Nicetown," I told him. I could tell in his eyes that he did not want the smoke I was ready to give him. After being teased in elementary school, I refused to be bullied. He backed away mumbling under his breath as the other kids separated us.

Kyle was from Greene Street which was right around the corner from my father's house. He always hung on Apsley Street, so he was considered to be from the block. In fact, he was more accepted on Apsley Street by the other kids than I was even though I had been born on Apsley Street. "They have more seniority than you," a drug dealer once told me. Like I said before, we moved into my mother's studio apartment when I was six years old. Prior to that, my father made sure we stayed in the house all the time.

As the years went on, Kyle and I had some epic battles on the court. Most of the time, my team beat his. I suspected that he was angry towards me because he was no longer the best player on the block. Between another kid named Ryan and Kyle, I always had to chump somebody for talking too much shit or messing with Wale. I guess this could be considered paying dues, but I just wasn't for the bullshit. I always felt like they wanted to be something that they weren't, which is a tough guy and "cool" like the *real niggas* around the way. But for Ryan, that image was quickly diminished before it started. I don't know what this next event was about, but when it happened, I could not stop laughing.

THE PUNCHLINE

I was sitting on the porch later that day when I noticed a guy walking angrily down the block. He was headed towards Ryan, and I could tell that shit was about to get real. Ryan looked stunned to see the guy. After one or two words that I was too far away to hear, BAM! The guy punched Ryan in the face out of nowhere. Ryan turned around crying as he walked home. Instantly, I started laughing! I was laughing so hard, I couldn't breathe. In the hood, shit like that was funny.

Ryan obviously told his father what happened, as his father came walking up the block with no shoes on and some knee-high tube socks. As Ryan and his father walked up the block, I was laughing even harder. Their goal was to confront the guy who just fired on Ryan. The guy was already gone by the time they reached the top of the block. He had already accomplished his goal; there was no reason to stay. In my mind, that was further confirmation that Ryan wasn't about that life. In Nicetown, you don't get punched in the face and then go get your father.

Ryan and Kyle were trying to be something they weren't. They were always trying to be "cool" and trying to impress the drug dealers in the hood. Think I'm exaggerating? Well, a few years later, Kyle was shot to death in a park in an alleged drug deal. Rest in peace Kyle.

PRACTICE MAKES PERFECT

After that game, Dre and I became good friends. We both shared a passion for basketball, so we decided that if we were going to make it to the NBA, we needed to practice. Since neither of us could afford a coach or a basketball camp, we decided to create our own basketball drills. I knew that I shot the ball well, so I wanted to focus on my dribble moves.

We didn't call it a crossover back then. We used to call it a "cut-up," which was a series of dribbles designed to confuse the opponent. I spent hours working on my in-and-out dribble, behind the back moves, and what would eventually become known as a crossover. We practiced every and all day in the summers. After school, I would take my book bag off and continue practicing.

When Femi saw me working on my dribble moves, he said, "You better work on that jump shot." "What's wrong with my jump shot? It goes in," I retorted. "Your form is terrible," he rebutted. "You shoot with two hands," he continued. Femi teased that most of the shots I made were bank shots, meaning that the ball hits the backboard before it goes into the hoop.

But my reaction to Femi's criticism could be accurately summed up in the words of JC, the battle rapper: "Why criticize the form if the shot is perfect?" I didn't care what my form looked like as long as I made baskets. To further make fun of my form, Femi started calling me "Ten Fingers." I ignored his taunts for as long as I could. Then, one day, while playing at the Hollow, I noticed my fingers spread as I released the ball. I made the shot, but all I could hear in my head was Femi teasing me: "Look at them 10 fingers" is what I heard over and over on the way home.

On the way, I stopped at a corner store to pick up Gatorade, and as fate would have it, I spotted an issue of *SLAM* magazine with Michael Jordan on the cover. I wanted to read the article, but I didn't have the money to get both the Gatorade and the magazine, so I stole the magazine. I know I shouldn't have stolen it, but that magazine changed my game forever.

In the article, Jordan talked about growing up poor with hardworking blue-collar parents. He talked about the work ethic he learned from his mother and father. He even talked about his favorite snacks when he was a kid: a honeybun and grape juice. I even learned that his favorite singer was Anita Baker. I had many things in common with Jordan. We had the same favorite snacks, and we loved the same music. I loved Anita Baker and had been in love with Toni Braxton since I was 12 years old. I'm sure many other people shared those similarities but having them with Jordan was amazing; I literally wanted to be like Mike.

While browsing the magazine, I looked at the many posters. As I looked at stills of Michael Jordan, I noticed the placement of his hands prior to shooting the ball. Jordan had the exact hand placement that I read about in my fundamentals of basketball book: his left hand on the side of the ball at the nine o'clock position and his right hand behind the ball with his elbow pointed towards the basket.

Other posters in the book showed him releasing the ball, which clued me in on how to follow through after shooting. Since Michael and I are right-handed shooters, I copied his form exactly. No more shooting the ball as if it were a medicine ball, no more "ten fingers." I put in hundreds of hours with thousands of shots to perfect this technique until it became second nature. Even when I didn't have a basketball in my hand, I would practice the form in the mirror to make sure it was fundamentally sound.

Using mirrors to practice my moves became a routine whenever I saw a mirror. Whether I was in a grocery store with my parents and looking at my reflection in the freezer section door or in a department store, dressing room, or bathroom, it didn't matter. I would practice my dribble even when I didn't have a ball. I called it the air dribble—sort of like that scene in *Above the Rim* where Shep was in his own world on the court by himself playing with no ball.

As a middle schooler, I walked the hallways, down the streets, and in stores pretending to crossover strangers who had no idea they were in my game. Wham! Wham! Those were the sounds that I made with every crossover move. Stewart often asked, "Why you always think you in a basketball game?" I explained, "The goal is to be prepared for any awkward movement a defender could make against me as I am trying to score." I also used my mirror practice to see what defenders saw as I tried to outwit them. I wanted to see what clues I gave defenders about what I intended to do to them. Basketball was very cerebral for me.

HOOPLA

If you haven't noticed already, I have always been a late bloomer in just about every aspect of my life. What I lacked in early experience, I prided myself on outworking my competition. If that meant an extra three hours on the court per day, then that's exactly what I would dedicate myself to doing. There was no room for complacency or procrastination, especially in sports.

Most kids started playing basketball and were in leagues when they were five or six years old. I was 15 years old when I played in my first basketball league. To give more context, at my Nicetown elementary school alma mater, games were played in a basketball league for kids aged 15 and under. I knew I was skilled enough to play, but this was my first time playing organized basketball.

The most uncomfortable thing about playing in the 15 and under league was that I was among the tallest players for the first time in my life. I grew up playing against people larger than me, and I patterned my game after a shooting guard. My thoughts of getting to show off what I learned about my natural position were quickly confronted with an uncomfortable reality. Coach Tony had other ideas; he wanted me to play center.

Coach Tony had never saw me play before. The league teams were chosen via a drafting system, which wasn't necessarily in my favor. All the coaches and players in the league lived in the same sections of Nicetown. They knew each other and had a good idea about who could play and what they could do. I was coming from Germantown after moving back to my mother's house. Therefore, he had no idea what my strengths were. Regardless, I was drafted to *Hoopla*, which was our team name.

I had never played center before, and it showed in the first game. From the sideline, I'm sure it looked like I had two left feet. As a natural wing player who could slash to the basket, I felt like my brain was on backward starting from the paint and flashing to the foul line. It was much more difficult for me to get into a rhythm and get a feel for the game. This league thing was going to be a lot more difficult than I anticipated.

On top of those challenges, I was constantly heckled because of my name and being Nigerian. As jokes were made about me, the entire gym would erupt with laughter. The goal was to intimidate me with jokes and threats from the tough guys from the hood. After all, I was playing with and against the very same people who teased me in elementary school. But I would not be deterred. I was experienced with being in a hostile environment, and my goal was to use all that negative energy to exact revenge on whomever we played. I wanted to make a statement, but first I had to conquer this new position.

While I was struggling to acclimate to a new style of play, Wale who was also on the team, struggled with never getting to play. To his credit, he came to every game and was enthusiastic throughout even though he rode the bench. He was 12 years old, playing in a league dominated by 15- and 16-year-old kids. Yes, we had a couple ringers in our league, but everyone was trying to get a competitive edge.

The best part about being challenged to play center was that I learned the importance of rebounding, which is another metaphor that translates to real life. Things are not always going to be comfortable. Life will not always go the way you would like, but you must be able to grab the ball of life and be ready to start again. That's the way I understood rebounding. In the same sense, you must be willing to ask for and accept help in order to allow yourself to see the game properly, which is how I viewed passing the ball. Over the course of that winter, I eventually hit my stride. Once I got comfortable, I began to use my creativity to make plays.

One of the turning points in the season came when the opposing team was in a full-court press. Both of our key ball handlers were being heavily guarded; therefore, the ball was inbounded to me. This was my moment to show what I could do. Once I got the ball, I felt completely comfortable and in my element. By getting the ball early, I was playing the guard position, and someone was going to pay.

I pushed the ball up the left side of the court quickly. I passed the first defender by switching the ball from my left hand between my legs to my right hand. I heard the crowd say, "Oh." After getting past the first defender, I was met by the second player who intended to trap me at the half-court line. The second guy's name was Vincent, I remembered him from elementary school.

What Vincent didn't know was that I had already anticipated what his defensive assignment would be. In the few seconds before he approached, I thought about all the possible ways to beat what he was trying to do. I felt like Dr. Strange in *The Avengers*. The scenario had already happened in my mind, and I knew what to do.

As he approached me from a perpendicular angle, I noticed his mistake. I quickly put the ball between my left leg from my right hand. I saw his body jerk towards my right side. Immediately, I faked as if I intended to go left. As he shifted towards my left hand, I immediately crossed the ball over from my left to my right hand, Tim Hardaway style. Vincent fell to the floor and rolled out of bounds ending up at the feet of the crowd. Everybody in the gym went crazy! "Oh shit," I heard the onlookers yell. "Yo, he fucked him up!" yelled another.

When I made it to the basket for the lay-up, the crowd exploded again. It was pandemonium. It got so crazy in the gym that we could barely hear the coaches' instructions or the referees. The game was stopped for a few minutes until everyone calmed down. I was loving it! It was a play that I will never forget, and I'm sure one that Vincent would like to. By midseason, moments like that set me up to be a starter in the all-star game.

COMING OF AGE

After the Vincent crossover, people started to look at me differently. I noticed they had more respect for my game, even though the heckling continued. A few games later, we faced our toughest test of the year to that point. We were going against the league-leading scorer a kid named Messiah Reames and his undefeated team. I went to school with his older brother, Omar. Messiah was about 13 years old and averaged nearly 30 points per game. He was also on a team full of guys who were very popular in the hood, which meant that I would be fighting the crowd more than ever. Most people feared him and his team, but I welcomed the challenge.

When we played them, it was an unexpectedly close game even though most people expected us to get blown out. They figured that we would succumb to Messiah's star-power and scoring ability. Every time they were getting a big lead, I would elevate my game, and my teammates followed. We figured a team approach would be the best way to beat one man. Messiah went off for at least 20–25 points, I don't know the exact number, but I know he was killing. I had about 15 or 16 points in that game, but we got the win, which was all I wanted.

As I mentioned before, I was voted to start in the all-star game for the east team. As fate would have it, Messiah was the star player for the west team. I expected the game to be super competitive, but I was wrong. It was a fun game that was played very light-heartedly, just like in the NBA. I enjoyed the game because I was not getting heckled as much. Messiah and I even exchanged some laughs as we playfully challenged each other in the game. I took this to mean that I had earned respect.

Hoopla advanced through the playoffs and made it to the championship. Do you care to guess who our opponent was? Yep, you guessed it, Messiah's team. This was the game where they wanted to exact revenge against us, the team that was not supposed to have stopped their undefeated streak. I still thought people felt like our team wasn't supposed to be in the championship, but I liked being an underdog; it gave me a point to prove.

THE REMATCH

From the very first tip-off, I could tell that they were tasting revenge. They were playing defense more aggressively than they had in the first game. They played us very physically, and we were ready for it. On every defensive possession, Messiah yelled, "Press! Press!" This game was intense. They wanted to prove that the first game was a fluke. I knew they wanted to take our hearts, but I was not about to relent.

Just like the first game, they went on some good runs, but we always fought our way back. The game was so close towards the end that the players on Messiah's team started getting frustrated at any call that didn't go their way. One kid named Lavar got so angry at a foul call that he began yelling at the referee, which earned him a technical foul and an ejection as he continued his rant. At the time of the non-shooting foul call, we were down four points with about 35 seconds left on the clock.

By rule, every technical foul gives the other team two free throws. Since Lavar earned two technical fouls, our team was awarded an opportunity to tie the game with four free throws. Guess who coach Tony chose to shoot the free throws? Yep, he chose the most heckled player in the league. As I approached the free throw line, I remember thinking this is the moment I had been waiting for. The other team tried to distract me, but I felt relaxed.

I stood alone on the court just as I often practiced. As I prepared to shoot the first free throw; Messiah and his teammates were standing on the sideline with their arms raised while making a loud and consistent sound. "Ahhhhhh," the sound gradually got louder and louder as I raised the ball to shoot. Once I made the first free throw, I knew we were going to tie this game. I made the next three free throws, and now we have a nail-biting game with 30 seconds left on the clock.

Messiah's team got the ball and wanted to hold the ball for one shot. As the clock winded down to about 10 seconds, they took their shot, missed, but the player was fouled. Messiah's teammate missed the first free throw. Coach Tony put Wale in the game because he had not played in any game for the entire season, and he wanted to reward him for continuing to come to the games. After Wale entered the game, the other team made the second free-throw. Now we were down one point. Coach Tony called a time-out.

I wanted to take the final shot so badly because I was already in rhythm, but coach Tony had other plans. Coach Tony wanted me to be the one to inbound the ball. I took the ball out and was able to run the baseline. We were covered intensely by the other team. The gym was so quiet you could hear a mouse pissing on cotton. Coach gave a hand signal for Wale to run to the other team's side of the floor in order to spread the defense out. Fortunately, nobody on the other team saw Wale. It was either that or they did not consider him to be a scoring threat since he had never played in any games.

Once Wale got to the other team's three-point line, I threw him the ball without a second thought. Everything felt like it was in slow-motion. It seemed like 10 years passed before the ball got to Wale. When Wale caught the ball, he took a few dribbles towards the basket as the time ran down. We were all on pins and needles. Wale went for a lay-up off the backboard. He made the shot AND got fouled. The crowd erupted! My whole team went crazy! It was like when Tom Brady threw the ball to Randy Moss for their record-breaking touchdown or when Malcolm Butler intercepted Russell Wilson at the goal line to win Superbowl XLIX.

After he made the shot, I stood there with my arms out as Wale ran towards me. He jumped in my arms as I carried him with his arms raised. In the most unthinkable turn of events; Wale had won the game for us. It was his only shot of the season and ironically the most important. Yep, the same kid who sat on the bench for the entire season, my brother. That moment was incredible because I got to share it with my little brother and win the championship on a play between the two of us. By now, you've probably heard of the "Philly Special" play the Eagles ran against the Patriots in Superbowl LII. Well, our play was the "Ige Special."

BASKETBALL ON THE BLOCK

Bringing that trophy home gave me a huge confidence boost. It was like a fulfilled prophecy in a fairytale. I carried that energy into every game I played. That meant the games on Apsley street got more intense. Every 2-on-2, 3-on-3, and especially 5-on-5 was the championship in my mind. Over the years, we played hundreds of games, too many to document.

The rivalry on Apsley street continued in the same way that it started. It was always the "cool" kids versus the outcasts. Kyle, Ryan, and Brandon were the cool kids. Dre, Brian, and I were the outcasts. Fortunately for us, we took basketball more seriously than everyone else on the block. Therefore, we won most of the games we played. Where I shined the most was in one-on-one games. Now, this may sound I'm giving myself a big ole pat on the back, and I can understand that perspective, but it's true. I almost never lost a one-on-one game, no matter who I played. I always had a point to prove.

I remember playing in a one-on-one game against my old head, we called Smoke. He was a first cousin to collegiate and NBA player Jerome "Pooh" Allen. Smoke was a great player in his own right; obviously, he grew up in a basketball family. In our one-on-one game, I was not going to be denied. No matter, how or where he guarded me, I scored. Jump shot after jump shot layup after lay-up. I could see that he was stressed as people from the block watched. Finally, he exhaled and said, "I cannot stop this dude. He's going to the league." Hearing that from my old head whose cousin was an NBA player was a huge confidence boost.

MANIAC

I did not have to wait long for the next challenger. Following the game between Smoke and me, Maniac decided that he did not like me beating Smoke. Maniac was known in the hood for certain extra-curricular activities. Without saying too much, let's just say he was considered a "real nigga." He was such a "G" in the hood that he had a nickname off his nickname, some niggas just called him "Ac." Most people were afraid of him in ways that had nothing to do with basketball. He had a reputation.

"You ain't shit," Maniac said. "You think you good, but you not," he continued. "You think you could fuck with me?" he asked. He even bet me

$100 that he would beat me in a game of eleven by ones. He wanted to play make-it-take-it. Never being one to back down from a challenge, especially as **everyone** on the block looked on, I accepted his challenge for a one-on-one game.

His game plan was very clear as soon as we checked the ball. He took it out first. Maniac was at least twice my age and easily outweighed me by a hundred pounds. It was like Shaq playing one-on-one versus Allen Iverson. As expected, he was posting me up by backing me to the basket and muscling his way for a score. I would love to tell you that I just shut him down, but that would be a lie. My goal was to play the best defense I could and try to make him miss a shot.

After scoring three or four times in a row, he eventually missed. I got the rebound, something I learned to do while playing as a center in the Nicetown league. I knew I could not let him have the ball again if I was going to win this game. I knew I was faster than he was, so my game plan was to make him expend energy by lateral movement.

The game plan worked well as I came back from a five-to-nothing deficit to lead eight to five. Maniac had a counter game plan, however. He decided that for every basket I scored, the harder he would foul me. Eventually, he decided to play dirty, pushing me onto the concrete as I went for a lay-up. When I called foul, he became angry and approached me as if he wanted to fight me. He gathered the rebound to take the ball out for his possession. Maniac continued his offensive assault, this time throwing elbows and pushing me on his way to the basket. I could tell he was angry that he could not stop me from scoring.

I continued my defensive game plan while thinking about how I could use his anger against him. He scored a few more times making the score tied at eight all. I got another rebound. "He is not getting this ball again," I promised myself. After I made two consecutive jump shots, it was game point, and I had the ball. He was pissed because his pushing, shoving, and verbal threats were no longer working. I could feel his anger.

Suddenly, Maniac was all over me trying his best to stay with me. Pushing and shoving to keep me in front of him. He was in desperation mode because there was a hundred dollars on the line in a game that he provoked. I knew he was going to foul me harder than ever if he got close enough to me, but I had a plan for him.

I backed up three steps which forced him to have to close the gap between us. With the ball in my left hand, I switched the ball between my legs to my right hand. I took a step to the right to create even more space, which he angrily and aggressively tried to close. Noticing his energy, I gave him a half crossover to my left hand and put the ball back in my right hand after going between my right leg. You follow so far? Neither did he. He took an even more aggressive step towards my right hand like I knew he would. That's when I hit him with the best crossover of the day, and everybody went crazy!

If I told you that Maniac went flying up the street would you believe me? He slid so far that he was completely out of my sight, literally. "Yo, he broke his ankles!" someone yelled. I drove to the basket and scored the game-winning lay-up. That's when everyone jumped up from the steps and went crazy again. Completing the play always drew cheers.

After the game, the only white kid who lived around our way approached me. His name was Elvis. Yes, people, I knew a white kid named Elvis in the hood. "I knew you were about to do something nice! I could tell," he said. Shortly after that statement, everybody came over to congratulate me, and Maniac was salty. Everyone was talking about and reenacting the crossover that I had just slain him with.

Me being the savage that I am, I asked him for the hundred dollars that he had bet me. "Take it from me!" he challenged. "You ain't getting shit," he added. I just laughed at him; I knew he wasn't going to pay his debt. Maniac got so angry that he threw the basketball at me! The ball missed and hit a nearby thrift store building. I laughed even harder, and that's when he reached in his pocket. I didn't know whether he was reaching for a gun or the money. Either way, I took off running. We all took off running. His nickname was Maniac for a reason.

What I knew that he didn't know was that because he outweighed me, it would be harder to stay with me in lateral movement. Everything I did in the game prior to the crossover was setting him up for that move. He helped me create that opportunity by being aggressive and angry. That play was a perfect example of letting hate kill itself. I used his negative energy against him, without developing negative energy of my own, a perspective I later practiced in all areas of life.

HIGH SCHOOL BASKETBALL

In high school, I had a very tough time making the team. I went to Simon Gratz High School in Philly. During my high school years, Gratz, as we called it, was the most dominant basketball school in Philly. I can say that without even a hint of bias because it's a fact; ask around. We were the New England Patriots of high school basketball in Philly.

We had the greatest high school basketball coach in the city, Coach Bill Ellerbee, and he was a master at the game. He demanded excellence from his players, starting with academic achievement. He was a very tough coach who played no games and gave zero fucks about your status or ego. Coach Ellerbee just wanted well-conditioned and intelligent players who knew how to follow instructions. If you want a more nationally recognizable coach to compare him to so you can understand the type of man he was, Bill Belichick.

In the history of Gratz, many great players graced the court including Aaron McKie and Rasheed Wallace who played in the NBA at the highest levels. Rasheed Wallace has held a basketball camp at the school every year since he made it to the NBA in 1995. The legacy of great players did not stop once I got there my freshman year. We had top-tier players on the Simon Gratz Bulldogs basketball team like Marvin O'Connor, a 6-foot-four shooting guard who went on to play for St. Joseph's University. Outside of Gratz, Marv is best known for dropping 37 points on Stanford University in the 2001 NCAA tournament, which were the most by any player against Stanford since Damon Stoudamire scored 45 on them in 1995. Marv also dropped 18 points in one minute against La Salle University.

Although there were great players on the team, believe it or not, that wasn't my biggest challenge. Most of the difficulties in making the team were not even about my game. The biggest challenge was my attendance in school or lack thereof and my immaturity off the court. I'll share a quick but true story that encapsulates my immaturity at the time.

THE SUBSTITUTE

One day during my freshman year of high school, we had a substitute teacher in Mr. Mortimer's World History class. The substitute for the day was a middle-aged mildly heavyset black male with thick glasses and a low fade haircut. He had a Pastor part in his hair—you know, the part in his hair like that of the great Louis Farrakhan. He wore a tight, light blue short-sleeved collared shirt and a pair of dark blue equally tight dress pants.

Anyway, this guy was our substitute for the day. In my high school, like most, when there is a substitute teacher in a class, it is full-on license to act a complete fool. I was more than happy to join the fun; in fact, I led it. I was jumping out of my seat, yelling loudly, and making jokes about our substitute teacher's appearance. "Yo, his pants so tight it looks like he painted them on," I yelled as the classroom erupted in laughter. "Look at his thick-ass glasses," I continued. "With them shits, he could count each one of my blood cells." When I wasn't making jokes about the substitute teacher's appearance, I was sitting on top of the desk and talking shit to my friends.

Everyone was acting obnoxious in the classroom; however, I noticed the sub kept staring at me with a look that felt like he wanted to catch a fade. A fade is a fight in hood terms. Eventually, he decided he had enough of my comedy routine. "You come here boy," he said with an authoritative voice. I began looking around the room to see who he was talking to. "You— I'm talking to you," he responded as he pointed at me. As I approached the desk, he asked for my student ID. I didn't mind giving it to him because he was a substitute teacher. The best he could do was write my name down and leave it for Mr. Mortimer upon his return. I didn't care.

When he saw my name, I noticed a sly smile on his face. I didn't understand what that smile meant. I thought he was about to make fun of my African name because I had been joking on him all class period. Then, he returned my student ID card and shook his head. It wasn't until later that I learned what his smile was about.

Later that night, my father told me that he had met one of the basketball coaches at my school the night before. He said they were both in a bar called Genesis in Nicetown, a place my father frequented. He said he happened to overhear that the guy was a coach on the team and decided to put a word in for me after talking with him. My father knew how much I loved basketball and how hard I worked at it; he told the coach that I was a player worth looking at and giving a shot.

Even after my father told me that story, I still wasn't putting any pieces together. To me, one thing had nothing to do with the other. It wasn't until I went to tryouts weeks later that I saw the substitute and people calling him coach. When I made eye contact with him, I thought my brain was going to explode. Suddenly, I cared. What kind of example did I set for myself and my family? There is no way in hell I am going to make this team now, I thought. I went on to play the worst game I ever had. I couldn't make routine shots and passes or make my presence felt on defense. I was too busy being worried about the negative impression I had made. After tryouts, I felt like I embarrassed myself twice once in the classroom and then on the court.

SUMMER LEAGUE

A few days after tryouts, I learned that Coach El was a math teacher at the school and also worked in the roster office. That means he knew about me cutting classes with Stewart all that time. Once I learned those things, I started to think that his presence as the substitute for my class was no accident. Here was God trying to give me everything that I wanted, even going as far as to have my father meet Mr. El organically in a space where he could discuss my love of the game. Silly and immature me screwed it all up. The embarrassment plagued me so long that I decided not to try out in the tenth-grade. I knew I had some growing up to do.

After my tenth-grade year, I decided to go out for the Gratz Summer League basketball team, which was governed by Mr. Ellerbee but not necessarily coached by him. The team featured all the players from the regular season. In order to make that team, I had to participate in a team sports conditioning program, that usually consisted of running track or playing another sport.

Coach Ellerbee was savage. Part of our conditioning to get prepared for the season was to run cross-country, which usually included running from the high school campus to the Belmont Plateau after school. We ran from

North Philadelphia to West Philadelphia, which was about 19 to 20 miles. Some days, we had to run back and practice after the run.

"It's raining hard outside," a teammate observed in hopes that we would be able to skip the run for the day. You think Coach El let us take a break on rainy days? Nope! "The faster you run, the least amount of raindrops will hit you," he responded. Pure savagery. I loved that about him. He set a standard that if we wanted anything, it was going to be hard fought until we get it.

I only played in one or two games, one of which was a blow out, which Gratz often did to their opponents. The players who got the most playing time were those who had been developed through the system since ninth grade. I was basically a walk-on. The second game I played in was coached by Mr. El, and he put me in the game in the fourth quarter. By that time, I had come to every single game on time, and I never complained about not getting any playing time. I was just happy to be in a space of discipline and basketball.

It was nearing the end of the summer, and finally, my number was called. "You, get up. You are going in next dead ball," Coach El said as he pointed in my direction. I was so excited. I mean too excited. Once the referee blew the whistle signaling a stoppage in play, I ran onto the court like Forrest Gump when he saw Jenny. "Hey, Hey come back here," Coach El said. I thought he had changed his mind about me going into the game or that I was delusional and that he wasn't pointing at me in the first place. When I got back to the sideline, he had a question for me. "Do you even know who you are going in for? he asked with a slight laugh. Seeing him laugh was about as rare as seeing Bill Belichick laugh. I laughed too because I forgot to even ask; I was just so excited to be put in the game.

On the first possession after I entered the game, I decided that I was going to play better than I had in tryouts a year earlier. I didn't know the plays for our team because as I said before, I was a walk-on who had not grown up in the school's basketball system. Our center, Brandon, got the ball from an inbound play nearing the three-point line. I decided to set a pick for him and rolled off to free us both of defenders. My instinct proved correct. After I rolled away from the play, I was wide open. Brandon who was now double covered for a split second passed me the ball all alone on the left wing of the three-point line. I promptly gathered myself and shot the three-ball.

It went in— nothing but net. It was the only shot I took all summer, and it got my name in the high school sports section of the newspaper. However, the assistant coach, Rolland, was not happy with the play because it was not a part of the system. At that moment, I could care less; the shot was a form of redemption to me. Later that summer, we won the summer league championship; it was the second time that I was part of a championship team.

With the momentum of being part of the Gratz summer league team, I decided that I was going to try out for the varsity team during my eleventh-grade year. I knew I was facing an uphill battle, but I decided to work extra hard on my game all the way up until tryouts.

THE BABY BLUE

Mr. El was known for traveling the city in a light blue van. We called it "the baby blue." After the summer league, I noticed Mr. El riding through my neighborhood more often. I don't know whether he drove through prior to meeting me or I was just noticing once I met him. Either way, it seemed like every time he drove by, I was at Happy Hollow playground practicing on my game. When he noticed me on the court, he would beep his horn as he passed by.

One day after a blizzard, I went to the Happy Hollow playground because I wanted to work on my game. However, the gym was locked, and eight inches of snow had covered the outside basketball courts. That day, I was not going to be deterred; I went home to get my father's shovel so that I could clear the snow off the court. It took me about two and a half to three hours just to clear half the court.

While I was about 75 percent done clearing the snow, I heard a horn beep. It was Coach El passing through. I waved at him and continued my mission. A few guys from Zeralda Street saw me shoveling the snow and said, "Yo, he going to the league." Those were some very encouraging words. I stayed at the court for another three hours practicing shooting. By the time I got home, my hands and feet were numb, but it was a good workout, nonetheless.

BELLFIELD AND LAWNCREST

Coincidentally, it was a good look for Mr. El to see me working so hard at getting better, and I felt encouraged. I wanted to show Mr. El my discipline and desire to get better. I learned from friends at school that Mr. El ran the Belfield gym, which happened to be about 10 minutes from my father's house. That's when I decided that I would be going to Belfield after school and on the weekends to get more exposure.

If I was going to make the varsity team, it was going to be through hard work, something I was willing to do for something that I loved so dearly. I began doubling up on my organized basketball play. I was playing at Belfield during open gym after school and playing in Lawncrest league in Northeast Philadelphia.

At Lawncrest league, which Dre introduced me to, I averaged 32 points per game, which led the league in scoring. It was at Lawncrest that I got my first dunk in a game on a regulation-sized basketball goal. The league had a no-dunking rule because they did not want to risk injury or having the backboard shatter. Therefore, if we dunked or grabbed the rim, it was an automatic technical foul, which awarded the other team a chance to shoot free throws and possession of the ball.

One week, the owner of the league was on vacation. Before our game that day, I went over to the game referee and asked him a question that I have never forgotten: "Ref," I called as I approached. "If I dunk in this game, are you going to call me for a tech?" The referee laughed at me. "If you get a dunk in this game, I will not call a tech," he answered. I guess he thought I couldn't dunk because he had never seen me attempt one. I knew that I could do it because I had dunked on other regulation courts, just never in an organized game. I decided to show him.

About midway through the game, I got a steal by playing the passing lanes, and we were on a fast break. I knew this was my opportunity. Once I got to the foul line, I pick up my dribble after two steps and took off. I slammed in a one-handed tomahawk dunk, and the gym went crazy! The game was stopped briefly because of the madness. I thought it was just for the dunk. It wasn't until later that my friend Dre told me that I dunked on someone. To this day, I don't know whether he was just gassing me up or not.

I never saw the other player; I was just laser-focused on getting off that dunk. I tell that story about the dunk because it was an epic moment in my basketball experience and something that I always dreamed that I would do, but on a bigger scale.

After the game, I went to the ref and asked him what he thought. "Holy shit!" he responded. "I didn't think you were going to really do it. I thought you were just blowing smoke up my ass," he continued. Though blowing smoke up his ass sounds suspect, we laughed about it anyway. For weeks, all people could talk about was that dunk, and that added another conversation to our porch gathering. I felt like a king.

What about the rest of the season, you ask? In the semifinals, my team lost to my friend Brian and the yellow team despite my season-high 40-point performance. They ultimately won the championship. In that championship game, Brian put on an epic performance that we still refer to this day. I was so proud of him. Perhaps that story will appear in another book.

Though most of my highlights came during the Lawncrest league games, it was Belfield that helped me move one step closer to my goal of making the varsity team. The hard work I put in on the basketball courts paid off, and that's what got me into my high school's summer basketball program after my tenth-grade year.

Over the summer, I also participated in the Rasheed Wallace basketball camp held at my high school gym. Former NCAA and NBA great Rasheed Wallace played for Coach Ellerbee. My junior year was my first time enrolling in the camp.

Being at a basketball camp was new to me. It was a very fun experience; the room was full of ballers looking to take their game to the next level, exactly where I always wanted to be. During the camp, we played in an intramural league. A teammate, Cornell, and I were the stand-out players during the camp; we were on opposite teams, and we had some epic battles. Throughout the camp, we took turns scoring 20 or 30 points against each other.

DIFFERENT LEVELS TO THIS

Once the intramural league concluded, Cornell and I were selected to the all-star team. The camp all-stars were selected to face the camp counselors; that meant we would get the opportunity to play against Rasheed Wallace. This was the moment I was waiting for. I was getting ready to test my skills against a proven NBA talent.

At tip-off, I was immediately guarded by Rasheed. One thing I noticed was how much taller he seemed on the court than he did standing next to him throughout the camp. I mean, he took up a tremendous amount of space on the court. I started mentally calculating how I was going to attack him and trying to determine how much space I would need to create to score.

After a few possessions of not shooting the ball and trying to learn his tendencies, he decided to back off about three to four steps from his tight coverage. That's when I decided that I was going to get my opportunity to put in some work. I got the ball on the wing of the three-point line and jab-stepped him. He barely moved. To create more space, I dribbled the ball towards him. As he backed off, I decided to take a step-back three-pointer, which was one of my favorite shots. Upon releasing the ball, Rasheed jumped to block the shot. Instead of blocking the shot, he caught the ball from midair. I was shocked. That's when I knew playing against NBA talent was a whole new level of skill and athleticism. It didn't stop me from attacking him though.

On one play, I managed to catch him leaning with a right-to-left crossover, which made the gym go crazy. He must not have liked that. As I drove towards the baseline on the left side of the court, I knew he would be ready to block my left-handed lay-up. I decided to use the rim for protection by opting for a reverse layup. Once again, his athleticism and size proved to be the deciding factor of the play. He reached both of his seemingly endless arms to block my shot.

Each time he blocked my shot or got the upper hand on a play, I learned something. I was more than happy to take in the lessons. Eventually, I managed to score a few jump shots over him, which were a boost to my confidence. Truthfully, he probably wasn't playing at NBA level. He just wanted to let us know that getting to his level was going to take a lot more work. We ended up losing that game to Rasheed and the camp counselors, but it was a very fun and informative game.

At the conclusion of the camp, there was an award ceremony. Although there was no most-valuable player award, I got the next best thing. I won an award that best defined my approach to the game of basketball—the most cooperative and most coachable player award. The prize was a trophy and one of the brand-new Nike Sports duffle bags, which were popping back then, and all the athletes rocked them. The bag was filled with school supplies. From that day on, I carried that bag with me wherever I went.

BULLDOG TRYOUTS

It was my twelfth-grade year and my final chance to make the varsity team. All the time I spent training over the past few summers was about to be put to the test. I came to the tryout ready to go and to show out, and that's exactly what I did. In that game, I had about five rebounds, two steals, and four assists. I only took four shots in the game, and I made each one of them. I remember each shot because that's how focused I was. It was like recording a live game using DVR. My first score came after stealing the ball from another player and getting a lay-up. The next score was on a fast break outlet pass from my teammate. My second shot was a jump shot from the three-point line, and the next one was a lay-up after crossing over a defender. I was very proud of my effort, and I was confident in my chances of making the team. I had to wait until the following week to learn my fate.

After a week of anxiety and barely sleeping, the team roster was posted at school. I searched that list five times looking for my name. Maybe they misspelled my name, I thought. The reality of being cut was devastating. I was crushed for the rest of the year. Especially, while watching us lose to Benjamin Franklin High School in the Public League championship that year. I know I could've helped our team win.

A month or so prior to graduation, I was called down to the roster office. When I arrived, I learned that I had mail, and Coach Ellerbee handed me the envelope. This was not just any mail; it was a scouting and recruitment letter from Ursinus College, a Division III school located in Collegeville, Pennsylvania, about 45 minutes outside Philly. I was puzzled because it was completely unexpected. I had never heard of the school and had to put two and two together to understand how they heard of me. Apparently, Coach Ellerbee called the coach and let them know that I would be a good player for their school.

Coach Ellerbee saw my reaction and pulled me aside for a conversation. He said, "It's very difficult to make this team. Especially, in the twelfth grade." I felt triggered and traumatized by the conversation because it was like reliving being cut. The conversation turned when Mr. Ellerbee offered more insight about why I didn't make the team. He explained, "Your basketball skill is not the reason that you did not make the team. You were good enough to play on the team, but I did not add you to the roster because you did not know the plays and had not grown in the system." I understood what he meant, and I felt relieved by the conversation because I spent most of the year feeling as if I was not good enough to play on the team. I needed that understanding because it offered closure and hope.

> "Through basketball I found my superpower. My superpower wasn't in being a great player, but in loving something enough to work hard at being better."
>
> —Kareem Abdul-Jabbar

COLLEGE BOUND

I met with my high school guidance counselor, Ms. Rowe, to discuss the next steps after high school. "What college would you like to attend?" she asked. "The University of North Carolina at Chapel Hill," I responded. After she looked at my grades, she told me it was time to set realistic expectations. My grades and SAT scores were not high enough to be admitted to UNC. I understood her point. As an alternative, she presented me with a packet of Historically Black Colleges and Universities (HBCUs) to which I could apply. The packet contained an application and a personal statement section. I only had to complete one application, and all the schools listed in the packet would be able to either accept or reject my application.

Fortunately, I got accepted by several of the HBCUs. I was offered a full scholarship by Florida Memorial College; however, I did not want to attend that school because they gave everyone at my high school a full scholarship. I wanted college to be a new experience, a place where I could grow. I did not want to attend Simon Gratz 2.0. In hindsight, however, attending Florida Memorial would have made the most sense financially.

Over the summer, I waited for the other HBCUs to either accept or reject my application. Letters came to my father's house one at a time. I received acceptance letters from Delaware State University; Cheyney University; Virginia Union University; Fisk University in Nashville, Tennessee; Southern University in Baton Rouge, Louisiana; and Virginia State University. I was very excited and happy to be accepted by these schools. Attending college had been a dream of mine since I was a little kid even though I tried hard to destroy those dreams with several stupid decisions. My dream was about to become a reality, but I had some serious decisions to make.

CHAPTER 6

HAIL STATE

THE DECISION

I remember arguing with my father all summer long about wanting to attend college out-of-state. His stance was that if I were away from home, I would be away from my support system. He wanted me to go to Temple University, his alma mater. My father was justifiably worried that if something were to happen, it would be difficult to help me because of the distance between us. I wanted to become a man. My argument was that I needed to spread my wings and see what I could do on my own.

Temple University is in the middle of North Philadelphia. I knew that if I went there, it would be hard for me to focus. I knew too many people who lived in the area. I also wanted to get out of Philadelphia because I had never been elsewhere. I knew that if I stayed in Philadelphia, I would get easily distracted as I did I high school. I wanted to be one of those students who went away for college; I wanted to live in the dorms and have a full collegiate experience. I was confident that I would come back home more experienced and mature.

Once Femi caught wind of the conversation, he said, "Virginia?! You want to go live on a farm?" I thought the statement was ignorant, but it showed the mentality of Philadelphians. We tend to think Philly and its surrounding areas are the center of the world, but I never thought that way. I was always willing to travel, especially after my father won tickets to Kings

Dominion one summer by playing shuffleboard. He and his friend could not go because they were finishing a construction job, so he sent Wale and me in their place. We had a blast!

I could not consult with my mother about my college choice because she was in an in-patient hospital recovering from an episode. Not having her involved in these conversations was devastating to me especially since her intervention during my high school years is what made college a reality for me. I took solace in knowing that she would be happy that we are even having these conversations. Even though she could not participate, her presence was definitely felt. My elder cousin Peach represented her by buying me a bedding set from Ikea to take with me.

After wearing my father down or his taking a "we'll see how this works" approach, I finally chose my school: Virginia State University. I made the decision so close to the deadline that classes were almost ready to begin on August 29, 1999. I had never visited any of the universities that accepted me; I had not attended any orientation visits because we were unable to afford the travel expenses.

Venturing to a new state where I would be living was both exciting and anxiety- provoking. To be honest, I was extremely thrilled to be going off to college and more importantly going to live on my own. I was a full-blown adult or so I thought. All the years of me telling my father that I was an adult and that I could take care of myself were finally going to be put to the test. What did this reality have in store for me?

I remember packing all the things that I was going to take with me to college. I had never packed for a one-way trip prior to going to college; we did not have enough money for suitcases or duffle bags, so I placed all my belongings in trash bags. I also had a huge chest that I bought from a local thrift store, which stored even more items. I packed everything! I did not want to take the chance of needing something and not having it available to me. It wasn't until later that I realized that I would never use most of the things I packed.

HIGHER LEARNING

The day finally arrived for me to leave for college; it was August 20, 1999, my birthday. My father drove Wale and me to 30th Street Station in downtown Philadelphia for me to take the Amtrak train to Petersburg, Virginia. Wale, who was 15 years old at the time, was beginning to tear up because I was leaving. Who could blame him? It was the first time we had ever been apart; he and I had done everything together. Maybe he thought I would never come back, or perhaps he was wondering what he would be missing out on. I promised to call home as often as I could; it was a promise I intended to keep.

When I boarded, I remember my father handing me a brown paper bag full of condoms. I took that as a green light. I remember the train attendant looking at me strangely because of how ridiculously I packed. We informed him that I was going off to college. He, an African American male, was more than happy to support the journey. Luckily, there were a few empty seats on the cars where I could place my excess bags.

"All aboard!" Once I heard that, I knew it was real. I said my goodbyes to Wale and my father as the train took off. I was headed to Petersburg, VA, to attend Virginia State University. I couldn't help but wonder what they were feeling; I felt both excitement and anxiety on the train ride. I had no idea what being without my family would be like. My life was literally and figuratively flashing before my eyes as I embarked on this new journey. I was thinking about every moment that led up to that day as I traveled from state to state, stopping for quick meals.

Six hours later, the train stopped at the Petersburg station. I had finally arrived. There was only one problem; I had no idea where the school was located. I had never visited. There were no attendants at the station to ask for directions. Even if there had been, how was I going to get all six of these trash bags and a huge chest to that location? There were signs along the train station advertising taxi cabs. Lightbulb! I called a yellow cab and informed them of my destination and that I would need one with lots of space. A cab came shortly. As I began to enjoy the ride and notice my surroundings, the cab came to a complete stop. I was puzzled. "You're here," said the cab driver. We had driven across the street; the school was visible from the train station. Had

I gone to orientation, I would have known where the school was. Instantly, a lesson was learned.

I began unloading my belongings from the cab. I noticed many students were coming and going to different locations. Everyone was moving in and trying to get situated. It was just like I'd seen on TV; parents were helping their kids navigate their college environment. But I was alone, left to figure things out on my own. I stopped a school official to tell them of my situation and inquired about where I would be housed. He instructed me to go see someone in the Student Life and Housing department.

Once I arrived at the Student Life and Housing department, I informed them of my situation. After waiting in a line for what seemed like an eternity, I was informed that I needed to go to another department before they would be able to fully assist me. They sent me to Admissions, who sent me to the Registrar Office, where I was informed that I was enrolled but that I had several holds on my account. The kind woman also informed me that I would be able to take care of all the financial aid affairs during *Validation*, which was starting on the following Monday.

Eventually, I was placed in Williams Hall, which was a male-only dorm at the time; I was placed in the basement in temporary housing. The room held about 10–12 bunk beds for students in similar predicaments. The purpose was to give us a place to stay until our financial affairs were taken care of and we were officially assigned a dorm. I didn't care about being in temporary housing; I had made it! I knew there was going to be a lot of running around from office to office to get my financial aid and other matters taken care of, but I had faith that it would all work out.

Over the weekend, I used that time to explore the campus and get more familiar with my new home. I was able to eat at the cafeteria, *the cafe* as it would be later known, because I had temporary paperwork. After meals, I sat on University Avenue or *the yard* as we called it, which was located in the middle of the campus. There were so many new types of people that I never encountered before, and they were all in social cliques. There were the people from New York, Washington DC, Tidewater, and various other places.

It was interesting to see how each group dressed and interacted among themselves. I mean, this was my first time living anywhere outside Philadelphia; it was a spectacle for me. I could tell that many of them knew each other prior to attending VSU. It was the first week for freshman, and they were already so familiar with each other. I remember thinking, "I don't know anyone here. I'm going to have to make some friends." There were so many women—I mean beautiful women, everywhere! I never saw that many beautiful women in one place at one time.

That's when I knew I was going to love this school.

VALIDATION

Eventually, Monday came—the big day when I was going to get all my financial aid and housing issues addressed. It was time to attend the validation process, which was taking place in Daniel Gymnasium. I woke up bright and early and arrived at the gym by eight o'clock in the morning. As soon as I walked in, I was handed a number, which coincided with my last name, and I was directed to the appropriate waiting section of the gym. I was assigned to the upper bleachers, and I knew it would be a while before I was called. It was time to get this done no matter how long it took, I thought, so I sat and waited with my paperwork in hand.

While I was waiting, I was looking at the various stations and layout of the validation process. I was watching other students and their family members navigate the system. I remember thinking, "This looks very confusing and overwhelming." The whole design looked like a huge maze. I watched people get good news about their statuses, and I saw people get bad news. I was becoming anxious as I wondered what my fate would be. To distract myself, I began observing people sitting in my section. I noticed a guy sitting in front of me with a huge sweat stain on his back; he was wearing a plain blue T-shirt. The sweat stain looked exactly like the Wu-Tang Clan's bird logo. I was laughing so hard at the thought of what Brian and Dre would say if they were here.

I continued observing the gym when I noticed a guy who had just entered the gym approaching from my left. He was making direct eye contact with me while he was moving through the rows like someone who forgot to get popcorn at a movie theater. I remember thinking, "This guy looks just like Nas," referring to my friend from high school. I could not get a clear look at him as people were standing up and sitting down to let him through. As he got closer and his face came into focus, I was pleasantly surprised; it was Nas. That's when I knew it was going to be on!

Nas, who arrived at the school 10 days earlier to report to football camp, said, "What's up, yo?" I think he was just as shocked to see me as I was to see him. I remembered him telling me in the last month of high school that he was going to attend Virginia State, but I never took him seriously. Most people talk about going to college shortly after graduation and seem excited about where they were going to attend. For one reason or another, very few of them follow through.

Once he sat next to me, we made small talk about how long we had been at VSU. We talked about our impressions of the school so far and most importantly the women. Nas assured me, "You ain't seen shit, yet. Wait until you see the Woo-Woos," referring to the school's most famous cheerleaders. I showed him the guy with the Wu-Tang logo-shaped sweat stain, and we both started laughing hysterically. I felt so much better going through validation with my boy from high school.

Our conversation was interrupted by a woman's voice: "163 through 173," she said loudly. Finally, our numbers were called. We were summoned down to the gym floor to begin the validation process. We held sheets of paper that cataloged our student account information including the discrepancies, such as having a financial balance, housing status, and various other holds.

The validation process was very confusing for a high school semi-dropout turned graduate like me. This was my first encounter with handling my own business. As I moved through the lines for what seemed like an hour in each line, I learned that this college enrollment thing was not going to be as easy as advertised. After talking to the various school office representatives at the end of each line, I learned many things.

In one line, I learned that I was not able to get a school ID because there were several holds on my account. In another, I learned that I would not be able to purchase books. I also learned that I would not be granted room and board. So, that temporary room I shared in Williams Hall would be more temporary than expected. Finally, I learned that although my financial aid had arrived at the school, it did not fully cover my expenses, which was the root of the problem.

I was puzzled because I was under the impression that once my financial aid was accepted, I would be covered even if by loans. That's when I learned that tuition for out-of-state students was three times higher than that of a Virginia resident. I inquired whether there were any scholarships or extra loans that I could apply for. The cashier said, "That will be $8,987.72. How will you be taking care of that today?" The question suggested that I had the money in my pocket and that I couldn't wait to give it to her. I immediately turned around as if Oprah were standing behind me and were willing to write a check for me. I responded, "It looks like you and I have the same question." The financial aid office representative gave several options, all of which were private loans. I knew that my parents would not have the credit or income to qualify for such loans. I left the gym with more problems than solutions.

After about six hours of waiting in lines and hearing bad news at the end of each of them, we left the gym. We accomplished all that we could for the day, learning about our school status or lack thereof. Nas and I concluded that our time at VSU might be much shorter than we thought. I called home to inform my father of the results and requested money, which I knew he did not have, but I had to at least ask. When he informed me that he would not qualify for the loans after he tried with Sallie Mae, I was convinced that I would be coming home.

The next few weeks were extremely stressful. Classes had begun, and my financial situation had not been solved, and I was on pins and needles. I was spending time in classes stressing about whether I would be sent home tomorrow or the next day. I stopped attending classes in favor of making phone calls and attending meetings to secure my enrollment. All the legwork provided me with new skills; I learned how to advocate and be resourceful while praying for a blessing.

I had private meetings with the directors of the various offices that were represented at validation. From those meetings, I was able to receive many forms of grants, work-study, and mini scholarships. I had to tell them my backstory and goals before they revealed they would be able to help through funding sources most people were unaware of. And wouldn't you know it, I was fully covered. I guess they used validation for people who were able to pay directly and saved the secret funds for people like me, or so I'd like to believe. Either way, I felt relieved. I got to stay in college.

TROJAN PRIDE

A few days later, I got my room assignment, and it was worth the wait. I was assigned to Nicholas Hall, which was in the Student Village or "The Ville" as we called it, which was located at the south end of the campus. The Ville was for upperclassmen, so it came with privileges that the other dorms did not have, most notably overnight co-ed visitation. Needless to say, that was all I needed to hear. More on this later.

Nicholas Hall happened to be right next door to Taylor-Williams Hall, an all-female dorm. In my opinion, many of the best-looking female students lived in Taylor-Williams during my freshman year, including some of the Woo-Woo cheerleaders. It was heaven. I remember moving my things into the room after getting my key. I was excited!

The door opened behind me a few minutes after I arrived, and a few guys with puzzled looks on their faces entered the dorm. They looked high from weed and smelled like they had a beer or two. I introduced myself to the one who entered first. "Wassup? My name is Adekunle; I'm your new roommate." "I'm Antoine," he replied. We shook hands. I guess he was used to having the room to himself because he began going over "the rules." I listened for a few seconds because I thought he was trying to put me on the game or enlighten me about the dorm rules. After all, he was an upperclassman, and I was a freshman. I was eager to learn.

When I realized he considered himself the main resident of the room, I stopped him mid-sentence. "And no phone calls after—," he was saying. "Yo, my man. I paid for this room; it's equally mine," I interrupted. Thinking of my struggle not only to get to college but to secure the room and board, I was willing to take it with fisticuffs. "I'm from Philly," I continued. He said, "You from Philly? I'm from PA too! My bad, bro," he apologized. "I just didn't want to be stuck with some lame ass nigga in here," he continued. The tension decreased as we engaged in small talk about each other and our home state. After unpacking most of my things, I left to go chill with Nas.

Nas lived in Puryear Hall, which was a freshman dorm located at the north end of the campus. I told Nas about my enrollment status. He told me that his financial aid also got covered. His mother was able to take out a private loan to assist him with staying in school. I guess God was looking out for us, I thought. We were both excited to have our financial holds removed and be fully enrolled. I also told Nas about my conversation with my new roommate. Nas said, "You want me to knock him the fuck out?" "Nah, I handled it," I told him. We headed to the cafe to eat dinner and spot some more women. The cafe was serving breakfast for dinner, and it was amazing.

After we left the cafe, we went back to Puryear. Nas told me that he wanted me to meet a friend of his that he met in football camp. He said he thought we would get along. We took the elevator up to the fourth floor to meet his friend. "Yo, it's me, Nas," he said. A dark-skinned, heavyset guy with a taper fade answered the door. "Wassup, yo? I want you to meet my friend Adekunle," he said. "Wassup, man? My name is Jerritt," he said as he extended his hand; I shook his hand and introduced myself.

Jerritt was from Charlotte, North Carolina. I told him that I thought it was nice to meet somebody from North Carolina because I am a huge UNC Tarheels fan. Once I said that, we connected instantly. Jerritt was all about college sports, particularly college football. We had long conversations that night. I mean, we talked about everything! We talked about what life was like for him being from a southern state, me being from Philly, and most importantly we talk about the girls at Virginia State.

Naturally, I started the game I used to play back in the day with Brian and Dre, would you fuck her? I explained the rules of the game to Jerritt, and then we started playing. Nas and I began naming several female students that we all thought were attractive. We named female staff members as well. No woman was out of bounds. Most our answers were a unanimous yes because there were so many beautiful girls at the school.

Nas was known for not really having a type of woman that he preferred. He often described himself as a "whoremonger." He had very few boundaries when it came to girls that he would have sex with. Some of the girls that we thought were disgustingly unattractive Nas did not mind smashing. I guess that meant that he was not as shallow and I was, but I saw it as me having standards. When I shot my shot, I shot for the stars. Nas was the ideal guy to take as a wingman on a double date. I knew that no matter what he would be willing to go. More importantly, he was usually willing to take one for the team.

In true Nas fashion, he started to name girls that were questionable to completely unattractive to make the game more interesting. After a few maybe answers and definitive no answers, Nas named this one girl asking me if I would fuck her. I immediately said "Ew" and made an ugly face. Nas started laughing and said, "I knew you were going to respond like that." Immediately, Jerritt responded "I'd beat!" in his thick North Carolina accent. Nas and I were crying laughing. We never heard that term used before, and it was even funnier with the accent. In that instant, I gave Jerritt the nickname "Beat."

A few minutes later, I met Jerritt's roommate; let's call him Tyler; he was from Ocean City, Maryland. We connected because of the conversations he walked in on about sports and women. We were discussing how bad, as in good, the DMV girls were. The DMV girls were from DC, Maryland, and Virginia, thus the acronym DMV. Before coming to Virginia State, I had not seen girls that beautiful and proportionately thick before. We all joked that there must be something in that DMV water. Of course, all the DMV driving analogies and sex-related puns were used. I told Tyler that my favorite woman, Toni Braxton, was from Maryland. Although Tyler had some weird energy, if he was cool with Nas and Beat, then he was cool with me. Just like that, we were a little crew.

Tyler is the first person to introduce me to the Internet. He spent most of the time on chat sites looking for girls both at school and in other states. I didn't have a computer in my house growing up, so all of this was new to me. He would have several windows open at a time talking to many different people on many different platforms. He would be on AOL Instant Messenger, Excite Chat, Black Voices, BlackPlanet, and Collegeclub.com, which was the Facebook before Facebook. Intrigued, I signed up for a few of those online services as well, more on this later.

It was 1999, not many people were walking around with digital cameras, and most people didn't have cell phones. We used to tease Tyler that he could be talking to a guy or someone's grandmother. I saw him type: ASL, so I asked him what that meant. "Age, sex, and location," he said. He told me that's how he knew whom he was talking to. "As if people don't lie," I retorted. One day, Nas, Beat, and I entered the room and Tyler had his shirt off taking a picture of himself with a webcam he recently purchased from RadioShack in South

Park Mall. We were screaming laughing! I guess he took my ASL retort to heart.

DR. NUNNALLY

After getting our finances taken care of, it was time to fully register for classes. We wanted to declare as accounting majors, but first, we had to take general education classes. Nas and I took many of the same classes, as did all the other freshmen at Virginia State. We took one class that changed my life forever. Freshman Writing was taught by Dr. Nunnally, an African American woman to whom I am forever indebted. Freshman Writing laid the foundation for every term paper, essay, and research project I would ever do.

I remember Dr. Nunnally tasked us with writing a descriptive paper on the topic of our choice. I chose to write about my journey to college. I worked very hard on the first draft. I stayed up for hours trying to make sure everything was right. Ok, that's bullshit. I wrote it the night before, a tactic that I learned in high school. I did stay up late, however, but that was writing to random girls online via the chat sites that Tyler introduced me to.

When I turned in the first draft of the paper, needless to say, many corrections were needed. Dr. Nunnally used a transparent projector of my paper to make an example of my work for the class. As she was reviewing my paper, I saw the mistakes I had made, such as writing the letter *u* instead of *you* when referring to a person. Using the letter *u* was a shorthand version of writing the word *you* that I learned as I honed my instant messenger skills. When Nas and I saw that mistake, we laughed hard and tried not to be noticed. Dr. Nunnally marked my paper with so much red ink that the paper looked like a crime scene. There were red slashes everywhere. I learned a few lessons that day.

The first lesson I learned was that Dr. Nunnally took her job very seriously, and she cared about my learning. She took the time to fully break down my paper and made me the example of the class, which was embarrassing to say the least. The second lesson I learned was to plan and take my time with my assignments if I wanted to pass. The third lesson I learned was to proofread my paper prior to submission. I didn't want to be made an example again. As was customary in her class, Dr. Nunnally allowed everyone to make corrections and revise their papers. I took the revision step very seriously; I made all the necessary corrections and proofread the paper. I had my friends proofread the paper as well before I turned it in for grading. I didn't want to take any chances.

The next week, I received a grade for my second draft. It was a grade that I did not think was possible. In fact, it was a grade that I had never seen in my life. In red ink on the top right corner of the paper, my grade stared at me. I got an F+++. I was puzzled. What does this even mean? I remember thinking. Apparently, I wasn't the only student to get that kind of grade. Some students got an F+ or an F++. I thought she was playing a joke, but little did I know it was no laughing matter. Instead, it was another learning experience.

I asked Dr. Nunnally, "What is an F+++?" "The question you should be asking is how you earned an F+++," she retorted. It was a fair question, but I was in no mood for the mystery. She said, "Your paper was really well written and very descriptive. I enjoyed reading it." "So how did I get such a poor grade," I asked. "For as well written in content it was, it was not properly written structurally," she answered. I began to understand her logic. The grade of F represented poor paragraph structure, and the pluses represented the good content that I had written. I stayed after class to learn more about MLA format, which is what we used in her class.

When I turned in my final draft, I got a grade of B+. I was hoping for an A+, but I was satisfied with the grade I got because it was earned. I learned many lessons on the way to that grade and had a greater appreciation of what it took to achieve it. I am very thankful to have met Dr. Nunnally because she either knowingly or unknowingly taught me the importance of the synergy an essay should have. I knew these were gems that I needed to hone and maintain long term.

PURYEAR HALL

As usual, I hung out at Puryear Hall between classes most of the time because our crew lived there. Other times, I hung out at Puryear because it was so close to the buildings where my classes were held. After I finished classes for the day, we would all hang out in Puryear for the rest of the day. At night, we would have stupid challenges like deciding which one of us could eat a whole pizza in one sitting. Nas always won. I had so much fun hanging out there that I wouldn't return to Nicholas Hall until 3:00 a.m. on school nights. After a while, people thought I lived in Puryear, including the residence life staff. I began to make friends in the dorm mostly because people always saw me there; I even earned a few nicknames.

The saga continued from high school. Most people couldn't properly pronounce my full name. After years of correcting people, I grew exhausted. I didn't want them to call me Ige because that's what I was called from grade school through high school. Instead of allowing people to call me Kunle like my family and close friends do, I decided to give myself a nickname for a change. I decided to shorten my name even further and told them to call me "K." I guess that decision in part was to also symbolize my fresh start. A new identity.

Choosing my own nickname was my way of controlling the narrative. Not too long after, Beat started calling me K-Hova and K-Hov. He called me that because I was easily the biggest Jay-Z fan at Virginia State in 1999. Jay-Z often referred to himself as Jayhovah or simply Hov back then. During the height of the Rocafella movement, I had all Jay-Z's albums, mixtapes, and

DVDs. I even used to make my own Jay-Z mixtapes, using collages of his features on other artists' songs. I knew every word of his lyrics, what album they were on, the verse, and track number to any lyrics he ever spit. I was fanatical.

I also earned another nickname without my knowledge. While waiting between my classes or Nas's classes, I'd sit in the lobby of Puryear Hall. I'd burn some time by watching BET or some other video channels. Eventually, I would fall asleep on the lobby couch. Almost every time I fell asleep, I was awakened by three female students from Norfolk who often spent time in Puryear. "Wake up, Sleepy," they would often say. It happened so often that they began to refer to me as Sleepy whether I was awake or not; Sleepy was my first non-derogatory nickname.

THE CAGE

The first weekend after classes, I went to the basketball courts. Basketball was always the best way for me to make friends *and* enemies. It was time to make some friends and enemies. I put on my shorts and summer league jersey and headed to the basketball courts. I didn't have far to travel because the outside courts were closest to the Ville. As I approached the courts, I noticed the scenery. It was a blacktop with a 15-foot high gate surrounding it. I called it The Cage, and it was packed! Every basketball player was running hard and sweating. I'm talking all courts full of 5-on-5 games featuring players from all over the country. It was like everyone was there to prove themselves on the court. It was competitive, just the way I like it.

Naturally, I had to get in there and test my game against a cage full of athletes. I remember my first play. I was on defense, and I was guarding a point guard who seemed to be pretty popular among the New York basketball players during the games. Now, I'm from Philly, and I'm very competitive. So in my mind, I'm representing my city, and there is an East Coast rivalry going on. That's the backstory I had in my head for this guy. I had a backstory for everyone I played against; that's part of how I gained a competitive advantage and motivated myself.

I'm sure he didn't know that I was scouting him as I watched his team win while I was waiting for my turn. One of the weaknesses that I saw in his game was that he liked to cross over from his left hand to his right hand. The problem wasn't so much the move as it was the speed in which he executed the move. It was slow compared to the people I grew up playing against. In the previous game, it was working for him, even though he was palming the ball, which is illegal. But this is streetball, and most people didn't make those calls.

While guarding him on a few possessions, I was waiting for him to finally try me with his move. On the previous possessions, he shot a three-pointer which was rebounded and tipped in by a six-foot-four muscular kid from New York who was wearing a du-rag. On other possessions, he passed the ball once he crossed the half-court line. I started baiting him to attempt his crossover by leaning to my right more heavily while guarding him. Then, the moment came. He thought he was setting me up by feigning disinterest in challenging me off the dribble, but I guarded him with a mission. That mission was to wreck his confidence in that move. I watched as he backed up two steps from the three-point line and began his dribble cadence. One bounce between his legs followed by a small crossover from right to left and then it came, and I was ready. Timing his crossover perfectly as I visualized in my mind while I was scouting him, I reached with my right arm at the height of his move and poked the ball loose. I ran around him from his right side to retrieve the ball and scored with a onehanded dunk on the other end of the floor. People went crazy. I went crazy.

That's how it went in the cage. We had some epic battles. I remember hitting this guy with a right-hand crossover, between the legs, and he slid off the court. I went to the cage as many times as I could to prove myself and earn respect. I wanted to make sure that my game transcended beyond my neighborhood and my city.

OUT OF SERVICE

One of the challenges of being an out-of-state student back in the late '90s to the early 2000s was keeping contact with my family. Back then, cell phones or other devices were not as readily available as they are today. Our only means of long-distance communication were collect calls, which cost my family money that we didn't have; letters, which took too long to solve immediate concerns; and phone cards.

For the millennials out there, phone cards were like getting a gift card from Amazon or Target. A person could purchase a card with a certain number of minutes for phone usage. For example, if I bought a $20 phone card, it may come with 300 minutes of phone time. I would call the 800-number on the back of the card and then enter the code from the back of the card. Once the call connected, my minutes would begin to decrease based on the duration of the call. Three hundred minutes sounds like a lot, but trust me, it's not.

The problem with phone cards was they were not cheap and as a college student, we were often calling home for money. That means that I had to have money to call home and ask for money. So, I wrote letters to my father to ask for money for phone cards, clothes, food, and other items. If I didn't have money and I needed something urgently, I would have to ask my friend Nas to use his phone card to call home.

This need created a hustle for me. I started selling ramen noodles, mixed CDs, and other items to make money. It took me a few weeks, but I was able to scrounge up some money to buy a phone card so that I could call home. I needed my family to know that I was ok and to tell them what I have been experiencing. Because the phone cards had limited minutes, I had to make sure every phone call was short and to the point. Often when I called, I couldn't talk to my brother Wale because he would be in school or outside playing, I couldn't burn minutes waiting for them to locate him.

Over time, phone cards became less popular as more people gained access to phones during the cell phone boom. Cell phones were easier to use and more accessible than phone cards, but many cell phone companies had limited service areas and more dead zones compared to service today So, when we talked to people, we had to sit by windows or outside, even in the winter.

Cell phones also had limited minutes back then. So, you might have a new cell phone with a monthly limit of 300 minutes per month; an overage would typically cost .25 per minute. A monthly cell phone plan still beat phone cards because it was a guaranteed 300 minutes per month. But cell phones really popped when the major companies offered plans with unlimited minutes on nights and weekends. That's when we would all be on the phones calling home or talking to girls.

OVERCOMPENSATING SAVAGERY

At Virginia State University, I really hit my stride when it came to women. Due to all the antagonism from other students in middle school and high school and feeling like an outsider, I approached dating with a different energy in college. I decided that I would not let my past be my future; besides, college was a fresh start. This was my chance to create a new identity, one that I would be proud of and one that allowed me to move with more confidence. Therefore, I became the late bloomer who wanted to make up for lost time.

Ironically, the first girl I started talking to was from Philly; let's call her Judy. I met Judy one night while leaving the cafe with Nas, Tyler, and Beat. She was with her friend Jessica. To keep it real, Jessica was by far the best-looking one. However, Tyler had already started talking to her. Being the wingman that I am, I decided to talk with Judy. We all began to walk and talk. Eventually, we ended up in front of Howard Hall, where they all lived. We sat on the stoop of the dorm and talked until around three in the morning. We all exchanged phone numbers at the end of the night.

From that day forward Judy and I began talking on the phone regularly until one day we got into a disagreement during our phone conversation. To be honest, I have no idea what we were disagreeing about after all these years. All I know is that she began screaming at the top of her lungs; it was so loud that her words became inaudible to me. I promptly hung up the phone during her screaming; she wasn't talking to me like that. It was our first disagreement, and I was not having it. I had to set some boundaries and a precedent for myself. That became my signature response if I didn't like something they did. I didn't have to put up with it; there were too many girls on campus for me to be stressing about one; that was my mentality.

Otherwise, I'd be a walking-talking doormat. She tried calling my room several times over the next couple of weeks to apologize. I never answered or responded to her voicemails. She even tried to send word through Nas and Beat that she was sorry, but I didn't care. Till this day, I have not spoken to her again. It was petty, I know, but I faced too much bullshit growing up to accept that from anyone.

Soon after, I started getting phone numbers from women all over the campus. I met women in the classroom, at parties, in passing, and in the cafe. I was trying to get as many as I could. Remember that bag of condoms my father gave me? It was time to put those to good use. At first, I started meeting girls on campus through collegeclub.com to set up late night smash sessions. Back in these days, people were into long chats on the phone followed up with phone sex. As I mentioned before, most people did not have webcams or digital cameras, and there sure as shit weren't any camera phones back then. Leave it to me and Nas to take it to the next level. So, when we met someone online most times, they had no picture on their profile. Have no fear Nas, Beat, and I had this down to a science. We decided that we would ask chicks to meet us at the Harris Hall fountain on campus. The Fountain was the perfect meeting place on campus. It was in between the female dorms and the student village, which is where I lived.

So, we had a system. Once the girl let us know that she was on her way, we would wait for her to begin heading towards the fountain. Then, we would post up around Harris Hall in a hidden location with a good vantage point to see her arrive so we could see her before she saw us. That way, we could evaluate and see if she was attractive or matched how she described herself online. Sometimes, we were pleasantly surprised, and other times we were like, "Aw, naw." Now, if the girl was not attractive, we would just go back to our dorm room and start over with whoever else we had been talking to. That meant that some poor girl waited at the fountain alone for a guy who never came.

I know what you are thinking: what scumbags we were, and you are right. We were savages before it became a Facebook phrase, even before memes. Using today's slang, after we "ghosted" the girls at the fountain, I usually had to ignore my dorm room phone for a few days as they would call over and over leaving angry messages. We didn't even think about it. It was routine.

Our goal was to reduce the Harris Hall ghosting incidents and get to our goals faster. After viewing so many online profiles, I learned about the tricks of the camera. One of the common tricks that ladies used was to angle the camera. I mean, they were professional photographers. If you think Catfishing began in 2012, you are sadly mistaken. I peeped the game quickly though. I was not going to holla at a girl that took pictures of herself at an angle that I would not normally view her from in real life.

As a rule of thumb, I knew that if a girl took a picture of only her head that meant she was probably fat. If she had on pounds of makeup, I wouldn't even click it. If she took an aerial shot of herself, it meant one of three things. She was probably fat, trying to emphasize her breasts, or more likely unattractive in person. Playing these odds allowed me to avoid leaving them at Harris Hall and got me more action. As savage as this sounds, everyone has a selection process that nobody knows about, even you.

As I mentioned before, I lived in a male upperclassmen dorm. Everyone in the dorm was allowed to have co-ed visitation, except me because I was a freshman. This is college, so we used some ingenuity. We started sneaking girls in through the fire escape doors in both Puryear Hall and Nicholas Hall.

I remember I met this chick named Courtney who was from Suffolk, VA. She made it past the looks test, and she brought a friend with her for my boy Nas. Long story short, I ended up fucking her on the floor of my dorm room while Nas smashed her friend on my bed. It was good times. In case you are wondering whatever happened to Courtney and her friend you are not alone. We never spoke to them again after that night. Like I said before, we were savages.

MS. CONNECTICUT

Then, there was this one girl from Connecticut; let's call her Cherry. I met her over collegeclub.com at the end of Freshman year in 1999. Cherry stayed in Eggleston Hall; she had a picture on her profile, so there was no need for the Harris Hall tactics. That profile pic did not do her justice; she looked so much better in person than she did on her profile with the grainy ass webcam.

She did work-study in the campus library; one night, we agreed to meet there after her shift. I walked her to her dorm so she could freshen up. I waited for her on the steps of Eggleston Hall. I guess she thought sneaking me into Eggleston Hall was too risky. When she came out, we took a walk around the north side of the campus while talking about all sorts of things. We talked mostly about what we thought of the school and, eventually, we walked off the campus and headed towards a small park area across the street.

We started kissing, and it escalated fast from there. Next thing I knew I was having sex with her on the picnic table between the Virginia State campus and the Appomattox River in the middle of the night. It was cold outside, but we didn't care. Well, I don't want to speak for her, but I was going in. She made noises like we were on an island all alone, and it felt that way. The louder she got, the harder I went. The next sequence can be best described by a bar from Houston battle rapper Scotty: "She felt so amazed. Then, I flipped her over and started backstabbing her. She felt so betrayed." That's right, I flipped Cherry over for doggy style, and I was in there to prove a point. Afterward, she snatched the condom off me and started performing fellatio. It felt like she also had a point to prove. It was unbelievable.

We made plans to keep things going once we returned from fall break, but that never happened. Cherry never returned to school. I mean, I was looking for her. I called her dorm room, and her roommate broke the news to me that she didn't come back for the Spring 2000 semester. I was damn-near heartbroken.

HARSH REALITY

"The wise man knows his fate. The fool merely finds it."

—Destiny, "Fate of all Fools"

As a result of not being able to afford books, chasing women, and experiencing freedom for the first time in my life, my GPA reflected my lack of focus. After the fall semester concluded, I had a .5 GPA. Yes, you read that right: .5. It was embarrassing and totally avoidable; I allowed myself to get distracted in the way that I was trying to avoid by staying in Philly. I was having more fun than I ever had in high school, while not taking advantage of the opportunity that I fought so hard for.

I worked harder to bring my grades up in the Spring 2000 semester. I didn't want to become the type of person that I consciously avoided—you know, the college student who went to college for a semester just to say they went to college. I did better, but I had a long way to go. My cumulative GPA at the end of the spring semester was 1.8. That meant that my collegiate career was in jeopardy, not to mention any hopes of playing basketball at Virginia State.

"What we don't appreciate we risk losing."

—Unknown

CHAPTER 7

THE TWELFTH OF JULY

The summer of 2000 was on the horizon, and it was the break that I needed. My goal was to go home and refocus. It was time to see my friends and my neighborhood to remind myself of where I came from and the struggles I had endured to get here. I needed to do a little less chasing women and basking in my newfound freedom and more focus on my education. I had enough shenanigans, and it was beginning to cost me the education my parents fought so hard for me to obtain.

ANCESTORS

My college experience wasn't all fun and games though. In November 1999, I got a phone call from Wale letting me know that our grandfather had passed away from congestive heart failure. No matter how old someone is or how logical the event is, you are never prepared for death; anyone who tells you otherwise is a sociopath. My grandfather's death was a tough pill to swallow. Even at the age of 18, I had a hard time understanding the loss. I knew if it was that incomprehensible to me, then I couldn't imagine the pain my mother and her siblings were feeling.

Two months later, in January 2000, I received a phone call in my dorm room. When I answered the phone, I heard a woman crying. I thought it was Judy calling again. "Hi Kunle," the woman said. When I heard that, I knew it wasn't Judy; it was someone in my family. "It's Aunt Sherri," she continued.

"I'm calling you to let you know that your grandmother died, " she said. When I heard that, I nearly dropped the phone.

My grandmother passed away of end-stage renal disease; I wasn't surprised because she had been on dialysis for most of my life. Even though it seemed like a logical conclusion given her ongoing battle, I was stunned. It was the second time in two months that I'd lost someone in my family. It was also the first time I'd heard from my Aunt Sherri since I graduated from the eighth grade, and hearing her cry broke me.

My mother attended both funerals and was present for each wake. However, each time triggered her to go into an episode, even while at the services. I couldn't help but feel for my mother. I couldn't imagine what it would be like to lose your parents regardless of their age. These were the people who had loved and taken care her for her entire life, and now she had to bury them. Life was so unfair.

HAVE YOU SEEN HER?

One of the biggest struggles I had in my life was dealing with my mother's mental health challenges. It made me afraid to leave the house because I never knew what would happen. I was always afraid that if she went into one of her episodes, there would be a disaster like a house fire or her falling down the stairs. There was always a threat of danger like the time when we came home to find that she was missing.

During the winter of 1996, when Wale and I came home, my Aunt Janet was at our mother's house with Femi. They both had very serious looks on their faces. I didn't know what was going on. "Did mommy come to your school today?" Femi asked. "No. Why?" I asked. "I ain't seen her since yesterday," Femi said. "We called the police and they said she would have to be missing for at least 24 hours before they can make a report," Aunt Janet said. "Femi called me to help y'all look for her," she continued. When I heard that, I thought my brain would explode.

When we first started looking for her, Femi tried to make Wale stay home. He said it in such an authoritative way, my Aunt Janet had to check him, "That's his mother, too." Femi was 21 years old; Wale and I were 12 and 15 years old, respectively. While other kids were searching their houses looking for Christmas presents their parents probably hid around the house, we were looking in local parks and ditches, hoping that our mother was still alive.

It was winter. If she was out there, she was probably cold and needed food. We looked in Wissahickon Park first, turning over rocks and boulders in search of our mother. I remember every site we searched gave me an eerie feeling. On one hand, we wanted to find her alive, but the longer we went without locating her, we knew the chances of it decreased. We did not find her in Wissahickon Park.

The next few days were brutal. We went to Fern Hill Park to continue our search. Unfortunately, there had been a series of murders in that park, and the victims were being found in trash bags. It was not the kind of information we needed to hear. Every time we looked in an area big enough for a human being, my heart dropped. By the time we got to the middle of the park, it was getting colder and darker. As snow fell, we approached an area with a huge ditch. Along the side of the ditch was a bunch of debris at the end of the park, and there were three large bags. I could not help but wonder if my mother was in one of those bags.

As we approached the embankment, it felt like it took two hours to get to those bags. Everything was moving in slow motion. The closer we got, the louder I could hear my heart pounding. By the time, we got close enough, my heart was beating so loudly that I couldn't hear anything except the ringing in my ears. Aunt Janet, Femi, and I made Wale stay back as we searched the bags. If my mother was inside one of those bags, it would be traumatic for all of us and something none of us wanted Wale to see. Femi tore the bags open; they contained nothing but debris and mulch. They must've heard our sighs of relief in every country around the world.

Afterward, we went to the Belmont Plateau, the same place where Coach Ellerbee made us run for conditioning at Gratz. When we got to the plateau, it was dark, and we were just wandering aimlessly looking for her. The search for my mother was called off for the night because we could no longer see in the pitch-black park. I had to brace myself for the possibility that she would either be found dead or not found at all.

KIRKBRIDE

We toured several hospitals trying to see if she had been committed, but she had not been admitted to them. We believed they were telling us the truth because they knew us as her family. We decided to try a hospital that she had never been admitted to, Kirkbride's Hospital, it was our last hope. The staff members there were unfamiliar with us and were unwilling to give us any information. When we showed them her picture, they still were hesitant about telling us whether she was at the hospital. Instead, they said, "She is ok," which was both the biggest clue we received and the best news we could ever asked for.

After a few more days, we received a call from Kirkbride's Hospital for the mentally ill; the call was from my mother. "Hey, how y'all doing?" she asked. She didn't sound like she was fully coherent, but it didn't matter to us at all. I can't even begin to describe what it was like to hear her voice again. I began crying tears of joy. I told her we were better now that we had heard from her. "We were all worried about you. Are you ok?" I asked. "I'm doing ok. I'll be home soon," she responded.

Apparently, she had been seen walking the streets during one of her episodes when the police found her and had her committed to Kirkbride. She had been receiving mental health intervention and medication for over a week. It was the best possible scenario. She told us that she wouldn't be home until she was completely well, which meant she would miss Christmas. Just hearing from her was the greatest gift of all, and she came home about a month later.

This wasn't the last time that she was forcibly committed. Over the next three years, we made several trips to mental health residential facilities to visit my mother. Many times, she sat in a catatonic daze almost as if she could see through us or didn't recognize us at all. It was unnerving to see her unkempt and smelling as if she hadn't showered in days. Though it was difficult to see and hard to understand, she was our mother, and we loved her regardless.

BACK TO APSLEY

Due to my mother's mental health challenges, she sent us to live with our father. With Femi going in and out of jail, Wale and I didn't want to leave my mother's house. We didn't want to leave her unattended. However, it was the best thing for her to reduce her stress. It was challenging for her to battle mental health and raise teenagers. Even back then, I understood why we had to go back to live with our father.

This move meant that we had to leave our friends in Nicetown and rejoin our friends in Germantown. We never got a chance to stay comfortable in a location for too long; instead, we were packing and unpacking, coming and going between our parents' homes. We lived in a state of constant worry and survival.

To make matters worse, Femi had been arrested on a drug charge. We had no idea when or if he would be out. That meant, my mother would be home alone most of the time because her then-boyfriend, Mr. Leonard, worked the late shift. Wale and I always worried about the possibility of her having an episode when no one was home to help her. She lived within walking distance of my father, so we decided that we would call and visit her as much as we could.

A NIGHTMARE ON APSLEY

In June 2000, my father was working as a Parking Manager at the Radisson Hotel on City Line Avenue in Philadelphia. They were preparing for over 3,000 students and family members to attend their prom, which was set to take place at the hotel. Suddenly, my father began to feel flu-like symptoms. He knew something wasn't right, so he asked his supervisor if he could go home for the day. The supervisor, thinking about being understaffed with 3,000 guests, reluctantly allowed him to go.

My father drove home safely but still felt sick. When he got home, he sat on his bed and turned on the news as was his routine. He took off his jacket and lay on his bed. Feeling tired and weak, he dozed off. Suddenly, in the middle of his sleep, he felt nauseated and began vomiting violently. He threw up so much and for so long that his stomach was completely empty. However, the vomiting didn't stop; he continued to vomit stomach acid. His condition was getting worse by the second.

My father had no idea what was happening to him as he became increasingly nauseated. He couldn't keep his eyes open because the house was spinning rapidly and violently. There he was, on his knees and alone in his house. He held on tightly to the bed as if letting go would send him flying like children on a carousel. He felt completely disoriented and unaware of time. It must've been the scariest moments of his life.

My father tried to reach for the phone, which was about two and a half feet from his bed. Every time he reached for the phone, it seemed like someone was pulling it away from him. The nausea was taking over his mind. He began praying over and over that God would save him and spare him. He was on the second floor of a three-story home with no one to help him. It was the worst possible place to be for a 52-year-old man with glaucoma, blind in one eye who could barely see, even without nausea.

After a long struggle reaching for the phone, he was able to open his eye for a split second. He grabbed the phone and struggled to dial 911. He was so disoriented that he kept dialing the wrong number. Every moment was crucial. By the grace of God, he was able to make the call. "911, what is your emergency?" the dispatcher answered. "HELP! HELP!" my father cried. "The whole house is spinning around me! I don't know what's wrong with me!" he yelled. Fortunately, he had the presence of mind to provide his address. If this were a movie, at this point, the struggle would be over. My father had no such luck.

My father knew his number could be called at any moment. Fearing for his life, he began trying to escape the house, but he was too nauseated to see and too disoriented to walk. He began to low crawl like a military soldier traveling under barbed wire. On his first attempt, he was inadvertently traveling to the back of the house before realizing he had been going in the wrong direction.

Fortunately, he was able to turn around, crawl down the stairs, and make it to the living room. The house was old, so he had to use a key in order to exit. So, even though he made it to the living room, he still needed a way out of the house. My father began reaching blindly around the room as he searched for his keys and prayed for a miracle. Somehow, he was able to not only find his keys but grab the exact key he needed from a ring that held 50 or more keys. To this day, I don't understand how he did that—must've been all that repetition as a carpenter.

After crawling to the door and fighting for his life with each step, he managed to pull himself up to the door and use the key to unlock it. As he opened that door, his right side became numb, and he collapsed into the hands of the paramedic who was getting ready to knock on the door. "I need you to walk, sir" the paramedic instructed. Between the porch and the sidewalk were two sets of stairs; walking was an impossible task.

It seemed like the paramedic thought my father was drunk. Every time my father took a step, he nearly collapsed. When they realized that he couldn't walk, they placed him on the gurney and carried him to the ambulance. "What were you drinking? What drugs were you taking?" they asked. My father could barely answer them because he was still vomiting periodically. "None. Nothing, " he said before vomiting again.

Once inside the ambulance, they rushed him to the emergency room at Temple University, which ironically, was the university he attended when he first came to America. Now, it was where he was fighting for his life. Upon arrival, they took him out on a gurney and rushed him into the ER. Even at the hospital, they were asking if he was on drugs or had been drinking. At this point, he was vomiting so violently, they gave him a bucket and pills for nausea.

He waited in the emergency room for what must've seemed like an eternity for him. A doctor arrived to run tests trying to determine the cause of his condition. They were still unable to figure out what was causing his dizziness, vomiting, and numbing of his body. My father was unable to explain because he was still completely disoriented. The doctors and hospital staff continued their routines as they searched for a cause.

There he was laying on the stretcher and praying for God to save him. Finally, another doctor approached. The doctor asked, "What's this guy doing over here all this time? What's wrong with him?" The hospital staff didn't know what to tell him, so he decided to examine my father himself. He ran the same tests as the other doctors and staff. That's when he realized what was going on. "THIS GUY IS HAVING A STROKE!" the doctor yelled.

"MOVE, MOVE, MOVE!" he shouted as he began giving instructions to his staff.

Once they realized what was happening and got a crew together to treat him, my father was placed in a hospital room. He was still nauseated and feeling like the room was spinning, but he was gradually improving. His symptoms calmed, and my father asked the nurses attending to him about the doctor who made his diagnosis and essentially saved his life.

"He was about six feet tall and had a beard," my father described. None of the staff recognized any doctor fitting that description. "Sir, there's no one who works here with those features," a nurse responded. After asking multiple staff members to locate the doctor who saved him, my father was convinced that it was an angel from God. "I knew it was help from above," he said.

I learned of the stroke when I came home from playing basketball. Wale called my father's house from the hospital to inform me of our father's condition. It was completely devastating. "Where you been? I been calling for hours," he asked. "I was at the Hollow playing ball, why? What the fuck happened?" I asked. Wale quickly filled me in. "He can barely move anything on his right side," Wale added. I wanted to visit my father in the hospital, but he instructed Wale to tell me to stay home so that people on the block wouldn't see the house as an opportunity. Even in times of crisis, we still had to worry about environmental threats. I stayed home wondering if he would be able to function properly when he got home.

My father remained in the hospital for another two weeks as he was dealing with hemiparesis and doing physical therapy. He had to relearn how to walk and use stairs. He nearly lost his life a week before his 53rd birthday.

I was very thankful that my father survived his brush with death. I never understood why the ambulance drove past Germantown Hospital and Albert Einstein Medical Center to take him to Temple Hospital, which was nearly two miles away. He could've died on the way. I felt for my father being home alone and having to struggle to save himself, and the situation was a lot for Wale and me to handle.

BASKETBALL CAMP

My father's recovery went well. He had medications for stroke survivors, and he also had support from his sister, my Aunt Keji and our neighbor Rob, a former police officer, who came to see him daily. Given all we endured during this time, I needed a break, and the only place I could find peace was on the basketball courts.

A week later, Wale and I were invited to attend the Charlie Ward Basketball Camp in Erie, Pennsylvania. Erie is northeast of Philadelphia—about six hours away. This was a Christian basketball camp that provided a week of spiritual enrichment and basketball skills. The trip was organized by a Christian community organizer and youth basketball coach we called, Coach B. Considering my father's support at home, we reluctantly decided to go to the camp.

It was my first basketball camp since attending the Rasheed Wallace camp at Gratz. I was excited to get in there and play some basketball, but Coach B had different plans for me. He decided that since I had two semesters of college under my belt I would be a camp counselor instead of a participant. It was a decision that he advised me of once we got to the camp. I resented that decision because I was 18 years old and so were most of the camp participants.

Coach B felt that I had a basketball advantage over the other players. He knew that I would not have come to the camp if I had known he wasn't going to allow me to play, so he lied to me. I resented him for it because he let my friends Dre, Brian, and Don play, and we are all the same age. Instead of playing against the best competition at the camp, I was a referee most of the time. Right off the bat, the camp experience sucked for me.

I had to watch my brother Wale and my friends participate in league play. It burned me up inside to have to watch from the sidelines while my friends were in the playoffs where I felt I should be. After all the league play was over, there were other activities to participate in. I played in the counselors' game for all of a minute and a half before I had to exit the game after getting elbowed in the throat by an opponent.

The next day, Coach B allowed me to participate in the camp's slam dunk contest. I was super excited! I breezed past the first few rounds because most people were missing their dunk attempts, so all I had to do was make a dunk, and I moved on. Once or twice per round, I had to perform a better dunk than an opponent. Then came the final round.

During the final round, it was a one-on-one between a six-foot-three camp resident and me; let's call him Devon. He and I went back and forth with dunks until we reached a sudden death round. In the sudden death round, the person with the best dunk automatically wins. He and I both got one attempt to perform our best dunk. A coin was flipped, and I had to go first.

I didn't know which dunk I was going to try until I started running. I wondered what Michael Jordan would do as I ran to the basket. I took off on my left foot about one step before the dotted line while approaching from the right side of the paint area. I decided that I was going to put Devon away for good. I cocked the ball, pause, with my right arm while doing the rock the cradle motion in full swing. When I got to the rim, I reached up with two hands and performed a hard two-handed dunk. Everybody in the gym went crazy!

When everyone settled down, it was Devon's turn. With his back to the basket, Devon turned around and performed a two-handed drop-step dunk. Everybody in the gym went crazy again. Afterward, it was time to declare a winner. All the camp counselors, except for me, deliberated for a few minutes before coming back with a verdict. "The winner of the Charlie Ward Camp 2000 dunk contest is Devon!" I was stunned; everybody was.

As if there wasn't plenty of things that frustrated me during the camp, this one hurt more than anything. I approached Coach B angrily. "How can y'all justify Devon winning?" I asked. "He is six feet three and did a drop-step dunk," I told him. "I did a twohanded rock the cradle dunk from one step in from the foul line. I'm six feet tall, and my dunk had a higher degree of difficulty," I added. I was furious, and so were many people in the crowd.

"All right Kunle, you know we can't let you win as a camp counselor. It would be unfair," Coach B said. I couldn't accept that response; I felt cheated. If he thought it would be unfair for me to win the trophy, why did he let me participate? Everybody knew I won that dunk contest. To this day, people still bring up how I got robbed.

After a very frustrating camp, it was time to go home. We packed our things and left the camp the following day. I was still fuming. I didn't say shit the whole six hours home. All I did was think about how I was tricked into going, denied an opportunity to play the game I love, and robbed of a championship.

THE FOURTEENTH OF JULY

When Wale and I got home late that night, I was still in a bad mood. Still thinking about the missed opportunities at the camp, I unlocked the front door and entered. At the time, we didn't know that walking through this door would change our lives forever. As soon as we entered the living room, I saw that my father was still awake. His bed was in the living room since his stroke two weeks earlier.

He must've heard me unlocking the door because he was already standing by the door waiting for us to enter. Once he saw us, he reached out both of his arms to welcome us home. I knew something was off because he was never this affectionate. That's when I learned why. "Kunle, Wale, I'm sorry to tell you that your mother died," he said. At that moment, I felt like my soul evaporated. I couldn't believe what I just heard. Wale and I both started crying immediately.

My father held us tight as we cried in his arms, still not understanding the magnitude of the moment. Apparently, she had passed two days earlier on the Twelfth of July. We came home two days later. All I could think about was never getting to say goodbye. She was only 47 years old. She was far too young to die. My whole world crashed in the most destructive way possible. We wanted to know how and why she died, but there were no answers for us. Wale and I cried together all night.

The next day, we went to my mother's house to meet my Aunt Janet and Femi to take care of her estate. When we arrived, Aunt Janet met us outside and gave us a hug. "I'm so sorry for your loss," Aunt Janet said. We had so many close calls with our mother, but in the end, everything was always all right, but not this time. When Wale and I entered the house, it felt so empty and so cold. It was the exact opposite of how it felt when she was home. It was like the house knew the difference and gave us cues.

Wale went upstairs into my mother's room and saw that she wasn't there.

A few seconds later, Wale came running down the stairs crying. Before I could grab him, he ran into the kitchen and kicked the back door open. That's when it became more real to us. Wale was trying to climb the gate in my mother's backyard to leave the house.

I ran out to the backyard and wrestled him off the gate as tears poured down my face. Wale was only 14 years old, and he was her baby. It broke my heart further to see him in so much pain. I never felt so helpless in my life. Crying uncontrollably, I wondered why God took her from us. My mother passed 15 days after my father's birthday, a week before Wale's 15th birthday, and just over a month before my 18th birthday.

THE DAY OF THE FUNERAL

This is the one day that never crossed my mind and the one day I want to forget. As a teenager, the last thing you think of is burying your mother. At any age, I don't imagine that anyone is ready to see their mother in a coffin. There I stood, angry yet void of emotion, looking at her lifeless and soulless body. With tears pouring down my face, I reached to touch her for the last time. Her hands were cold and stiff. I couldn't help but think of all the times I had given her trouble and stress while wondering whether I was responsible for her death.

At funerals, we see family members that we haven't seen in years. It's a time when people who could've served you soup when you were sick bring flowers after your death. Funerals are where people make promises to offer support. They really mean it but seem to forget shortly after, as if your loss and needs just fade away. It's where people try to console you and tell you everything is going to be ok. To me, that was bullshit. It only got worse.

Seeing my mother in a coffin created a deep sadness that evolved into an uncontrollable rage over time. I don't care who it was, but everyone was going to pay for this pain. Thinking about the fact my mother died alone with no one around who loved her deepened my depression and increased my rage. Watching everyone cry and mourn was too much for me to bear. I felt nauseated and blacked out. I don't know how long I was out. All I remember was suddenly hearing the raindrops that poured on our heads as the six of us carried her casket to the hearse.

After the wake, we got into the hearse filled with family and flowers. Why is it called a "Wake" anyway when she is deceased? It just seemed like a cruel joke. The wheels on the hearse began rolling on a drive that seemed it would be decades before we reached the graveyard. Can you imagine driving to a location knowing that you are going to be putting your mother into the ground? All I could do was think of everything she'd ever done for us, seeing her smile, and wondering what she experienced in her final moments.

UNANSWERED QUESTIONS

My father tried to calm us, which was an impossible task. "Your mother came here two days before she passed," he told us. "She walked from her house to tell me to make sure that all of you are all right," he continued. My father said that she told him she knew that he would take good care of us. Hearing those words made me wonder what was on her mind. Did she know that she wasn't going to live long? What did she feel? It was the last time he saw her.

After the funeral, the unanswered questions still plagued my mind. The autopsy revealed that she was diabetic. I remember wondering whether she knew that she had diabetes. Did she have an episode and forget to take her medicine and go into diabetic shock? Did she take the wrong combination of medications? There were too many questions living in my mind. The death certificate listed her cause of death as natural causes, which made no sense to me. Even after her funeral, there was no closure for us.

Later, one of our neighbors said she had been seen walking through the neighborhood naked. Someone eventually called the police to have her committed on a 302. The neighbor said when the police came, they were really aggressive with her after handcuffing her. According to them, she was handcuffed and dragged down the stairs of her house and her head was hitting the steps very hard on the way down. They wondered if it contributed to her death.

Because of what history has shown me, I still get scared when life is going too well for too long. In nine months, I lost both of my mother's parents, my father had a life-threatening stroke, and less than two weeks later, I lost my mother. We were a doctor's diagnosis away from being orphans. I was filled with so much anger and rage. Just about everything made me upset. I became introverted and antisocial. It would be years before I could understand the pain I was feeling.

> *"Make up your mind that no matter what comes your way, no matter how difficult, no matter how unfair, you will do more than simply survive. You will thrive in spite of it."*
>
> —Joel Osteen

HER LEGACY

I have many memories of my mother. I could go on for days about how much she supported me and pushed for me to be great in education. Instead, I think of the many things we did together in the short time that I had her on this earth, like the time she opened a water ice stand on her porch in Nicetown. Water ice was popping in the summer, and we had a leg up on the competition by having the vision to make ours a little bit differently.

My mother involved us in the marketing of the water ice. She trusted us to know what the kids wanted. At the time, the Teenage Mutant Ninja Turtles were at their height in popularity. We decided to use our flavors to make ninja turtle water ice. We used the green watermelon-flavored water ice and topped it with either the cherry, orange, blueberry, or grape flavors to simulate the color scheme of the ninja turtles. It was a huge hit among the kids in the hood. "Let me get the Michelangelo," kids would ask referring to the watermelon water ice with the orange flavor on the top. It was great.

Part of her soul still lives inside me, filling some of the hollowness I feel. I still catch myself saying and doing some of the things she used to say and do. That includes watching *Columbo* reruns and watching *The Fugitive* with Harrison Ford; she loved those shows. The original *Fugitive* TV series was something she grew up on and passed down to us. I remember we took her to the theater in 1993 to see the movie when it came out.

I think about the times when she took us to *The Bazaar*, a festival for families in Philly back in the day, and all the theme parks. Memories like sneaking cheesesteaks into the movie theaters to avoid buying $5 hot dogs as we went to see the *Teenage Mutant Ninja Turtles*, often come to mind. The simple times like her going to the corner store to buy us all burgers and fries before watching *Welcome Back Kotter* at night. There are hundreds of other memories that I keep near and dear to my heart. Most of all, I remember her intervening and making sure I didn't become a high school dropout.

I thought I'd never see her again until one night she appeared in my dream. I saw and heard her so clearly that it felt real. I could hear her voice without her even moving her lips; it was odd but nice to hear her one last time. "I'm all right, and it's not what it seems," she said. Soon after, she disappeared, and I rose from my bed looking around the room hoping she was there. They say losing someone you love can play with your mind.

Maybe it *was* real. Maybe it was my subconscious screaming at me; I wasn't sure either way. Every so often, I could feel her in the room and smell her in the air. Even though I knew better, I thought I saw her on Broad Street and Erie Avenue near Maxx's Cheesesteak Shop where she used to go shopping. Even if my mind was playing tricks on me, it was still nice to see her.

My mother had life insurance, so even after death, she was taking care of us. She was normally the most spontaneous one, but she had the foresight to make sure we would be ok. It wasn't a tremendous amount of money, but it was clutch at a time in our lives when we were most vulnerable.

Thanks to her, I was able to pay some of my school tuition and purchase a reliable car. I was 18 years old, so some of that money when to stupid stuff like clothes and sneakers—things she would've provided for me if she were alive. She also left us her house. Of course, I would give everything back to have her here with me, but that's just me being selfish.

I trust that God has a plan for something greater. Be that as it may, I won't act like it doesn't break my heart that she will never get to meet her grandchildren if any of us decides to have them. They will never get to know what a great person she was and how much she would've loved them. She would've done everything for them, but her job on this earth is done.

She saved my life and got me through high school and to college. I made a promise to her that I would graduate from college with a 4.0. My goal was to get my diploma and dedicate it to her; she more than earned it. I like to believe that she was just tired of suffering from her mental health challenges. I'm glad she is no longer suffering. She is survived by her boyfriend Mr. Leonard, her three boys, siblings, and other family members who loved her.

We are her legacy. DMX once said, "To live is to suffer. But to survive well… that's to find meaning in the suffering." We were the meaning in her suffering.

A reason to live, A reason to die

You niggas choose

Before you do, here, try on my shoes

I gotta prove niggas wrong cuz they hate my success

I got a whole lot of shit to get off my chest

Want my brother out the bing, but I can't do a thing

They keep on giving him numbers, like it's a lottery game

A reason to live, a reason to die

You see the tears in my eyes?

I look out for my brother, but I ain't got a job

I gotta prove to myself it's destiny I survive

I'm infected by the streets, it captured my soul

The only thing to reach for is money or gold

A reason to live, a reason to die

You niggas decide

Living in a place that's corrupted with violence

And losing my elders put my family in silence

Aunt crying the blues, when she delivered the news

And I'm 18 years old yall

What could I do?

A reason to die

A reason to live, A reason to die

Come home see the funeral with tears in my eyes

Cars drive by, bullets fly, see three friends die
Three a magic number, I remember the summer
The same number, of bullets my brother caught on the corner
He got cases in court
A reason to live? Nah, hold that thought
My pops working hard, two jobs, to keep the bills paid
Then he passed out from working hard on a summer day
He out struggling, doing the best that he can
As his son, I'm too young, to even give him a hand
His heart froze, muscles tight in his throat
We don't know what it is, but doctors call it a stroke
He needs help, that's a reason to live, I can't lie
But when you lose your mom, that's a reason to die
And he took her to heaven, so Lord I thank you
And I know from heaven, God sent me an angel
A reason to live

Song: *A Reason To Live,* **Artist:** *Me,*
Album: *The Death of J. Storm* **Year:** *2003*

CHAPTER 8
VIRGINIA SLIM

Still mourning the death of my mother, I was trying to make sense of my life. I knew I had to do something to make her proud of me, something to honor her. My first goal was to return to school and get myself back on track. I know that she was proud of me for making it to college, considering how I nearly dropped out of high school. I needed to mature fast if I was ever going to realize my dream of graduating college but it's hard to dream when all you know are nightmares.

Over the summer, I had gotten my driver's license. I needed a car to get around not only in Philly, but in Virginia. My father took me to an auction he frequented and bought me a car. It was a 1991 Buick Century. It was black and already had a sound system provided by the previous owner.

I spent most of the summer driving to and from places that I would normally walk. Having a car made me less resistant to running errands for my father. Most of the time, I was driving to and from basketball parks to participate in leagues and pick-up games. Other times, I was riding around with my friends doing nothing but feeling "cool" because I finally had a car.

YEAR 2 – ACADEMIC PROBATION

Once summer ended, it was time to return to Virginia State for the Fall 2000 semester. I was super excited because I had a car, which means I could get around without taking cabs or begging for rides. This time, my Aunt Tina on my mother's side decided to take the drive to Virginia with me because I had never driven a long distance before. I'd like to tell you that we shared the road equally, but she damn-near drove the whole way. I let her do most of the driving because I was still nervous about the four-and-a-half-hour drive. I had just gotten my license, and I was worried that I'd fall asleep at the wheel.

On the way, Aunt Tina tried to ease my anxiety about driving long distances. She told me a story about how she once changed her stockings while driving. Thinking about my aunt changing her stockings is not something I wanted to do, but I let her continue talking. "How you been doing since your mom passed?" she asked. "I been trying to make sense of it," I responded. "I just want to make sure that I make her proud of me." "I'm sure she is," she replied. "Are you enjoying college so far?" she asked. "Yeah, I love it here. I am just trying to make sure that I can stay. It's expensive." I told her. "That's why I am coming down with you, to help sort it out," she affirmed.

The conversation got weird again when Aunt Tina decided to start talking about sex. "I hope you not down here drinking and participating in orgies," she said. "I know what goes on in college dorms," she continued. In my sick little mind, I started thinking that my aunt used to get busy in her day. I told her that I didn't spend too much time worrying about the women on campus, which was complete bullshit. I also told her that graduation and basketball were my main focus. "That's good," she replied.

Once we arrived at the school, I had to go through validation once again. This time, I had my aunt with me, and I was on academic probation. Validation went the exact same way as before. Only this time, there was a lot more push back in giving me financial aid due to my grades. Aunt Tina explained to the financial aid director that I was still mourning my mother's death. Aunt Tina even brought my mother's obituary and showed it to them. The school was still pushing a hard line about my academic performance. When Aunt Tina started crying and pleading for them to give me another chance; they obliged, and all my financial holds were eventually sorted out.

Aunt Tina could never know how much I love her for taking care of me and making sure that I got school taken care of. Although I told her that I appreciated her for taking the time out of her life to get me squared away, there is still no way to accurately measure my gratitude. So, if you are reading this Aunt Tina, I love you!

THINGS DONE CHANGED

If I wanted to stay at Virginia State, I needed to make sure that I brought my grades up. I decided to use my mother as a motivator rather than allowing her death to continue to kill my soul. I knew it was easier said than done, but at least I could try.

I knew I needed to get my act together. Just like when I was a kid, my way of getting my act together was to get organized. I knew I couldn't stay up all night with Nas and Beat anymore. My goal was to make sure that I could create time to get my work done for my classes.

However, I had quite a few harsh realities awaiting me upon my return to campus. When I arrived, I learned that all three of my squad mates were no longer attending the school. Tyler moved back to Maryland. Beat moved back to North Carolina to work and to attend North Carolina Central University. And Nas had transferred to Norfolk State University, which was about 80 miles from Virginia State. His goal was to pursue playing Division I college football. Just like that, I was alone at Virginia State again. It wasn't like my freshman year because I still knew a lot of people, but there was still a huge void without my boys.

On one hand, it was very hard to deal with not having my guys around. We had so much camaraderie and so much fun. Every day without them was difficult for me. I still hung out in Puryear Hall because that's where everybody I knew lived or hung out, but it wasn't the same without Nas and Beat.

Often, I would walk by places where some of our memorable moments happened and smile before feeling sadness.

I recalled one day during the past winter when Nas and I were looking out the window of Puryear Hall and saw what looked like the whole female student body heading toward the dorm with buckets of pre-made snowballs. Their plan was to set off a snowball fight against the male students. That plan worked. Quickly, we alerted as many guys we could find, so we would have a line of defense. We all started making snowballs and went to war with them.

I still have flashbacks of Nas throwing a snowball at one female student. The funny thing was the woman he threw it at ducked, and it hit another female student in the face. I damn near peed on myself I was laughing so hard. That snowball fight began at Puryear Hall, moved towards the cafeteria, and ended up near the library. The snowball fight lasted for hours, and it was all in good fun. In the spring semester, we paid them back with a water balloon war that was just as epic.

Without my guys, I felt empty. On the flipside, now I had the time I needed to get my work done, more than enough time.

NICHOLAS HALL 2.0

During the fall semester of 2000, Nicholas Hall had a new cast of characters. We had Corey from New Jersey, Randy from Philly, Charles from Atlanta, and Darrell from Virginia whom we called Picasso because he looked like a Ninja Turtle. We also had Eddie, whom we called "Ed." Ed was from Philly but had in Virginia for lived several years; he hung out with a guy named Brandon, who was from Virginia. Brandon didn't live in Nicholas, but he might as well have for as much time as he spent in our dorm.

Corey was the guy who introduced me to downloading online music from sites like Napster, Kazaa, and Limewire; he was also one of the best-known bootleg CD vendors on campus. He was very business-minded. Later, he started selling food on campus after the cafe closed; the guy was a legit hustler. I thought Corey was a little on the sweet side, by the way he walked, sucked his thumb, and the colorful eye contacts he would wear. I didn't give a fuck though; he was a cool dude.

Corey also had lots of female friends that came to his room, but he wasn't smashing them. Some of those ladies were BAD, in a great way, and not trying to have sex with them was foreign to me—especially, during this stage of my life when I was trying to fuck everything moving. I figured since he wasn't trying to smash them, then he could put in a good word for ya boy. I mean, somebody had to beat them guts, and I'd rather it be me. As a result, he threw a few assists, and I gladly took those alley-oops like he was Gary Payton and I was Shawn Kemp. On those nights, I was the Reign Man.

Randy is a somewhat quiet hyper masculine guy who played tight-end for the Virginia State football team. Randy was almost a Rob Gronkowski sized guy. Now, I mentioned Randy was quiet, but he had his funny moments. When he thought someone was doing too much or causing too much attention, he would say, "Yo you DRAWIN," in his signature deep voice. We all laughed because it came out of nowhere. The non-Philly people found it especially funny because they were unfamiliar with the term. "Drawin" is a Philly term used for just about anything, but it began as an adjective to describe someone attracting too much attention or being extra. The word evolved to mean many other things over the years, see *Urban Dictionary* for more meanings.

What really got under Randy's skin was his roommate, Tormell, who was from the DC-Maryland area. What was it about his roommate that got under his skin? I'm glad you asked. His roommate was gay. As immature as I was during this time, I had all the jokes. And I do mean, ALL the jokes. Remember when I said Randy played tight end? Just mentioning his position, tight-end, made me burst out in laughter. "Yo Randy, what route you running tonight?" I would ask him before he entered his room to go to sleep. "Does your roommate know you like the tight end position?" I would ask him. "You ever thought about being a wide receiver?" I'd joke. The rest of the team would laugh so hard they couldn't breathe! Randy would tell us that we were drawin, and then we'd laugh even louder.

One day, the whole crew was hanging out in the Nicholas hallways. We were just shooting the shit and bonding over real-life stories when we heard a door slam out of nowhere. BOOM! We all turned around at the same time. "What the fuck?" we all responded. That's when I saw Randy, and he was pissed. Before anyone could ask what happened, he gave it to us. "Man, that nigga DRAWIN!" he yelled. "Who?" I asked. "That nigga Tormell, he responded. "What he do?" Corey asked. "He in there laying in the bed with another nigga hugged up with they shirts off and they feet out," he responded. Man, you would've thought Richard Pryor was doing stand-up in the hallway. We laughed so fucking hard. The laughter lasted for what felt like an eternity. When I was done laughing, my back was hurting. The jokes came nonstop, but I couldn't get them out because I was laughing so hard. We never let Randy live it down.

Charles was a six-foot-six freshman who was recruited to the Virginia State basketball team. He was a very free-spirited, silly, you-only-live-once type of guy. Literally, his motto was "fuck it." He was very spontaneous. All he cared about was basketball and getting "crunk," which was the thing deep south people did back then. It's similar to the phrase "turning up," which is more commonly used nowadays. If you came up with an idea no matter how risky or ridiculous, Charles was down. That made for some nice pranks and funny moments. Like the time Charles was tired of being hungry after the cafe closed, so he decided to stuff his empty book bag with all the pastries served at dinner. He didn't care if they were all smashed up in his book bag, as long as he had them.

Charles had a knack for saying and doing the funniest stuff. One time, we were all talking about how nicely shaped this female student's butt was. Being the horny guys that we were, we all began to lust over what we would like to do to her. You know, stuff like "I wanna hit that doggy style," or "I'd smash that raw and smack her ass," the usual immature and thirsty comments. Out of nowhere, Charles said, "Man her ass is so fat, I just want to punch that bitch in the butt. I bet it will never stop shaking." We were all dying laughing.

As I mentioned before, we all loved the DC-Maryland women at the school, but not so much the guys. The DC guys didn't like northern guys too much, especially because we were after their women. The guys from DC dressed the same; they wore black shirts with cartoon characters painted on them with silver colored glitter. They paired those shirts with a black bandana tied around their heads that also had glitter lettering on it. They wore grey sweatpants and Foamposite sneakers. I thought they looked like a bunch of Oakland Raiders fans, but Charles had the best analogy. Charles considered their country accent with their style of dress and said they looked like Pirates.

We all laughed at the moniker because it was very vivid. From that point forward, we referred to them as pirates.

I was no longer alone at Virginia State; the Nicholas 2.0 team was always together at football games, basketball games, parties, and rolling 15–20 deep to the cafe.

THE RECEIVING END

By now, it should be clear that we were all a group of trolls. If there was a way to troll somebody, we were all down for an opportunity to create moments that we could laugh about and hold us over until the next one. It didn't matter who the person was that got trolled. Anyone was fair game, like the time they finally got me.

There was a very beautiful and voluptuous woman on campus that I was damn near in love with. Let's call her Natalie. At the time, she was easily one of the finest women that I saw in person. Of all the women that I shot my shot or spit game at, I just couldn't bring myself to get at her. Approaching her seemed like a major leap, even for me, a person who had been overachieving with ladies way out of my league. For whatever reason, I was intimidated by her.

I remember describing her to the crew when we inevitably began talking about the fine ladies on campus. That's when I learned that both Ed and Brandon not only had classes with her but knew her personally. From there, I was constantly trying to get them to put a good word in for me, I just had to have her. At first, they would tell me how approachable she was and encourage me to just step to her. I wasn't buying those tickets though. That's Philly slang for I wasn't believing that. Eventually, they said they would put out a good word for me, and I was ready to take it from there.

One Saturday, we were all venturing to the cafe at dinner time to do the usual eat, shoot the shit, and find women to holla at. We were all in line figuring out what we were going to eat. I had a funny feeling that I couldn't shake. It just felt like something was off. I paid it no mind as I went to the juice machine before returning to the table we had secured for the team. As I walked back to the table, I noticed that all the crew had already made it back to the table, except for me. That was odd because we usually went back together.

On my way back, I saw the table had only one seat available. How nice of them to save me a seat, right? The whole crew watched me as I approached. I wondered what the fuck was up. As I got closer, I noticed that we had a special guest at the table. It was Natalie. Remember that empty seat they saved for me? It was next to Natalie. That's when I knew what they were planning.

At that moment, it was like everyone and everything in the cafe was moving in slow motion. They were in full troll mode. Ed said, "We have a guest; aren't you going to say hi?" Everyone turned and stared at me. Natalie looked at me and smiled; she knew that I liked her because Ed and Brandon had told her. She also knew about their plans to troll me, and she was on board. I was so fucking shook I didn't know what to do. I'm sure my anxiety showed up on the Richter scale. I could barely talk past saying, "Hello Natalie." I played it as cool as I could, but there was no way that I was going try to holla at her in front of my whole crew. If I were rejected publicly, they would never let me live it down. The stakes were too high. I couldn't tell whether she was genuinely interested or just playing along with the gag. That's when I decided to dead the dream of getting at her. I decided to take the "L." It was the only way to get me, and they got me good. We still laugh about it till this day.

NORFOLK STATE UNIVERSITY

By spring 2001, I got a new car, a 1992 Infiniti Q45. It was a V8 with a silver sleek design. It was much better than my 1991 Buick Century. Stepping my car game up was like graduating from the get pussy school. I was trying to over-overachieve.

On the weekends, I would fill up my Infiniti Q45 with gas and drive to Norfolk State University to chill with my best friend Nas. Nas was trying to make Norfolk State's football team as a walk-on. We spent most of our time playing basketball or shooting the shit about life. Nas showed me around Norfolk State University and the city while trying to talk me into transferring to NSU. As we strolled the campus, of course, I was scouting for women to holla at. Nas introduced me to a girl from Philly he had been dating, her name was Chloe. "Yo, see if she got a friend for me," I asked. "Aight bet," he responded. Once we got back to his dorm room, we ate the nastiest pizza I ever had in my life from a local chain that I will not name because I'm not trying to get sued.

One weekend in the spring semester of 2001, I took the road trip to Norfolk State to chill with Nas and to meet Chloe's friend who she and Nas were matchmaking for me. I had a fresh low haircut with waves and was wearing my Michael Jordan UNC throwback jersey with no T-shirt, letting my well-toned arms show. A pair of grey Nike sweatpants and a pair of white and Carolina blue Jordan 11s completed my outfit. I pulled my silver Infiniti Q45 into the parking lot of Nas's dorm and hopped out.

When I arrived, I saw a beautiful sista with medium length hair, wearing a grey Norfolk State T-shirt, blue jeans, and black sneakers. She wore glasses, which I thought were extra cute, and she had a nice smile that was accented by her dimples. This wasn't going to be a Harris Hall situation, I thought. "This is my friend K I was telling you about," said Nas. "How you doing?" I asked. "My name is Kunle, but people call me "K" for short. What's your name?" I asked. "I'm doing good; thanks for asking," she responded. "My name is Shantel," she said with a smile.

Later that night, there was a party off-campus at a place everyone called the sweatbox. It was a very small club that got so hot everyone would be drenched in sweat, hence its name. During my conversation with Shantel, I learned that she did not like going to clubs. "How come you not going to the sweatbox?" I asked. "It's just not my scene," she said. Aside from the fact that she was also from Philly, it was another connection that we had. "I don't like going to clubs either," I responded. Instead of going to the sweatbox, we chilled outside the dorms getting to know each other.

After a few months of talking on the phone and going to see her every weekend, we decided to be together. Just like that, I had a girlfriend.

MISSION COLLEGE

During the Fall 2001 semester, Shantel and Chloe decided to move off the Norfolk State campus. Given that all my Nicholas 2.0 crew went in different directions, I had a decision to make. Carl moved back to ATL to attend college. Eddie took about a year off; Randy went back to Philly, and Corey moved off-campus. Brandon still lived on campus at Virginia State, but I barely saw him. Once again, I was alone at Virginia State University; this routine was getting old, fast.

I decided that I was going to move in with my girlfriend and her roommate who also let Nas move in. The four of us were under one roof in a two-bedroom apartment called Mission College Apartments. The apartment complex was two blocks from Norfolk State University. The goal was to live in Virginia off-campus for a year so that I could establish residency and attend Norfolk State while lowering the cost by paying in-state tuition. There was only one problem with that, neither Nas or I had a job.

Living with Shantel and Chloe had its great moments but was not without its challenges. It was a new situation for all of us. Technically, it was our very first apartment. With so many strong personalities under one roof, there were bound to be confrontations. Add in the dynamics of two pairs of friendships plus two separate romantic relationships, and it got nuclear at times. Sometimes, Nas and I had to break up fights between Shantel and Chloe. Other times, each couple played therapist to the other. We were young, Adele voice, and we loved each other, so there were great bonding moments too.

Shantel and I had a very strong connection. Not only were we from the same city, but we liked the same music and loved to watch sports together. While at Mission College, we spent nearly every waking moment together. We never wanted to be too far from each other; that's how strong the bond was. When we had money, we had money together; it didn't matter if it was only enough for two chicken wings and a biscuit from Church's Chicken, we ate it together. Even when we were broke, I never felt like I was missing out on too much because I had her. She was the closest person to me and my first true love. We shared many big moments together.

Quick story, I remember driving to Military Circle Mall in Norfolk with Shantel and Nas to cop Jay-Z's *The Blueprint* album. I was a huge Jay-Z fan, and this album was highly anticipated. We were so excited because there was good energy in the air, and as soon as I heard his lead single titled "Izzo," I knew that the album was going to be a classic. On the way home, we listened to the album enjoying track after track. By the time we got to the sixth song titled *"U Don't Know,"* I yelled out, "Yo, I knew this album was gonna be a classic!" The crazy thing about that was the best songs were yet to come.

What's the significance of this story you ask? Well, this was in 2001 before everyone was walking around with cellphones as mainstays in their pockets; in fact, not too many people had them. We had no idea what news we were going to hear when we returned home. When we arrived, everyone rushed us with concern. "Are you ok?" everyone yelled. "We were so worried about y'all," they added. We had no clue what they were talking about or why everyone was so concerned.

Before I could understand what was happening, I saw Chloe and a group of her friends all huddled up around the 25-inch television and crying. Now, I mentioned that it was 2001, but I neglected to mention that it was September 11th, the day of the terrorist attacks on New York City. Chloe and her friends were watching as the planes flew into the twin towers and people jumped to their deaths on national television. Some of her friends were from New York and had family that worked in the towers. When they saw we were ok and all the hugs were over, I realized we could've been killed. No one knew when or where the next attacks were going to happen. If we had died, we would've died together and that would've been the best case scenario to me, taking my last breath with Shantel beside me.

ABACUS COMMUNICATIONS

I couldn't live with a woman and not be able to contribute, so I got on my grind to get a job ASAP. My first job was at a telemarketing business that specialized in harassing people to buy magazine subscriptions during a time when the Internet was starting to make everything digital. Even back then I knew it just a matter of time until the telemarketing service for magazines would be obsolete. On top of that, I hate the idea of calling people and trying to convince them that I was worth talking to and that I had something that they needed. The truth is, I didn't. They didn't need these outdated magazines when they could just Google anything of interest to them. When I factored in being hung up on, yelled at, and threatened several times daily, I knew it was time for me to go. It wasn't worth the stress, and it certainly wasn't worth the $6.25 per hour plus the commission that nobody ever got. Regardless, it was a job, and I was going to keep it until I got another one.

After working at the telemarketing place for about a week, Shantel let me know that Ticketmaster, where she worked, was hiring. Ticketmaster was a reverse situation compared to the magazine place. At Ticketmaster, people called in looking to buy tickets for concerts and events they already had interest in attending. I liked that. It was also a higher paying job at $7.25 per hour. The only problem with working at Ticketmaster was now I would be living with Shantel *and* working with her as well. I knew that being with her all hours of the day without either of us having separate identities would be problematic. So, I decided that Ticketmaster was going to be short-lived as well.

Fortunately, I found another job that Shantel put both Nas and me on to, Abacus Communications in Virginia Beach. Abacus was a third-party call center for Sprint PCS, which is now known simply as *Sprint*. Yep, the same cell phone carrier that some of you use today. Shantel had left Ticketmaster and taken a job at Abacus where she worked long enough to finish the paid training before going live on the floor. She then took a job at the Greyhound Bus company doing customer service, where she worked long term.

At the time, Abacus paid $7.50 per hour for training, and $8.50 once we were on the call floor. Nas and I were both excited to be working in a more stable environment. The cherry on top was that we could now afford to get our own apartment together as roommates.

SEWELLS POINT ROAD

Nas and I saved up enough money for a security deposit and the first month's rent before we began apartment shopping. We applied to several places and got many rejections because I did not have enough credit to meet the requirements, and Nas had bad credit. We still had a few more applications pending, but it was feeling hopeless. I did not want to overstay my welcome at Shantel's.

One day while interviewing for a nice apartment, we received a phone call from a more ghetto apartment complex that had accepted us. The beauty of the phone call is that it came mid-conversation as the lady from the nicer apartment was rejecting us, so she was there to witness it all. We accepted the offer from the lesser apartment and were on our way to go review the lease. "Wait, one second," the lady from the nicer apartment said. "I am on the phone with my manager, and they want to accept your application."

It was funny that two minutes before, we were getting ready to leave after another disappointing interview without an apartment, but after that phone call, we had options. The change of heart was noted. We decided to stay with the nicer apartment because it was simply the better option. Either way, God came through and made sure we got the apartment we originally wanted, Apollo Arms Apartments on Sewells Point Road in Norfolk.

Nas and I already knew how we were going to furnish the apartment. We decided that we were going to get furniture for every room, except the living room. That way, if we were to have female company, they would have to visit us in the bedroom. It was basically a test. We knew that if they were willing to come to the bedroom late at night, it was going down. It sounds ridiculous now, but in our 19- and 20-year-old perverted minds, it made perfect sense. It was especially true if we were on the outs with our girlfriends, which happened periodically.

Where did we find said girls, you ask? Well, we had a multitude of ways. One way was Nas getting on the party line and chatting with girls; once he landed one, he made sure she brought a friend. The party line used to be popping back then; that was before online dating sites like Match.com or Tinder. The people you found on the party line were hit or miss, both figuratively and literally; they were somewhere between people who genuinely wanted to date and backpage.com. Keep in mind there was no way to know what a person looked like because there were no profiles, just conversation. Thus, there was a lot of catfishing going on, like that time Nas and I went to holla at chicks at Hampton University.

HAMPTON

Hampton University was known to have some of the best-looking women back then. So, when we heard that the girls that Nas was talking to went to Hampton, we just knew it was going to be on. We knew the chances were high that these ladies were going to be highly attractive. We took showers and got dressed and ready to meet these ladies. When we arrived at the dorm, we called them at the front desk of their dorm to let them know that we were downstairs. "We will be down in a minute," they responded. That's female terms for another 30 minutes to an hour at least.

We waited about another 20 or 30 minutes as we watched ladies go in and out of the dorm. We were trying to use our Harris Hall skills to figure out which of them were the ladies we had been talking to over the phone. It was a Friday night, so you know these ladies were all dressed to go to parties and clubs. The more bad ladies that came out of the dorm, the more excited we got. Every time we saw one, Nas and I would make eye contact and just nod our heads yes and no with a smile. Yes meant that we would smash, and no meant that we wouldn't pull out; that's how bad they were. If a lady got a yes and a nod, that meant they were wifey material.

A few more minutes passed, that's when I turned and looked into the dorm lobby and saw this huge and I mean Stay Puft Marshmallow Man huge lady coming to the door. No disrespect to her, but she was the biggest woman I had ever seen in person. That's when I knew exactly who Nas had been talking to on the party line. Let's call her Tammy. I started laughing so hard I damn-near peed on myself. Not at Tammy, but at Nas. Only Nas would find a way to find her out of all the chicks that Hampton was known for. Nas looked pissed, but even he had to laugh as well.

When Tammy finally came through the door, Nas and I were playing it cool. I knew Nas was disappointed and no longer wanted to have sex with her. Tammy's friend, let's call her Natasha, was extremely attractive though, so I was winning. The four of us walked and talk for most of the night before heading home. A few days later, I got a phone call from the Hampton ladies. "We are on our way to your apartment," Natasha said. "Cool," I responded as I gave them directions. I figured Nas had contacted with the two ladies and invited them over.

When they arrived, I let them in. I showed the Tammy to Nas's room and took Natasha to mine. Tammy was so big that she had to walk through Nas's bedroom door sideways. I don't know what went on in Nas's room, but a few minutes later Tammy knocked on my door to ask Natasha if she was ready to go. When I answered the door, she saw that I didn't have my shirt on, and Natasha wasn't wearing pants. Tammy realized what was about to go down, so she returned to Nas's room.

When Tammy left the room, I tore Natasha lil fat booty ass up. After I finished fucking Natasha, I hit her with my favorite line. "What you about to do?" I asked. "I want to go check on Tammy," she responded while pulling her panties up. When Natasha knocked on Nas's door the check on Tammy, I went to the kitchen to rehydrate after putting in work. Tammy came out of the room looking disappointed. Natasha told me Tammy wasn't feeling well and that she wanted to take her back to Hampton. That's was lady talk for this didn't work as I planned so I'm ready to go. "Aight, I'll see y'all later," I responded as I gave Tammy a hug.

When they left, I went into Nas's room and asked him what happened. "Nothing," he responded matter-of-factly. "What do you mean nothing?" I asked. "You think I smashed that don't you?" Nas asked. I burst out laughing uncontrollably. When I gained composure, I asked if he did. Nas said, "You drawin. No, I didn't smash." "So, what happened?" I asked. "After she knocked on your door and knew that y'all was about to get it in, she came in here thinking we was going to have sex," Nas responded. "And it's all your fault." he continued jokingly. "What did you do?" I asked. "Man, I rolled over and went to sleep," he responded. I was crying laughing. I told Nas I thought he was the one that invited them over, but he said he didn't. He told me they invited themselves over. Long story short, I guess this is one of the few times where Nas didn't take one for the team.

When we weren't smashing random chicks from the party line, we were knocking off chicks in our call center and anywhere else we met them. Remember those girls from Puryear Hall that nicknamed me Sleepy? Well as fate would have it, I ran into them at a 7-Eleven around the corner from our apartment in Norfolk; they were from Norfolk and were home from Virginia State for Christmas break. It was nice to see them again. I gave them my phone number and told them I lived locally. I told them to hit me up if they wanted to come through. They came through the same night. Of course, I smashed, but that was the first time I got head from a girl with a tongue ring. The head was good, but I don't think that the tongue ring had anything to do with it. I just think she was a master psychologist, that means the head was crazy!

CHAPTER 9

ALL FALLS DOWN

There is a scene in *The Sopranos* where Carmella was trying to get her husband and main character Tony to plan for his future. Tony was known for living in the moment and seemingly just going along for the ride. Although he had plans for things, he kept his wife in the dark about them for her own safety. I mean, the guy is a mob boss. Carmella was trying to get Tony to leave his mafia life behind before he got killed or was sentenced to life in prison. In that scene, Carmella was tired of living in the unknown, and she says some of the realest shit ever to him. "Everything comes to an end!" she yelled. It was a reality that Tony spent his entire life trying to avoid coming to terms with. For so many other reasons in *my* life, I just wish someone loved me enough to tell me that same shit.

THE SOUND OF THE POLICE

Nas and I were bored one day and decided to buy some BB guns. We ran around our apartment shooting them at each other, just having fun. The ones we bought looked very realistic and even had realistic weight. Out of nowhere, we had a bright idea of trying to see how real our BB guns looked. We decided to go to the Norfolk State campus during open-gym basketball. For whatever reason, we brought the BB guns with us.

When we got to the gym, we knocked on the door. A student came to the door and said, "Y'all can't come in here unless you have your student ID, so get the fuck out" while buffing up like he was going to beat one of our asses if we didn't listen to him. It was just the excuse we needed. We both simultaneously lifted our shirts to show the BB guns we had stashed on our waists. The guy looked so terrified as his face went pale. He closed the door, and we ran off laughing; it was funny to us.

Before we could exit the campus, we heard a voice. "Excuse me? Guys?" the voice called. We continued walking. Then we heard a walkie-talkie radio describing our outfits. Before we could take off running, we heard "Freeze. Hold it right there!" The voices we heard were two female Norfolk State school police officers. "Put your hands on your head! Get on your knees, now!" the officer demanded. Once Nas and I got to our knees, the two officers confronted us with their guns drawn. "That sucka dude at the door punk ass called the police," I remember thinking.

The crazy part about it is, I wasn't scared of the gun being drawn on me. I'm from Nicetown; I've had guns pointed and shot in my direction several times. What really scared me was both officers being so nervous and shaking. I mean, they were more scared than we were, and they were pointing the guns. One officer particularly was shaking so intensely that it worried me that she would accidentally shoot and kill one of us. When they finally searched us and realized that we only had BB guns that shot yellow plastic pellets, they seemed to relax. We explained to them that we were just playing around and was not going to hurt anybody. They gave us a lecture about safety and let us know that we could've gone to jail. Afterward, they let us off with a warning.

STUPID IS AS STUPID DOES

Even in the best relationships, there are problems, and ours started with proximity. We were around each other so much that we started to get on each other's nerves. Everything became an argument, and those arguments got more and more heated over time. Like the time when I came over to Shantel's house unexpectedly.

I hadn't heard from Shantel in a few days, which was unusual. Normally, I wouldn't trip but I couldn't shake the eerie feeling I was having. I decided to hop in my whip and head over to Mission College to see what was up.

When I arrived, I knocked on the door and Chloe answered. "Hey K, what are you doing here?" she answered while barely cracking the door. I noticed that she didn't want me to see what was going on in the apartment, which I thought was suspicious. "Where's Shantel?" I asked while looking through the crack in the door. "I don't know where she is," Chloe responded.

Through that little crack in the door, I saw Chloe's friend Ben with his cousin, Shantel's ex-boyfriend. "What was her ex-boyfriend doing there?" I thought. I became skeptical about Chloe's story. Both she and Shantel knew I didn't like either one of those dudes, and the feeling was mutual. "I need to see if she is here," I said. Chloe knew that I was onto something and decided to prove me wrong by letting me in the house. When I walked in, I looked in Shantel's room and noticed she wasn't there. I knew something was up, so I decided to stay. I went to the kitchen to grab a knife while I sat in Shantel's room. I was in the house alone with two dudes that I had issues with. I had to make sure that I wasn't going to get jumped by these bitch ass niggas.

When Chloe saw that I had a knife, she called Shantel to tell her that I had come to kill her. Not only was that far from the truth, but it also meant that she knew where Shantel was. I put the knife back in the kitchen as I left the apartment. I knew she had to be close by, and there weren't too many places for her to go. I sat on the staircase while I pondered where she had gone. I looked across the parking lot at her friend's apartment, and I saw her silhouette in the window peeking at me. It was nighttime, so she was easy to spot.

Apparently, Shantel had the same eerie feeling that I had, and she knew that I might come to the apartment—either that or Chloe called Nas and found out that I wasn't home, so she put two and two together. She decided to run over to her friend's apartment before I got to hers, clever.

I called her cell phone to let her know that I saw her and that I just wanted to talk. She knew I was upset about her ex-boyfriend being at her apartment. Chloe had her believing that I came to kill her, so now she was scared to a higher degree. The whole situation was a mess. After lots of conversation and assurances, she agreed to come outside. She had her two friends accompany her. "I didn't come to hurt you," I told her. "You can even drive my car to where ever you want to talk," I added. She knew that I was serious about not wanting to hurt her once she heard that. I had never allowed anyone to drive my car before, especially her. She still had her friends follow my car until she felt safe. I didn't care, I just wanted to stop the charades.

We drove and we talked the problem out. I expressed to her how disrespectful and deceitful it was to have her ex-boyfriend at her house. Of course, Shantel blamed their presence on Chloe. She knew there was tension between him and me, so explaining the knife took less energy than I expected. Shantel blamed me for not trusting her and called me jealous. Was I jealous? Maybe. I was so paranoid when it came to other guys being around her. I knew that I loved her, but I also knew I wasn't ready for her. "How would you feel if you came over to my apartment and my ex-girlfriend was there?" I asked. "Especially if it were an ex-girlfriend that you had issues with," I added. I think she got the point after a while and eventually, things got worked out.

That wasn't the first or only problem in our relationship. Things got much worse over time. Our arguments became physical—to the point, we would fight each other. If there is anything in the world that I am ashamed of in my life, it's our physical altercations. I'd love to tell you that she started them, but I'd be lying. Even if she did, it was my responsibility as a man to walk away, and sometimes I didn't. I couldn't shake the rage I carried. It was like Sam Rothstein and his wife Ginger in the movie *Casino*, without the drugs and booze. We never left bruises on each other, but we did plenty to damage each other's hearts.

At this point in my life, I was on some real Jody shit. If you don't get that reference, go watch the movie *Baby Boy*. Jody, the main character played by Tyrese, and his girlfriend Yvette, played by Taraji P. Henson had a relationship that mirrored Shantel's and my relationship. There was so much love between us, but one of us was not mature enough for the other—that somebody was me. Shantel was my heart of hearts and, like every other woman who mattered to me, I found a way to fuck it up. I have carried that skeleton in my closet ever since.

"Fear God in your treatment of women."

—Prophet Muhammad

BACK TO PHILLY

One day, while working my shift at Abacus Communications, I became incredibly sick. I felt very faint and weak. I went to my team leader and let her know that I was feeling really ill. She informed the director on site. The director told the team leader that she didn't want to send anyone home because she needed everybody to stay for company numbers. I didn't give a fuck about company numbers because I could tell this was no normal feeling of illness. I went to talk to the director personally to urge her to reconsider. She told me that she was going to talk to her superiors and get back to me in a few minutes. Those few minutes turned into about an hour, and I felt sicker with each minute that passed. I mean, this is a job where I had put in hundreds of hours of overtime and stayed every time they asked me to—and they had to deliberate on whether I could go home or not. I decided that I couldn't take it anymore, and I just drove myself home before I would be unable to do so.

As the days passed, my illness got worse, and no matter what medication I took, it didn't get better. I called Shantel begging her to come to take me to the hospital. I laid on the bed with a fever and chills, sweating profusely; I could barely move. I felt like I was going to die. Shantel told me she couldn't leave work but would get to me as soon as she could. "Help me, I'm dying," I told her. I thought I was going to check out before she got to me.

By the time Shantel arrived, I was barely conscious. After I was checked out by a doctor at the hospital, it was determined that I had a very bad case of pneumonia. I wasn't bullshitting about being near death. "You are very lucky. Had it been any longer before I saw you, you wouldn't have made it," the doctor said. The doctors took really good care of me, and after a few days in the hospital, I began to recover.

Since I left my shift early and without permission, I lost my job. I didn't care about losing the Abacus job because I left for a legit reason. However, I could no longer pay my rent or utilities. I decided to pack my things and move back to Philly to live with my father until I could get back into Virginia State for the fall 2002 semester. Nas understood the situation. He decided to stay and keep the apartment. He eventually moved in with his girlfriend at the time, Angel.

TROJAN AGAIN

After a few months living with my father, I returned to Virginia State for the fall 2002 semester, which started very much like my first semester. There was a shortage of housing on campus due to a massive influx of students, so for the first time in my Virginia State career, I would not be staying in Nicholas Hall. Instead, many of us had a choice of moving off campus or being placed in the nearby Ramada Inn as a part of room and board. Since living off campus was not a viable option for me, I chose the Ramada.

THE DANGER ZONE

Quick story about the Ramada in Petersburg, Virginia. When I stayed there in the fall semester of 2002, it was during the DC Sniper's reign of terror. One of the lesser-known facts about his violent tour is that he actually stopped in Petersburg. Where exactly did he stop? He spent the night right outside the window of my room at the Ramada Inn. I lived on the second floor and had a direct view of his 1990 Chevy Caprice which had Alabama license plates on it. This was obviously before anyone knew who he was or what car he drove. The night he arrived, not only was his car spotted, but I saw him several times going in and out of the Ramada. He kept taking and eating ice from the ice machine in the hallway, which was very peculiar. At the time, I didn't think too much of it. I figured the guy was homeless and down in the dumps.

Once he was apprehended in Maryland, a few days later, I learned how close to danger I was. The next morning while on my way to catch the shuttle to campus, I was approached by a news reporter asking, "Do you know who John Allen Muhammad and Lee Boyd Malvo are?" I remember it clear as day because it was raining, and I did not want to stand in the rain for an interview. "No, I don't," I responded. "Well those are the names of the DC Sniper and accomplice," the reporter added. Before I could ask why he was telling me that, the reporter continued. "He was spotted right here in the Ramada parking lot a couple of days ago, and there were reports of a strange man using the ice machine." That's when it hit me. I used to have the newspaper article saved, but after moving so many times, I cannot seem to find it. I'm sure the local news station in Petersburg still has the footage of me looking stupid during the interview.

BACK ON CAMPUS

When I returned to VSU this time, nearly all my friends from Nicholas 2.0 were gone. There were no more distractions or excuses for me not to get busy and start making progress towards my goals. I had two goals. My first goal was to get back on track academically, and my second goal was to make the Virginia State basketball team.

As the semester went on, I knew I was doing better with my grades than I ever had at Virginia State. Also, I had been hitting the gym and gearing up for basketball tryouts. When the day came, I was prepared. Just like in high school, I played a decent game in the tryouts. Also, just like high school, I was cut. It was very disappointing to experience déjà vu, but at this point, everything was déjà vu, not just the outcome. In both high school and college, I was goofing off and getting distracted by things that were not associated with my goals. By allowing those distractions to become my focus, I took time away from pushing in the directions that meant the most to me. It was heartbreaking, but I recognized the pattern of my life. I was always late to the party.

I decided that just as I did in high school, I would use this opportunity to focus completely on my game. Not only that, I would make sure that I worked on my game at the place that would get my abilities noticed, Daniel Gymnasium. That's the gym where the Virginia State basketball team played. It was logical for me to practice at the place I wanted to play, but with the added chance that the Coach Benjamin would see my ability and effort. However, it didn't quite turn out that way.

OPPORTUNITY KNOCKS

One day, I was in the gym running suicide drills and defensive slides for cardio. When I heard a voice, "Who's winning?" I looked up and saw that it was Patty Delbridge, the Women's Basketball coach. I hadn't noticed that she was around, nor did I know if she had been watching or just passing through. "I am," I responded. "He's tough, but I'm going to outwork him," I continued. Coach Delbridge laughed. What she didn't know was in my mind my response was a metaphor for anyone more talented than I was. I was laser-focused on being the best every day, and I approached the court with that energy every day.

Over the next few weeks, I saw Coach Delbridge passing through the gym. I did my best to pay her no mind while I practiced. One day, Coach Delbridge came through while I worked on shooting drills. "Did you try out for the team?" she asked. "Yes, ma'am," I responded. "What's your name?" she asked. "Adekunle, but most people call me K," I responded. We exchanged small talk about the origin of my name; then, she went on about her business, and I continued shooting.

A couple days later, I received a call from the men's basketball coach, Coach Benjamin, inviting me to do conditioning and participate in team workouts. I am not ashamed to say that I damn near peed on myself when I got the call. I was so excited. Coach Benjamin explained to me that if I were to make the team, I would be considered a walk-on and would not receive an athletic scholarship, but I would be eligible for one the following season. I was not deterred. Hip-Hop artist Nas said, "All I need is one mic," and all I needed was an opportunity. In fact, this was the opportunity of a lifetime, and I knew it would only knock once.

Given that I did not make the cut directly after tryouts, I don't know what prompted the phone call. I used to play basketball with a few of the guys who were on the team; perhaps there was a word-of-mouth situation. Did Coach Benjamin call Coach Ellerbee for a reference as I often asked him to do? Or did Coach Delbridge put in a word? I never really found out how it happened, but I was surely thankful, and I had no intentions of screwing it up.

The next morning, I was up and ready to go at 4:00 a.m. The schedule for the day, which became routine, was, to begin with a timed jog around the campus. We followed the run with breakfast at the cafe around 6:30 a.m. or 7:00 a.m. Then, we would do stretching, weightlifting, drills, and then scrimmaging. The routine felt familiar because it was similar to the basketball program at Gratz High School.

Finally, I was a part of a major team, and I soaked in every minute. I lived for every moment. I enjoyed putting on the weighted vest and doing agility drills. I loved the morning runs, the stretching, and weight training. The one thing I really lived for was the scrimmages. It was fun matching wits and abilities with guys who were trained in organized basketball, guys who were a part of the system. The opportunity to showcase my talent in front of Coach Benjamin was the cherry on top.

A DOLLAR SHORT

A few days before the season began, I received a notice of my financial standing at the school. The letter stated that my account had a hold for over $4,000 and that it would need to be cleared before I could return for the spring 2003 semester. It was a very deflating letter that came at the worst possible time. Reading it made my heart feel like it was going to jump out of my chest.

I instantly began racking my brain about how to come up with the money. I made several phone calls to family members, but nobody could afford such a price tag, not even collectively. I went to the financial aid director to see if there were anymore scholarships, grants, or loans that I would qualify for, but my efforts were to no avail. My financial aid had been maxed, and I still had an outstanding balance for the upcoming spring 2003 semester. I could not work because I did not have a car because I had sold my car to help pay for the fall 2002 semester. Even if I had a car, it was impossible to work and play basketball at Virginia State.

My final attempt was to see Coach Benjamin. I met with Coach Benjamin and told him of my situation. "That's a tough situation. What are you going to do?" he asked. I told him that I had come to see if there was anything that he could do to help me. "There is no more money available for the basketball program until next year; I'm sorry," he told me.

Over the next several days, I applied for private loans and credit cards. All of them were denied either because I had no credit or my father's credit wasn't good enough to get approved. I was on the verge of realizing my dream of playing ball for Virginia State, but it was being ripped from my grasp, and there was nothing I could do to help change the situation. I was a dollar short and a day late. All I could do was cry. I was literally watching my dream turn into a nightmare.

With no means of covering the $4,000 cost to return to school, fall 2002 was my last semester at Virginia State, and it ended unceremoniously. My life flashed before my eyes. I thought of all the time I had wasted and the years of eligibility that were being wasted as well. I literally cried all the way home to Philly, having no one to blame but myself. By the time I got to Maryland, I had no more tears to cry, but my broken heart remained.

> *"The world equally distributes talent, but not opportunities."*
>
> —Unknown

DOOMSDAY

At the lowest point in my life and just when I thought things couldn't get any worse, I got a phone call from Shantel. I knew by the tone of her voice that it was going to be something that I didn't want to hear, but I listened anyway. "I don't think I can do this anymore," she said. I knew exactly what she was talking about, but I played dumb anyway. "Do what?" I responded. "This long-distance relationship. I want to move on," she added. When she said that, it felt like my heart was going to explode. I tried to convince her to stay, but I could tell she had already made up her mind. When a woman is fed up, R. Kelly voice, but fuck him though.

The anger and rage I carried had taken its toll on her and our relationship. I wanted to ask her why, but I knew all the reasons except one. Aside from our long-distance difficulties, our arguments, and physical fights, there was another reason, one that I wasn't prepared for. Eventually, she told me that she was seeing someone else and that she was going to cheat on me if she stayed with me. Everything went silent when she said that; I could only hear that buzzing sound like when a bomb goes off in the movies. I wondered if she had sex with the guy that night— probably so, but there was nothing I could do about it, and that's what hurt the most.

It was my first real breakup and another major loss for me. There was no one to blame for this breakup but me. I knew I was a shitty boyfriend, but that didn't keep me from being angry at her. Even though I meant well, I didn't deserve her. I deserved to be broken up with—for what I did and the things she didn't know about. All is fair in love and war. Shantel had no plans of coming back to Philly, so moving on seemed easier for her. She told me to promise her that I would finish college; that's when I knew that she would never speak to me again. It felt like she gave up on me and didn't think that I was serious about finishing school. I accepted the challenge and made the promise.

Over time, I tried to call her, but she kept ignoring my phone calls and letting her roommate tell me that she didn't know where she was. I never felt so powerless in my life. I hated her and vowed to never say her name again. Actually, it was really me that I was angry with. I should've practiced more self-control or made better decisions. I knew the way I treated her was not how I felt about her; it was how I felt about me and my life. I pondered each poor decision and bad move over and over as the heartbreak became increasingly severe. I beat myself up for years to come and vowed to never let anyone close enough to hurt me again. Yep, you guessed it, my depression came back like "did you miss me?"

> *"Even the strongest feelings expire when ignored and taken for granted."*
>
> —Unknown

That night at Chloe crib
I could've sworn you was cheatin'
And you knew that's what I thought
That's why you in the blinds peakin'
They was trying to get it through
That I'm the wrong dude to be with
The only thing that you remember
Is our last time speakin'
You remember me sayin'
That "I would never deceive you" I told you "
God gave me eyes so I could see other people"

That's when it hit you, now you trippin'

Cuz I was dead wrong

And the story of our life

Is another sad song

So, instead, you Re-bel and Re-pel

All my phone calls

I roll out with Fe-males, Re-tail

Using phone cards

We ain't speak for like a week

So now, I'm out getting cheeks

I have 'em spend the night now

Cuz I could answer their beeps

Drove to Charlotte, visit Beat

Chill with Nas and the peeps

As we cruise around the city in a Chero-kee Jeep

You ain't hear from me in hours

Voicemail, you keep trying

Now you on the phone crying

While your mom's implying

[That it's midnight. Do you know where your man is?]

Song: *"Midnight,"* **Artist:** *Me,*
Album: *IDENTITY II: The Nicetown Diary* **Year:** *2005*

CHAPTER 10

A MOMENT IN SPACE

HILL HOUSE

After coming home from Virginia State in December of 2002, I moved back in with my father. A few days later, I linked up with my friends from the neighborhood, Nas and "Buff" aka Eric. Eric and Nas met at Simon Gratz High School where they both played on the football team. Eric went by the nickname Buff based on his physique as a kid. Aside from Nas, he was always much stronger than the rest of us. I probably should've been saying pause for constantly calling another man Buff, but whatever.

Eric was working as the lead chef at a nursing home in Bensalem, PA called *Hill House Manor*. Eric hooked Nas up with a job working in the kitchen when he returned from Virginia, and Nas put me onto the same job when I returned from Virginia State University. So, there we were—three of Gratz's finest working in a nursing home. I was very happy for the opportunity because that meant I was able to earn money to pay my bills. It also kept my mind occupied on something productive rather than my depression and the bitterness I held toward Shantel. Even though I was happy to have a job so that I could shed the financial neediness that had come to be my life, I still lived with demons. Bitterness and depression were eating me alive daily. I was constantly beating myself up. What if I had not been so arrogant? If I had stayed in Virginia, would it have worked out? I hated myself for carrying so much rage which, in turn, led to poor and impulsive decision-making. There were many nights when I cried without sleep. I wasn't feeling sorry for myself; I was hating myself because I knew I had done everything I could to earn each of those tears.

A GOOD WOMAN

I wanted to rid myself of the misery I felt, so, I got on the BlackPlanet website and began browsing women's profiles. I wanted love, but what I really needed was validation from a woman. That's when I came across the profile for a beautiful woman who I came to know as Carla. I worried about bringing my baggage into her life, but I couldn't help myself—I needed to not feel dead inside.

Carla was biracial—a mix of Puerto Rican and Caucasian. Carla was very well proportioned. She had a great spirit and a huge heart. Aside from being visually appealing, to put it mildly, she was a recent college graduate. She was definitely the kind of woman I needed in my life, but clearly one that I didn't deserve. You think I was going to let a little thing like that stop me from living in the safety of my selfishness? If your answer is yes, then you clearly haven't been paying attention for nine chapters. Shame on you.

After several phone conversations and in-person meetings, Carla and I began dating. There was one problem though: I never actually claimed her as my girlfriend. After what happened with Shantel, I was too afraid of committed relationships and couldn't be bothered with titles like *boyfriend* and *girlfriend*. Carla understood where I was coming from and did not want to rush me. She knew I was a broken soul.

"I feel so bad for you," she would say. "I wish that I could go back in time and heal your heart," she continued. I believed every one of those words she uttered. However, I was still incapable of allowing anyone true access my most vulnerable place. The worst thing a man can be is broken, and I was shattered beyond repair.

As we talked about our backgrounds and goals, I told her I wanted to return to college. I told her that I had promised myself and my mother that I would graduate from college. I even told her that I had promised Shantel that I would finish college—that promise I intended to keep.

When I told Carla that Nas and I were considering Lock Haven University, she got extremely excited because Lock Haven happened to be her alma mater. Ever the helper and willing to prove that she had my back, she talked about all her connections at the school. She was willing to use her resources to help me, that's how much she cared for me. I was happy to have her in my corner, but having her devotion scared the hell out of me.

LOCK HAVEN UNIVERSITY

In August 2003, Nas and I applied to Lock Haven University and were both accepted. We were both excited to be back in school and have another chance to graduate. I couldn't wait to get busy working toward my future career. I promised myself that this time I would be more focused and eliminate the distractions that challenged me when I attended Virginia State. Who the fuck was I kidding? Nas and I wanted to get at all the "hoes" we could.

Lock Haven is a predominantly Caucasian school, which was a huge change for me since I came from Virginia State, which is a historically black university (HBCU). Enrolling in Lock Haven was my first time attending a school where the student body was primarily Caucasian, and that meant one thing to a dude from the hood like me: white bitches. I wanted to try as many as I could. I decided that I was not interested in making friends with the guys at the school. I was 22 years old, and I didn't care for hanging out with the bright-eyed, easily impressed, 18year-olds. Besides, I already had my best friend, Nas.

Since Lock Haven is located where no so-called black people lived, I decided I was not getting my hair cut there. I'm from Philly, and we are very prideful and serious about our haircuts. I felt the same way when I attended Virginia State; however, since that was an HBCU, I was willing to teach the barber what I wanted. Shout-out to Smiley for keeping me fresh at Virginia State! At Lock Haven, I would take no such chance. I decided to grow my hair out and get cornrows.

The transition to Lock Haven required a lot more acclimation than I had anticipated. Virginia State was so rich in culture, activities, and school pride, and there were extremely beautiful melanated women on campus. I found Lock Haven to be extremely boring. It was in the middle of nowhere—I mean nowhere. As a young black man, I was constantly experiencing racism by what I called the "small town, small minded" townies whenever I ventured off-campus.

Nevertheless, my goal was to find out about all the white women who were down for the brothas. On the first night, we went to a school gathering at the student union building. We figured that's where the best-looking women in the school would be. When we entered, there was hip-hop music playing, but nobody was dancing, and people just standing around with cups in their hands. It was weird to me. Why come to a party to stand around and talk? If it were Virginia State people would be dancing to music. It was a culture difference, I guess.

Once I got to see most of the women the school had to offer, I was disappointed. In hindsight, I should've been disappointed that all I thought about were the girls. We were so disappointed that Nas and I spent time talking to guys who were also new to the school. I admit some of the guys we conversed with were cool, but I was just passing time and not trying to make friends.

A NEW FRIEND

The universe has its way of putting things or people in your life that will change you for the better. That same night, I met a Nigerian kid named Alex Oyewole. Alex was an 18-year-old freshman from West Philly looking to make his mark in the world. Through conversations, I learned that we had a lot in common like being Nigerian and from Philly for starters. I also learned that he loved hip-hop and had recorded songs of his own.

After the conversation concluded, Nas and I were headed back to the dorms. We noticed that Alex kept following us. "Where y'all about to go?" he asked. "We going back to the dorms," I responded. "Y'all mind if I go with y'all?" he asked. When he asked that, Nas and I looked at each other as if we were both thinking the same thing: What kind of man asks if he can go back to the dorm with two men he just met, pause. I knew he was young, ambitious, and wanted to belong. I could relate to him because I knew the feeling. Rather than perpetuate what was done to me over the years, I decided to let him tag-a-long.

Alex wanted to continue our conversation about hip-hop. He expressed his admiration and fandom of the hip-hop group *The Diplomats*. His interest in The Diplomats was reflected in his style of dress. I mean, he looked like he jumped out of the television from one of their videos. He was wearing extra baggy jeans that sagged, a black T-shirt, and a colorful blue and white baseball jacket. His durag was untied and hanging under a blue and white baseball cap.

True to his West Philly roots, Alex had bootleg rap DVDs handy to show us. Nas and I were not interested in watching street DVDs. Joe Budden has a song called "Who Killed HipHop" in which he explores possible theories of how it happened. In the song, he asks, "Was it street DVDs like Smack, showing you just how stupid your favorite rapper would act?" Joe not only posed a good question, but perfectly illustrated my perspective on those DVDs. I just saw them as a waste of time. Alex strongly disagreed. He continued to press us to watch the DVDs. Alex saw the DVDs as a way to view up-and-coming talent. He also saw many of the acts as pure comedy. He either thought they were funny because of how corny they were or how they were acting in the video. I thought they were very immature. Alex never relented in his insistence that we join him, so to appease him, we decided to watch the DVDs.

We began by watching "Smack" and "Too Raw for the Streets" that presented Philly-based artists. This was during the height of the popularity of Beanie Sigel and State Property and the emergence of 50 Cent. Meek Mill, a 14- or 15-year-old rapper at the time, was also on the DVD.

I remember watching some of the artists on the DVD and laughing. Some of the guys on the video were so terrible that I would be crying laughing. However, if you were to press mute and watch the same video, you would think they were killing it by the way they performed. I'm sure they thought they were the hottest rappers in the world.

Watching those DVDs was also the first time I watched a hiphop battle on camera. We were watching Reed Dollaz vs Trigga, which was an easy battle for Reed after he hit Trigga with the Rambo line. We spent most of the time laughing at Trigga; we just thought he was goofy. We also watched Bugsy vs Cash Dollaz which happened in front of Beanie Sigel, and the epic battle between E. Ness vs Hollowman. Alex got me hooked on battle rap. All these battles can be found on YouTube today, which did not exist back then.

Afterward, Alex and I stayed up late debating about who was the better lyricist, Cassidy or Joe Budden. Both artists were titans on the mixtape scene. Alex was pro-Cassidy because he is from Philly, and he thought his punchlines were really good. I was pro-Joe Budden because I felt his lyrics were wittier and required more thought. I guess this was a preference debate, but I viewed it as maturity level difference.

When Alex realized that I preferred Joe Budden, he laughed, "You like the *Pump It Up* guy?" I began to put Alex on to Joe Budden's mixtape and features he had done on other artists' songs. After listening to the music for a couple of hours, I could tell Alex had changed his opinion about Joe Budden. "He iight," Alex responded. That was a stamp of approval from Alex. He was never too impressed about anything except Jay-Z, which was another commonality we shared. This Alex kid is cool, I thought. And from that day forward, I had another good friend.

CARLA

Carla wanted to keep in contact with me while I was at Lock Haven, but I didn't have enough money to keep my cell phone on without interruption, so she added me to her plan. Periodically, she would call me and give me leads about who to talk to on campus to get things done. She even introduced me to her former supervisor who hired me for work-study during my second year.

After a month or so, Carla informed me that she would be taking the three-hour drive to Lock Haven to visit me and a friend she still had at the school. The weekend she arrived, there was a party at "The Diamond Club," which was a really whack hole-in-the-wall-you-had-to-live-here-to-find-it kind of place. When Nas and I got to the party, I saw Carla for the first time in a month. I greeted her with a hug and a kiss, but I decided to give her space and time to party with her friends.

Once I dipped out of the party, I went back to campus. I got a call later that she wanted me to meet her friends and that she was going to prepare my favorite meal, which was fettuccine with shrimp at the time. I didn't really want to go because that meant all her friends would associate me as her boyfriend, which I wasn't. As I said before, my insecurities and selfishness would not allow me to claim her. I ended up going anyway because it was good to know who her friends were, and I did not want to embarrass someone who cared so much for me.

I had a great time at the party, but I was constantly correcting people. "We are just friends" is how I responded when someone called me her boyfriend. "Sure, whatever you say," was usually the response I got from them. When the party ended, we went back to my dorm room and had sex. The next morning, she drove back to Philadelphia.

A BAD LOOK

A few months later, I began messing with a Caucasian girl. Let's call her Amanda. Amanda was a sweet and kind-hearted person, the type of person that was always willing to please people, but she was not my girlfriend either. However, she did a lot of nice things for me, and we had fun when we were around each other, which was often. I thought she was a really cool person, and she was. She thought we were going to be a couple, but I knew we weren't.

"What was wrong with her?" you might ask. Or if you have been paying close attention, you might ask, "What was wrong with you?" Both are fair questions. In this case, I always had a feeling about her. I never knew exactly why, but I always felt a different kind of internal opposition to her. I'd love to sound noble and pretend the opposition was about my love for Carla, but this isn't a Tyler Perry movie.

From the outset, I knew exactly what I wanted. I got with her just to have a consistent person to have sex with. Carla is not my girlfriend, I reminded myself. "Technically, I am not cheating on her," I'd justify. "I am not responsible for her wanting to be my girlfriend when I told her otherwise." With Amanda, the problem was this: Everyone got with her to have sex. When I say everyone, I mean EVERYONE. You might think I'm exaggerating or "slut shaming," as Amber Rose would say, but walk with me.

In a predominantly white school, information was at a premium among the so-called black students, and it spread quickly—so quickly that it nearly gave me a concussion. For instance, one day, Lex and I were getting lunch in Bentley Hall, the cafeteria, when we ran into another brotha who played for the school football team. Let's call him Marcus. We greeted each other as we usually would when we ran into each other, a nod or a handshake and kept it moving.

Except this time, he had more he wanted to share. "Let me talk to y'all right quick," Marcus offered. As we sat down, he began to whisper. "I see you hanging with Amanda," he said with a sly smile. Immediately, I thought he wanted to express his jealousy. Before I could respond, he continued to reveal his purpose: "Y'all should fuck her." I was even more confused, but he wasn't done shocking me yet. "We used to train her," he added. By "we," he meant the football team. Stunned, I had no response for his bombshell. I just smiled awkwardly and nodded. The confidence in his voice and the smile on his face let me know he was "dead ass," as my New York brothas would say. That means really serious, if you are a nerd.

After that revealing conversation, I was trying to process what I just heard. With our food in our hands, Lex and I walked back to the dorm room we shared. When we arrived, I sat at my desk with my food for a good 15 minutes unable to eat a thing; I was deep in thought. "You heard what he said, right?" Lex asked. Lex wanted to know how I felt about it. "Yeah, I heard him," I responded. Still stunned, I was trying to figure out my next move.

Once I finished processing Marcus's revelation, I realized I felt embarrassed. After replaying his comments in my head over and over, I realized he had been under the impression that I knew about her. After all, she had quite the reputation. However, I was new to the school, and I wondered who else knew about this. As I stated before, I was hanging out with her often. As a man, you don't want to be seen in a certain light with the town pump. Still think I'm being harsh?

"Reality bites, like a thousand mutts."

—Jay-Z

AND. HERE. WE. GO!

I decided to do what I now don't recommend any man ever do in a situation like this. I decided to confront Amanda with what I heard. Just by the look on her face, I knew it was true. She couldn't even deny it, especially coming from the source. That reality made me nauseated, but it didn't stop there. Being the glutton for punishment that I am, I continued with more and more questions.

After weeks and weeks of questions and shocking revelations, I learned a whole lot about what I am still trying to forget. Long story short and with no exaggeration whatsoever, I learned that she had sex with 303 people at our school alone; notice I didn't say she had sex 303 times, and I'm not including me, in case you are wondering. After a while, I literally stopped counting. To put it into context, she was in her sophomore year.

My mind went crazy figuring out the math, which was like an average of 75 people per semester. Even worse, I had to consider the demographics, which turned out to be nearly every so-called black dude on campus. Literally every so-called black athlete had sex with her. Football team or basketball team—it didn't matter. Come one, cum all.

I never knew she was into sports like that. That reality hit me harder than Mike Tyson hit Trevor Berbick when he ended the fight in the second round of their 1986 bout. I won't go into the details that I learned about her because I don't want to beat a dead horse here. Let's just say, I could never look at her the same. And of course, I got myself thoroughly tested. A few months later, I learned that she left the Fallon Bar one night and had sex with Marcus. Go figure.

"Looking for love in the club, now I can tell that you're blind."

—Adekunle Ige

CARMA

Yes, I know I spelled *karma* unconventionally. Prior to Amanda and me parting ways, things came to a head with Carla. Carla's friend, Zaria, who lived in the same duplex as Amanda, phoned Carla to tell her about my affiliation with Amanda. Needless to say, she knew all about me and Amanda. That's when Carla called me, while I was with Amanda.

Carla confronted me about Amanda. Of course, I lied. Zaria was upstairs and could hear the entire conversation. Carla was pissed, and of course she did not believe me. I gave all kinds of reasons. "Amanda is my friend," I told her. Which was truthful, but obviously not the whole truth. I even invited her to come visit me at the school to prove my point.

Carla took me up on that offer and came to the school the following weekend. She spent time with her friends, probably deliberating what to do with me. My guess is the plan they came up with was for Carla to have sex with me. Their logic was that if I wasn't having sex with Amanda then I should be pretty quick in bed, not having had sex since the last time with Carla.

Later that night, we ended up having sex. Apparently, I lasted far longer than she had expected, and that's when she knew. Not only did I have sex with Amanda, but I had sex with her earlier that day. I'm sure Carla didn't know it was the same day, but she had all the evidence she needed. For her, there was no turning back. I tried to tell her that I masturbated before she came because I didn't expect us to have sex, but she wasn't buying. Carla was not stupid.

Carla was a great woman, just one that I knew I would eventually hurt. I wanted to be able to come out of my funk and be the man that she deserved, it just never happened. My heart was smashed to pieces and everyone had to pay, whether intentionally or unintentionally.

> *"The biggest coward of a man is to awaken the love of a woman without the intention of loving her."*
>
> —Robert Nesta Marley aka Bob Marley

LEX CALIBUR

Once second semester hit, Nas went back to Philly because he was having a son. He decided that he would not return to Lock Haven so he could be there for his son. It was definitely an admirable thing to do. Parenting from three hours away would be difficult. Nas's decision, albeit the right one, reduced our trio to a duo. Alex and I had to hold it down.

When Alex learned that I rapped, he not only wanted to hear my music but to play his music for me. We took turns playing each other's music. We had different styles. Alex was more into spitting four-bar setups for punchlines. I was more of a street storyteller. Both of us had great hip-hop approaches and qualities, but it became clear that we could benefit from each other's perspective.

As usual, Alex and I spent time debating which was more important, punchlines or the story. Listening to Alex's mixtape, which is what he played for me, I thought he reached for reasons to add unnecessary punchlines. He thought my stories were not exciting enough without punchlines. Since I had access to a studio in Philly, I invited him to come through to record a song during fall break.

The lyrics in my songs reflected my ignorant attitude, personal demons, and harsh realities from my neighborhood. I came up with the concept of a song that would feature my cousin Face and Lex. The idea of the song was to represent our neighborhoods in the most authentic way. I pitched the song to Face and Lex over the phone, and they both loved the idea. We all began writing our verses.

On the day of the recording, Lex brought over a beat CD full of instrumentals. He already had a beat in mind for the song and a concept we all agreed on. Once Face and I heard the beat, we knew it was going to match, and we were excited. We titled the song, "Who Hood?" After we finished recording, we were super hyped and loved the song, and we knew we needed to work together more often.

In 2004, Lex and I decided we would also work on our solo albums and do features for each other's songs. Lex worked on his first album he titled *DisLexSick* a play off the word dyslexic, while I worked on my second album titled *Identity*. Let's address the elephant in the room, we are not mega famous artists where you could follow our musical catalog. Given that music was such an integral part of our lives, it's impossible to leave out. Once both albums were completed, they were considered cult classics to those that were able to hear them.

THE COMPLEX

Around January of 2005, Lex and I had a friendly competition going when it came time to record our latest albums. We found several websites where freelance producers were selling original beats for affordable prices. It was like a race to see which of us could find the best beats. Meanwhile, we spent most of our time writing rhymes and preparing to make the best music that we could. We let each other hear beats we acquired, but not the rhymes. We wanted to shock each other with the ideas we were putting on the page.

Lex and I finished collecting our beats and writing our rhymes. I couldn't wait to return home to Philly and begin recording. Lex had other plans; he decided to test out a new engineer on campus named Moshe. Moshe recorded his own rhymes and produced records for his friend A.L., another rapper on campus. When Lex learned of this, he decided to try recording with him to have a different sound from that of his previous work.

"I can't wait until you hear it," Lex said. "I'm telling you this is going to be crazy," he continued as he listened to the new songs through earphones. He wanted me to hear the album in its entirety once it was completed. Those were the same sentiments I shared about my upcoming album as I rapped my rhymes in my head while listening to the instrumentals. We both were anxious to hear each other's reactions to the new music.

Once Lex completed the album, he gave me a copy to review. Lex's album *The CompLex* was amazing. I could see that he had taken me up on the challenge of adding more content and stories to his lyrics. The format to his album reminded me of the blueprint I laid from my previous album *Identity*, but with a Lex twist. Not only did he have in-depth and personal songs with storylines, he kept his signature punchline-heavy style. It was amazing to see him grow and mature as an artist. To me, that album is a masterpiece. At 20 years old, he already had a timeless album.

SUMMER SCHOOL

Over the summer of 2005, Lex and I were attending classes. We didn't have a place to stay, so a mutual friend allowed us to stay at his off-campus apartment while he was in Philly. It was about a mile from the campus, but it wasn't that bad of a walk. We couldn't use the bedrooms, so we slept in the living room— alternating with one of us on the couch and the other on the floor.

One night, Lex and I were having one of our usual hip-hop debates. This time we were discussing who we thought won the battle between Jay-Z and Nas. As the conversation progressed, we started talking about what it would be like if the both lyricists joined forces. "What would it be like?" I wondered. "What kind of songs would they make?" We pondered all night about the endless scenarios that would cause them to end their beef. We stayed up so long, I lost track of time. Finally, I went to bed because I had work-study in the morning.

The next morning, I got up before Lex did and made sure not to make too much noise as I prepared for work. When I got to work, I got busy on the projects that I needed to complete that day. Once I completed the projects, I continued writing lyrics to songs I planned to record for my new album. I knew this album was going to be something special, and I could not wait to record it.

On my way home from work, I was listening to a beat CD that I made for my album. I was walking and rapping my lyrics in my head. When I got home, Lex was sleeping on the couch. I wanted to tell him of the progress I was making musically, but I decided not to wake him. Tired myself, I decided to take a nap on the living room floor.

When I woke up, I noticed Lex was still knocked out on the couch. He was still laying in the same position as he was when I left for work and when

I returned home. It had been 8 to 10 hours, and he had not changed positions. That's when I knew something was wrong. I got up from the floor and grabbed his arm to wake him. His arm was cold and solid. His body was stiff, and that's when I knew. He was gone.

9-1-1

I quickly grabbed my cell phone to call the ambulance. I was so stunned that I couldn't even dial the number correctly. It took me three tries to dial 9-1-1. Crying hysterically, "Somebody help me!" I told the dispatcher. I think my friend is dead," I continued. I knew there was nothing they could do for him because he was already in rigor mortis, but I was still praying for a miracle.

When the ambulance and police arrived, I took them to the apartment where Lex was laying. "I think you should step outside sir," the EMT said. "You are not going to want to see this," he continued. I stepped outside the apartment and sat on the staircase crying uncontrollably. "CLEAR!!!" the EMT yelled. The only thing clear to me is that my life would be changed forever. I couldn't believe that my best friend was gone. I didn't understand. There was no reason for him to die. I was heartbroken.

That's when I heard the phone ring. It was his younger brother, Henry. I knew it was him because of the ringtone. The song was "Standing Ovation," which was the final track on Lex's *The CompLex* album. I cried harder and harder because I knew that Henry had no idea why Lex wasn't answering the phone. I knew that he would never get to speak with his brother again.

Henry must've been alarmed because he kept calling, and the song kept playing over and over. After a while, I started to feel as if Lex were trying to send me a message. The ringtone was the chorus of his song. The chorus lyrics were:

> *"Thanks for holding me down or corners and blocks/Thanks for all of your love, support, and the props/Thanks for everything, especially the standing ovation"*

I took that as a message as a sign he was thanking me for taking care of him and being a good friend to him. Lex was not only my best-friend, he was my Nigerian brother. His mother often considered and referred to me her son. Henry is also my brother; they are family to me.

BREAKING THE NEWS

After pronouncing Lex dead at the scene, the police took me down to the station. They wanted me to tell them what happened, which I willingly did. They took pictures of my hands on both sides to make sure I wasn't hiding any scars. They had to rule out the possibility that I had harmed him, since there was no obvious reason for his death.

I probably should've asked for a lawyer, but I didn't because I knew I didn't do anything wrong. However, the questions they were asking me were very offensive. "You sure you guys didn't have an argument?" the officer asked. "What did you use, a needle? We are going to find out either way," he continued. It was like being on *The First 48*. I was so offended because harming Lex was a complete impossibility. I tried to take the interrogation in stride because I knew they had to investigate, and I was too busy mourning Lex. Finally, they had me complete a written statement that sequenced my day and any relevant events.

To test me, they wanted me to call Lex's mother and tell her of his passing. That was something that I could not do. I still had not come to grips with that reality myself. It had just happened a few hours before, and I was too distraught. The police officer decided to make the call.

Immediately, I could hear his mother cry. I started crying even harder. "Where is K? Is he ok?" she asked while sobbing. "I want to speak to K," she repeated. "She wants to speak to you," the officer said as he handed me the phone. "Hello," I answered. "Where's Alex?" she asked. "He passed away," I responded. We both began crying uncontrollably. Henry grabbed the phone. "What happened?" he asked. "I don't know," I responded. I told Henry exactly what I told the police. "We are on our way up there. We will see you in a few hours," he continued.

FAMILY ARRIVAL

Lex's mother and Henry soon arrived at the city morgue. As you would expect, his mother was hysterical, as any parent would be. The officer decided to test me again. "We need you to go in there and identify him," as he gently pushed me toward the door. I refused. I'm the one who found him; I didn't need to identify him. I didn't want to see my friend on an autopsy table. I wanted to remember him as he lived. I also did not want to have the image of his mother crying and screaming in my head after seeing her son that way.

When his mother and Henry entered the room, things got worse. Lex's mother completely lost it; we all broke down crying. Trust me when I tell you that there is no pain like hearing a mother mourn her baby. It echoed in my head for months. I gave Lex's mother a hug, but I had no words to share. I was still wrapping my mind around having to console my friend's mother for losing her son.

A FAMILIAR FACE

Because Lex passed away in the apartment where we were staying, I was homeless; the apartment was now a crime scene and had been sealed off by the police. Having nowhere to go, I called Amanda. The phone rang and rang and rang. She was clearly upset with me and uninterested in talking to me, I understood. I left her a voicemail telling her that Alex was dead and that I had come from the police station. A few minutes later, she called me back.

Amanda came to pick me up, and on the way to her apartment, I filled her in on what happened. If you are thinking that I had sex with her, you are wrong. I stayed on the couch for a few days trying to figure out where I could stay long term.

One morning, I was awakened by Lex's voice. "Yo, K," he called. It was loud and unmistakable. I jumped up immediately. While clearing cold from my eyes, I heard him say, "I'm iight." It was very chilling, I had goosebumps on my arms. I knew he was trying to tell me that he made it to the other side safely. I'm glad I got to hear him one last time.

Once Carla heard of Lex's passing, she gave me a call. I was still angry with her for parting ways with me, and I was emotional after Lex's death, so I did not respond to her nicely. "Who told you?" I asked angrily. She was taken back by my anger. "I just wanted to say I'm sorry to hear about your friend," she said. "I hope you are ok," she added. I said, "Thank you," and we ended the call.

THE INVESTIGATION

Lex's family left the morgue and arranged for his body to be taken back to Philly where his funeral would be held. Life was turned upside down for all of us. I needed to get some clothes, so I had to contact the police to see if I could get permission to enter the apartment. They were happy to oblige; it was another opportunity to question me. The officer escorted me to the apartment and allowed me to get my clothes, unfolding each piece to make sure I wasn't trying to hide a murder weapon.

Periodically, I would be called back to the police station to "clear up something" or to "tie up loose ends." All of those *Columbo* episodes were useful. I knew exactly what they were doing. They wanted to see if my story was going to remain consistent. I always went to the station when asked because I knew I was telling the truth, and it was verified that I never left work-study prior to the end of my shift. I have at least 10 people who saw me there.

The police were considering a theory that I had perhaps injected him with something prior to going to work so that I could create an alibi. All their theories were insulting to me. "Nobody that ever encountered Lex and me would ever say that I would harm him," I said confidently to the officer. "That's why I keep showing up because I have nothing to hide," I continued. In hindsight, I should've gotten a lawyer because there are plenty of innocent people in jail.

I couldn't afford a lawyer, so I did the next best thing. I enlisted Dr. Marshall, our Criminal Justice teacher, to assist me with the police interactions because I knew they thought I was responsible for Lex's death. Dr. Marshall had been a police officer for 12 years in New Orleans prior to becoming a professor at Lock Haven. I needed him to make sure that they didn't try to railroad me.

A few months after the autopsy, it turned out Lex had a rare heartbeat irregularity called a heart arrhythmia, which happens when the heart stops beating or skips beats. Typically, the heartbeat picks back up and continues to beat normally. In Lex's case, his heart stopped and never restarted. The diagnosis made me recall that Lex used to complain about being tired and dizzy. Those are two symptoms of heart arrhythmias. I'm still not sure what caused the condition in Lex's case, but I can say definitively that he was not on drugs or alcohol. He was against both.

It was estimated that he passed away around 10:00 a.m., which was about two hours after I had already been at workstudy. When I returned home, he had passed about 8 to 10 hours earlier. That's why he was still laying on the couch in the same position when I returned home. I literally took a nap on the floor without realizing that he lay lifeless on the couch.

Upon learning of this revelation, the police officer offered his condolences. He stopped calling me down to the police station every other day. He would even wave at me when he saw me as he patrolled the city. I took that as an apology. I think he felt bad for me, especially after learning I had been telling the truth the whole time.

MEMORIAL

A few weeks after the investigation, I worked with the school administration to have a memorial for Lex. The memorial was held at the student union building, ironically the same place where I met him. It was summer, and most of the students were home with their families. I had no idea what kind of turnout we would have. But I was pleasantly surprised that the most important people with real connections to him showed. Our friend Raquel came all the way from out-of-state to attend. It really touched my heart.

At the memorial, I decided to decipher Lex's lyrics from his most heartfelt songs. Lex was maturing in real life, and it was reflected in his music. It was important for me to let people to hear how much he had grown. It was also important for people who did not know him as well as I did to understand how great of an artist and more importantly what a wonderful person he was.

When people heard the direction of his music and lyrics, everybody started crying. All the teachers, administrators, and students spoke about their best memories and lasting impressions. I knew he was a special person when I met him. I just needed him to know that he was loved by many.

PAYING HOMAGE

Part of why Lex and I were so excited about the music we were making is because we planned to reveal what we had been working on at the upcoming school talent show. When the time came, Lex had already passed. So, I decided to work with Moshe, the engineer who worked on Alex's album, to create a song montage that I could perform for him at the talent show. Moshe was more than happy to oblige. After all, he lost his best friend A.L., also a rapper, that same year to cancer.

My goal was to create a visual representation of Lex's life by making his songs come to life. In order to do it in an authentic way, I recruited people who deeply cared for him to take part. I recruited a girl named Precious, who knew Alex since high school and a girl name Samantha we used to kick it with. Both of them played vital roles as we acted out one of Lex's songs on stage.

I called a girl that Alex was dating at Penn State University to attend the tribute segment. Shout out to her for coming through! The auditorium was packed as people were waiting to see the show. There I was on stage without Alex in front of the entire student body and staff—a place where we had planned to perform together.

At first, I was going to rap Lex's songs over his beats, but I thought about it and felt it would be more impactful for them to hear it directly from him. So, I lip-synced and acted out the picture he was painting on each record played. I could tell that people enjoyed his music. It was an emotional set. People were crying during part of the show.

By the time the last song, "Standing Ovation," came on, everyone was on their feet clapping and dancing. Afterward, there literally was a standing ovation. It was amazing. I just wish he could have been there to see it. I'm sure he knew that I would do this for him. Maybe that's the message that I was supposed to get as the song played when Henry was calling.

LOST

After attending Lex's funeral in Philly, I returned to Lock Haven. Shortly after, I was able to acquire on-campus housing to finish out summer school. That meant that I moved out of Amanda's apartment. When I got on campus,

I did not know what to do with myself. I was literally lost. I was completely unable to function normally by myself. I had spent so much time with Lex that my entire routine was based around our friendship. I remember trying to take a nap and couldn't sleep. I would wake up and go to the gym that was only a stone's throw away from where I lived. I would play basketball for what seemed like hours. Then, I would go back to my dorm room, take a shower, and a nap. Once I woke up from the nap, I realized it was not even noon yet. The days just felt three times as long, and I felt three times as lonely.

Once nightfall arrived, I would walk the campus or in downtown Lock Haven while listening to music. "I wonder what Lex would think about Kanye West's *Late Registration*," I thought. "Would he like Lupe Fiasco?" I wondered. All the conversations I would normally have with him became wonders and what-ifs.

Ironically, a few months after Lex's funeral, our final conversation became a reality, and it shocked the hip-hop world. In November of 2005, Jay-Z brought out Nas in New York for summer jam, and the two performed together. The two lyricists had ended their beef that spanned more than 10 years. I cried like a baby because Lex did not live to see it become a reality.

"Sometimes you can't see God, but there is never a time when God doesn't see you"

—Adekunle Ige

ONE LAST MESSAGE

After I moved toward the acceptance stage of grief, I began recording my album. I decided that it would be my final album since I had lost the love for it after Lex passed. Prior to his death, the album that I kept so secret from him was going to be called *The Rapture*, the title was inspired by Anita Baker's classic album.

In light of Lex's death, I decided that the content of the album needed to change and match where I was mentally. I scrapped a bunch of songs; then, I wrote and recorded new ones. I used a two beats that Lex gave me to record some of the newer songs. I wanted him to be a part of this album. I knew his spirit had never left me.

I couldn't think of what to name the album because it had changed so much since the original idea. One day, I was in my dorm room when I noticed my silhouette on the wall. I was literally standing at the perfect angle. It looked exactly like my album cover for *Identity*. Only this time, I had cornrows under my fitted hat instead of a low cut. That's when I created the new album cover. I named the album, *Identity II: The Nicetown Diary*. I think Lex was responsible for that message too.

The final song on the album was a tribute to Lex. It was titled, "One Last Message." On the song, I used a sample of his voice that I got from recording his voicemail message after his death. I used it to open the song. The song was designed as if I were leaving him a voicemail. There are all kinds of hidden messages and references in the song that only he and those who were close to us would pick up on. I wanted it to be a conversation. I also wanted to let him know all that he meant to the world and for those that never got to meet him to understand.

At the end of the song, I used an actual voicemail that I left Lex on his home phone in Philly. That message came from Henry who randomly sent it to me wondering if I would want it for memories. He wasn't even thinking about music. Following the message, I played a montage of my favorite Lex verses and lines. I closed it appropriately with "Standing Ovation" as it marked the close of my rapping career and the celebration of his life.

"You got a best friend? Me too. Mine is in heaven. My bro L-E-X '05 May 27th."

You was my nigga, nah
You was more like my brother
Different fathers, different mothers
But we still found each other
You were never a lost cause

A bright kid with ambition
And a hungry ass dude
Couldn't stay out the kitchen
Nah, no time for jokes
Just had to loosen up folks
If I didn't I might cry, this is my way to cope
With losing a golden child, my right hand
My nigga, ayo Lex, The CompLex
Is right here my nigga
I could see you now, black fitted, jacket and kicks
You so impressed by your hat
Cause it had Gucci print
I'm mad I never got to rate what your albums about
Or to pause you for saying
"Give the game mouth to mouth"
But your rhymes were introspective
"I've Ever" was magic
You had a song for everything
That's Lex Calibur mastered
We all mourned your death
Happy for you, while tragic
You're in the heaven's with God And by the way, it's a classic

Song: *One Last Message,* **Artist:** *Me,*
Album: *IDENTITY II: The Nicetown Diary* **Year:** *2005*

Sometimes to question God is the wrong thing to do
Like, why the struggles and the pain? Is this a game to you?
And then I wonder,
How come the good die young? Do you consider them good?
Or is that just what we want
To think about those that are no longer here
Lord, I got a couple cliché's you need to hear
They say tough times don't last, only tough people do
Is that why I stand alone knowing no one but you?
And then I wonder,
When will the drama ever end?
With these girls diamonds and pearls
what they want me to spend
And what I'm about to say may sound evil
But now I'm starting to realize why you stayed single
They say if you don't know your enemy
Then you don't know your friend
Convince me Lord,
Give me a reason why Lex's life had to end
Why'd I have to hug his brother and see tears from his mom?
I guess the Lord knows best, words that's keeping calm
Then I wonder,
People dying, mom's crying, and it happens in days
While I'm trapped like a rat that's locked in a cage
And it stays on my mind
Prison is packed with blacks

Why is that if justice is blind?
I think I predicted your answer
I guess I'm in my prime
So, I have a question for the cliché of all-time
How can we have faith in which we cannot find?
'cause I heard, when you're out of sight
Then you're out of mind
And then I wonder...

Song: *For The Record,* **Artist:** *Me,*
Album: *IDENTITY II: The Nicetown Diary* **Year:** *2005*

CHAPTER 11

SELF-DISCOVERY

It was July 2005 and I was still reeling from Lex's death two months earlier. I needed to figure out what to do with myself. I was left at a crossroads. Since it was the summer, I had to use that time to refocus and get myself together. The loss of my best friend and my time at Lock Haven University needed to mean something. Once again, I was put into a position of having to beat the odds, both physically and mentally, but it wouldn't be easy.

I couldn't shake the depression and intense feelings of loneliness following Lex's death. At the rate I was going, it would be a matter of time before those feelings would destroy me. Staying in my dorm room staring at the wall or watching reruns of *Law & Order* wasn't helping much. I needed to get out and reconnect with the world. Since there were hardly any students on campus during the summer, I decided to meet up with a few people I knew who lived off-campus.

GOING THROUGH THE MOTIONS

One day while eating dinner alone in Bentley Hall, I saw Don approaching my table. "Yo, you should come chill with us, so you don't have to be alone," he offered. "We be chilling off campus at Lisa's house downtown by the river," he continued. I knew Don and a few other guys he chilled with, but I didn't know Lisa. I wasn't really in the mood for being social, but I told him I would think about it.

I knew that I couldn't stay cocooned in my own misery forever, so I decided to check them out and get some nighttime air. When I arrived at the house, it was exactly what I expected it to be. A group of guys were hanging out at Lisa's smoking weed and drinking liquor, two things that I didn't do. They were all shooting the shit about the times they got so drunk and did something stupid or the time they got so high they did something else stupid. It wasn't my type of company, but I didn't know anyone else who stayed local during the summer, and I needed to avoid being alone.

After hanging out at Lisa's for a few weeks, I had a routine. I decided I would chill in the house with them while they were drinking and playing video games. Then, when they started smoking, I would go into the backyard alone and listen to music in my Discman. I didn't want to smell like weed. It brought back memories of the dudes back home in Philly that I saw while chilling on the porch. Those guys disgusted me and not because they smelled like weed, but because their other actions were destroying my community.

BEING SOCIAL

One night, I was in the backyard jamming to Nas's *It Was Written* album when the damnedest thing happened. Out of nowhere, Lisa came out to the backyard. When she approached me, she gave me a kiss without warning. It happened so fast that I couldn't react. "I'm going to the store. Do you want to come with?" she asked. I was down to take the walk. I had nothing else better to do plus I needed something to stop my mind from racing. Don and the rest of his friends stayed at Lisa's drinking and smoking.

The store was only a few blocks away, so it took us no time to get there. We made small talk about what our majors were and how boring the city of Lock Haven was. I waited outside the store listening to music until she was ready to go. She picked up a pack of cigarettes, a bottle of liquor, and some other items. It was time to head back and see what everybody else was up to.

On the way back, Lisa told me that she wanted to take a scenic route by walking the trail next to the Susquehanna River. I had no qualms with that since it was on the way to her house. It was a nice night and for the first time in months, I wasn't feeling depressed.

After a short walk, we sat by the water. The moon was clearly visible over the river and only the sound of the water flow could be heard. It was a peaceful summer night. Apparently, Lisa was enjoying it too. Without saying a word, she began rubbing my penis through my basketball shorts. I looked over at her as she smiled. She could feel my erection as it grew. It didn't take long for it reach maximum strength either. It looked like I stole a cucumber from that store.

I pulled down my basketball shorts without wasting a single moment. Lisa began performing fellatio. Notice, I said *fellatio* and not oral sex or *head*. There is a difference, or at least to me. Oral sex sounds clinical and basic. Head is when the girl is going crazy on it, making lots of noise, but isn't really doing anything. Ladies, ask yourself are you providing oral sex, giving head, or performing fellatio?

The way Lisa was getting busy it was like an art to her, one that she had clearly mastered. The way she sucked, licked, and caressed my penis it was like she cared more about it than I did. I loved every minute of it. Apparently, Lisa was the penis whisperer. Let me explain what I mean.

During the fellatio session, it felt like my soul was leaving my body. My eyes were open, but I literally couldn't see or hear anything. She was performing an exorcism. It was like I left earth. I imagine that she wanted me to warn her before I came, but I would do no such thing. It was freeing to let it all go. Soon after, my body felt cleansed and relaxed.

My hearing returned a few seconds after the orgasm. I heard her slurping it all in. Gradually my vision returned, and the moon looked close enough to grab. Lisa looked at me for a few seconds as if she were deciding whether to swallow it all or not. She decided to spit out the sperm. "Why didn't you warn me?" she asked. "YOU just snatched MY soul. Why didn't YOU warn ME?" I thought. I told her that it was so good that I couldn't talk, which would normally be game, but it was true. It was the first time I ever orgasmed from fellatio.

Afterward, we walked back to Lisa's apartment. Everyone was gone by the time we arrived. I guess we had been gone longer than I thought. "They probably just went to chill at someone else's apartment," I said. I wanted to sit on the couch and watch some TV, but she would have none of that. She grabbed my hand and guided me to the bedroom. Fully aware of the moment,

I put on a condom. It was time for *me* to snatch *her* soul. I was Shang Tsung that night. If you don't know who he is, google him.

When I finished working her out, I was ready to go home. I exited her bedroom and I saw Don sitting on the couch watching TV. I guess he heard her moaning and screaming, but he said nothing. He didn't even give a sly smile or the bro thumbs-up men give when we know one of us got some. In fact, it looked like he was hating. Maybe something else was on his mind. Either way, I didn't care. Needless to say, I left happy. I went to the store with a busy mind and returned to Lisa's house with a clear head, all puns intended.

Later that night, I called Nas who was working security at King of Prussia Mall in the Philly Area at the time. I told him about the head games she played. See, these immature puns are not going to stop. While telling him the story, he asked if he could put me on speaker phone so the other security guards could hear. I guess they were bored on shift and could use a good story. I wanted to share the paranormal activity I experienced, so I agreed.

"Yo, she sucked the skin off my dick. My shit was inside out when she finished," I said excitingly. There was an eruption of laughter. "Y'all think I'm bullshitting. I couldn't hear or see shit for like five minutes!" I said. The eruption was even louder. "It felt so good that I wish she sucked y'all off," I continued. After that last line, I couldn't get another word in because they were laughing too hard, good times.

FALL 2005

Fast forward a few months and the fall 2005 semester was in full swing. I was busting my brain in the books trying to make something of myself. Unlike years in the past, I was void of all distractions. I decided that it was time for me to focus on getting out of Lock Haven University. There was nothing left for me there. I needed to graduate not only for myself but for Lex since it was something he would never get to accomplish. To add further motivation, I had promises to keep—one for my mother and one for Shantel. From then on, my life took a turn.

HURRICANE KATRINA

When hurricane Katrina hit New Orleans at 8:00 a.m. on August 29, 2005, it was devastating. The saga dominated headlines for months as the death toll seemed to rise by the hundreds daily. If you are not familiar with Hurricane Katrina, do your googles. My mentor Dr. Marshall, yep the same guy who made sure the cops didn't railroad me after Lex's death, offered an opportunity to help. He got permission from Lock Haven University administration to organize a trip to New Orleans, his home town, to provide support to Hurricane Katrina survivors.

I volunteered immediately. I couldn't stand how it seemed like the government didn't care and portrayed victims as criminals when all they wanted to do was survive. I knew all about loss and pain, I could relate to that. Several other "black" students and I signed on for the trip. We would be away from our families during Thanksgiving but for a much greater cause. It was a trade none of us thought twice about.

When we arrived in New Orleans, we didn't stay in a fancy hotel; we stayed in the Covenant House shelter. The water was so toxic that we had to use gallons of bottled water to brush our teeth and take bird baths. Immediately, I felt for the survivors. It was a small inconvenience for us, but it was everyday life for them.

Once we got to our work site, I noticed the devastation was about three times worse in person compared to what was shown on TV. There was both obvious destruction and subtle horror. We had to wear surgical masks due to the intense mold in the air. On the way to the breach site, we noticed an entire neighborhood was gone. I mean houses completely gone. The few houses left bore signs warning of the number of people who had died inside. There were tricycles and smashed cars stuck in the top of trees, leaving me to wonder and pray that the children made it out safely. That's when I realized that none of the media outlets accurately depicted the terror these people went through.

When we arrived, we went to the site where the levees supposedly had broken. I'm no conspiracy theorist, but if you saw what I saw, you would have doubts too. That concrete looked like it was blown away by a cannon, but I digress. Magnolia Projects, the original home of hip-hop artists Jay

Electronica, Juvenile, and Turk of the Cash Money Millionaires, had water marks of over 30 feet high. Imagine that.

I knew that offering to support the people affected was the correct decision. As a team, we passed out food and supplies to the homeless and survivors who lived nearby. We collaborated with the New Orleans Police Department to clean mold, repaint buildings, and other tasks. I am happy to say that on a small scale, I had a hand in helping the city rebuild. It was the only time in my life I was willing to help the police.

When we made the trip, I was expecting devastation and suffering, but I wasn't expecting to see the next thing I saw. We went to Bourbon Street nearly every night after we arrived, and they were partying as if nothing had happened. Those parties were popping-popping; I'm talking chicks sliding on poles, and every bar was filled. It was beautiful to see that the city's spirit was not broken.

When we returned to campus, it was back to the grind. I was even more motivated and focused than I had been when we left. The experience in New Orleans really changed my worldview. It reminded me that no matter what we are going through, there is always someone who has it worse. Though it sounds cliché, I needed that message more than ever. It was time to make use of that energy and make something of myself no matter what it took.

KEEPING MY PROMISE

The most challenging class I had at Lock Haven was Social Work Applied Research taught by Dr. Tabler. It was a very demanding and time-consuming class. To make matters more challenging, most people could not stand our professor, because she was very rigid and didn't take any shit. She was my kind of teacher. Thanks to my math teacher in high school Ms. Horan who was similar, I understood Dr. Tabler. She had people in class scared to talk or do anything off script. Not me. I always had good timing and could sneak in a joke every so often that made everyone in the class laugh, even her.

The most valuable lesson I learned from Dr. Tabler, besides the research techniques, was to be proactive. While my other classmates were cramming or feeling overwhelmed by a large number of assignments that were due daily, I was completing assignments a week in advance. I used the syllabus as a blueprint of what we were going to be tasked with next. Therefore, I always had time to do whatever I wanted on the weekends. The approach was so successful at eliminating academic stress, that I applied it to every class I had thereafter.

I finished the spring 2006 semester strong and even made the Dean's List for the first time in my life. Can you imagine that? I'm the same guy who had a .5 and 1.5 GPA who had trouble getting off academic probation. The following semester was my last and my best one yet. I had straight As and earned a 4.0 GPA for the semester. That accomplishment fulfilled a promise I made to my mother after she passed. I was now a college graduate, which meant I fulfilled the promises that I made to myself and to Shantel.

Given all that I had gone through, it was a hard-earned feat. I was more excited than I had been for anything in my life. I was the first person in my immediate family to graduate from college. To me, I was breaking barriers. To my father, I was matching the potential he already knew was there.

Wale and my father came to see me walk the stage. They couldn't have been more proud of the accomplishment. I wished that my mother had been present to see the fruits of her labor. Had she not saved my life in high school; I would never have made it to college, much less graduate. I cried thinking of what it would've been like to see her smile on that day. I knew she had been watching me, and I'm sure she was proud.

"Things are not happening to you; they are happening through you."

—Adekunle Ige

STARTING MY CAREER

After graduation, I moved back home to my father's house. Like most college graduates, I was having a hard time finding employment. Nas knew I needed a job, so he hooked me up with a security gig at King of Prussia Mall to hold me over until I found a job in my major. I was thankful to have a job, so that I can pay my bills, but I knew I wasn't going to stay for long.

Around July 2007, I got a job interview for a case manager position at

Northwestern Human Services in the behavioral rehabilitation services unit. My job was to make home visits and organize services for children with mental health challenges and their families. Based on my experience with my mother, I knew the trauma of dealing with mental health and challenges families faced.

Working in the professional field was new to me and reality struck quickly. Suddenly, I was responsible for productivity time, audits, and case conferences. It took a while for me to adjust to the expectations. I remember tossing and turning at night wondering if I had done everything properly. After sharing my concerns with my supervisor, she laughed and offered words of assurance. "You must be used to working assembly line type jobs," she said. She told me not to worry and that many people come out of college with the same anxiety. "Hang in there; you are doing a great job, and we are happy to have you," she added. She could not have known how much those words eased my mind.

There were some great professionals to learn from. I began picking the brains of mobile therapists and behavioral specialists to learn more about their jobs and the credentials needed to obtain them. Those positions required a master's degree, and the pay was more than double my current pay. I thought even longer term when I talked to the psychologists who served my clients. It was helpful to see a path and longevity beyond case management in this career.

As time passed, my supervisor's words began to ring truer. I was far more comfortable and became more self-directed. I became one of the experts in child and family intervention. The experience taught me that I was valuable and could make good decisions to positively impact the people I served. It was rewarding and most of all, it gave me the confidence to access my innate strength—a confidence that I wanted to add to my professional arsenal going forward.

FISHER'S CROSSING

I didn't think it was appropriate to be a college graduate with a full-time job in my career field and live in my father's house. As soon as I got enough money for a deposit and first month's rent, I got my own place at Fisher's

Crossing Apartments. It was my first solo apartment, and it was liberating. Making my own moves and decisions was something that I dreamed about since I was a kid. It was a feeling that I could get used to.

I also got my first car note. I traded in the 2000 Mitsubishi Galant I bought from eBay. The car had served me well for the few years that I had it, but it was time to move on. I bought a red 2003 Honda Accord Coupe. Here I was, moving as an adult. Life was getting good, but little did I know it would get even better.

FORGIVENESS AND LETTING GO

Around December 2008, through my friend Nas, I ended up running into a familiar face. "You never gonna guess who I saw today," Nas said. "Who?" I asked. "Your boo-boo, Shantel," he responded. "You Drawin'. Get the fuck outta here," I retorted. Shantel had been a sore subject for me since our breakup five years earlier. It was the first time I'd heard her name in just as long. "I'm dead serious. She works at a Walgreens not too far from here," he continued. The last thing I remembered was her living in Norfolk, Virginia. "Why was she back in Philly?" I wondered. "She asked if me and you were still friends," Nas added. But when he said that, I didn't know how to feel. It was the closest I'd been to her since 2003.

A week or so later, I was face to face with her for the first time in five years. I was nervous. It was literally my first time seeing her since breaking up over the phone. How was I supposed to act around her? So many thoughts ran through my mind, and my anxiety levels were raised. However, the experience was nothing like the worrying response I was having. The truth is, it was nostalgic to see Shantel again. The best part about it was seeing her at the high point in my life. I had evolved over the five years since we last spoke. I cannot lie; it was like seeing her for the first time again. My heart warmed for the first time since the breakup, and I could feel love.

The first thing she said to me was, "You still look the exact same." I tried to tell her the same thing, but she interrupted, "I know I don't look the same," as she patted her stomach, indicating that she had gained some weight. "You still look good despite," I added. She still had the same big titties and beautiful smile accented by her dimples. She was still rocking the same style of glasses.

Shantel brought her daughter with her. When I saw that beautiful little three-year-old girl, I thought she looked exactly like her mother. It was a conversation Shantel and I used to have when we were together. I used to tell her that if she ever had a daughter, she would look exactly like her. Here I was seeing the words that I said and the scenario that I predicted in real time.

While I had the opportunity, I needed to remove five years' worth of burden from my heart and let Shantel know that I'm not the callous person that my past actions showed. I apologized for all the wrong-doings that I was responsible for during our relationship. "Don't worry about it. I forgave you a long time ago. We were young," she said. There is no way Shantel could've known how badly I needed to hear that. I tortured myself and refused to allow any woman to get close to me since our breakup. After Shantel's words, I literally felt my heart beginning to heal. To be honest, I always knew I would see her again, and I never stopped loving her.

Shantel told me she was a married mother and had moved on; she no longer held a grudge against me. I wish I could've said that same. I had held a grudge for the entire five years since our breakup. I was honest with her. I told her that I spent the last five years hating her for two years because she left me, then hating myself for another two years for mistreating her and being angry and confused for the last year.

Shantel and I hung out a few times. We got the group together again for the first time since our breakup, everyone except Chole. Apparently, Chloe and Shantel had some issues over the years that included fistfights and court hearings over money owed from their apartment. I wasn't surprised when Shantel shared that information. The two of them had several fistfights that Nas and I had to break up when we all lived in Mission College back in the day.

Brian and Nas came along with Shantel and me as we took a trip down to Penns Landing. We walked and talked about where we were in life and what we were looking forward to. I told Shantel that I kept the promise she asked of me five years earlier. "I graduated from Lock Haven University with a bachelor's degree in social work," I told her. I shared that I had a job working as a case manager for children with behavior disorders. We talked about the irony of me being a person that struggled with rage and then becoming a person who reached back to help others who struggled with similar challenges. I told Shantel that I was also was planning on going to graduate school. She seemed proud of me.

After a good time by the waterfront, we all decided to pack it in for the night. On the way home, Nas thought it was a good idea to draw on me for the rest of the ride. He had all kinds of jokes about Shantel returning to my life. His grandest joke was playing Ne-Yo's song "Do you" on high volume over and over again for the rest of the ride. I couldn't even be mad at him; it was creative considering the song was a literal depiction of my thoughts and the situation.

I called Shantel a few days later to see what her plans were for the holidays. She told me that she would be moving back to Virginia with her husband and daughter in the coming weeks. She told me she wanted to see me one last time before she moved, so I invited her to my apartment. I wanted her to see exactly how much I had changed and how I was living.

When she came over, I gave her a tour of my apartment. It was a humble space, but the point is, it was mine. The last time she saw me I was living with my father and out of school being unproductive. I can't lie: My feelings for her were strong and I felt the same energy from her. Truth be told, this woman still had my heart. I resisted any urge to try anything with her. I needed her to see that I respected her. If I had tried something and we ended up having sex, I knew it wouldn't go far after that. She was getting ready to move back to Virginia with her husband. Seeing her leave after reopening my feelings for her would've been devastating; my heart would never have recovered. My ability to resist my urges was the strength that I needed to rid myself of the demons that plagued my soul since our breakup. Instead, I gave her a warm hug and a kiss on the cheek. "Be safe," I told her as she left.

Today, Shantel and I are friends on Facebook. We speak every now and then. Both of us left the past in the past. I'll always love her, and I'm thankful for her forgiveness.

"Be loyal to your future, not your past."

—Unknown

GRADUATE SCHOOL 2008

After working at Northwestern Human Services for a year, I decided to go to graduate school. I applied to three schools in Pennsylvania: Immaculata University, West Chester University, and Marywood University. I didn't get accepted to Immaculata, and West Chester wouldn't offer me advanced standing. Marywood accepted me in two programs, Master of Social Work and Master of Public Administration. The cherry on top was that they gave me advanced standing. That meant I would be finished with the program after a year, instead of the traditional two years.

Marywood's school colors were green and white just like the flag of Nigeria. It was meant to be. My decision was made. The school was in Scranton, which was more than two hours away from where I lived. That meant I needed to move, so I did. I moved to Allentown in Lehigh County. The school was still an hour and a half away, but it was the best that I could do and the most that I could afford.

Unfortunately, I had to leave my salaried job because of a conflict of interest. The conflict came when I decided to do my internship at NHS in the Outpatient Therapy building a few blocks down. Due to some stupid rule, the higher-ups decided that I couldn't do both. I didn't understand the decision because I would be working in a totally different building, performing completely different tasks, and working under a different supervisor. There was nothing I could do about it, so I had to get a new job.

THERAPEUTIC SUPPORT

I found a job at a place called Horizons Behavioral Health in Southampton. I was working as a therapeutic support staff or TSS for short. This position was per diem, which was scary for me because the hours were not guaranteed. The hours were assigned by the client's medical provider, which meant if I wanted increased hours then I needed to have several clients.

Fortunately for me, there was a client who had behaviors so severe that he required 35 hours from his TSS. The client was a 5-year-old boy who suffered from oppositional defiant disorder and ADHD. The boy, let's call him TJ, was attending a preschool program, which was where he was having the most difficulty. The case manager offering the case told me that all his other TSSs had quit and that TJ did not like working with men. She offered me the case because it was one that nobody would take. The consensus was that TJ was not going to make it through first grade. I willingly accepted the challenge.

Even though I worked as a case manager and was familiar with clients with mental health challenges, I had no experience with direct service. The first day I came to see TJ at school, I didn't interact with him, I just observed. I wanted to see him in his natural environment without any distractions. My goal was to see how he handled frustration and to recognize his triggers.

A few minutes into my observation, TJ grabbed a chair and threw it across the room. Soon after, he began ripping up a paper and tossed it to the floor. I refrained from intervention to observe how Ms. Karen, his preschool teacher, intervened. I noticed she was highly stressed and could barely deal with him. The whole class stopped and stared at TJ's tantrum.

I saw the entire event unfold. TJ was playing on the computer. He was enjoying the game that he was playing; however, it was time for him to transition to another activity. The kids were being rotated on and off the computer because there were only two in a room for about seven kids. TJ felt cheated; he thought he was being pulled off the computer too soon even though he had been given extra time to prevent the very tantrum he had.

Ms. Karen thought his tantrum came out of nowhere. I explained to her what I observed and made suggestions. The next day I came in with an oven timer. The goal was to set the time on the clock so that it would ring when the desired time was over. That way, TJ could see how close the bell was to ringing and mentally prepare himself for his next transition. I instructed Ms. Karen to use the timer with all her students so TJ would not feel singled out. It worked like a charm.

TJ had a rough home life. His mother stayed out all night partying. The few times she did show up, she looked like she spent the night in the club. As a result, TJ was being cared for by his grandmother. His father wasn't always present in his daily life. When he was sent to school, his lunch box was packed with cheese doodles, cookies, and candy. There was not a single fruit, vegetable, or sandwich in his bag. I felt bad for the kid. I knew that all these things were the reasons he had so much rage.

I worked with TJ for nearly a year. His behaviors decreased significantly over that time. It wasn't an easy task, but it was worth every minute. He and I bonded to the point that he would look at me before reacting to stimuli that would've typically caused a tirade. When he looked at me, he noticed that I had already been looking at him and paying attention to the situation. Over time, it took little more than a head nod or a finger wave to prevent his outrage.

Ms. Karen told me that I was the best TSS she had ever seen. "Most of them just come in here and don't do anything when he had his tantrums," she said. "Every time he was having a tough time, you were right on it," she added. I thanked her for the compliment. I told her that she had a tough job. She had to worry about seven or eight other children, and I only had to worry about one.

The knowledge and confidence that I gained while working at NHS helped me use my instincts with TJ. I learned that TJ just needed someone to care and spend time with him. There were times when he would just cry in my arms instead of destroying the classroom. Those were significant wins because he was accessing his real emotions and not masking them with rage. I spoke with his grandmother about his diet and how it contributed to his behavior in school. Soon after, his lunch box had one piece of fruit, a sandwich, and a bag of chips.

I worked with TJ all the way through his second month in first grade. By that time, he no longer needed me as a support. It was hard to terminate from a client who felt like a son to me, but I knew it was the best thing for both of us. I know I wasn't supposed to get emotionally attached to him, but he was such a sweet kid underneath all that rage. I'm happy to say that TJ did just fine in first grade.

A NEW HUSTLE

After closing the case with TJ, I picked up a few more clients to cover the 35 hours I lost. Based on my work with TJ, my name spread to other agencies and suddenly, I had a constant stream of clients. I never forgot about TJ, and I brought the same dedication to all the clients I've had since. I enjoyed making a difference in the lives of my clients and families. I was often invited to birthdays and holiday parties. Unfortunately, I had to decline them because it was against agency policy. I typically thanked the families for the gesture and sent a card to the client.

Maintaining my schedule became increasingly difficult. At this point, I was going to school an hour and a half away, interning part time, and working nearly full time. Needless to say, I didn't have time for much else. I used the strategy that I learned in Dr. Tabler's research class to make sure I was never behind in work. I typed all my assignments ahead of time while watching all the football games on Sundays. I had to make use of every minute.

VERNON PARK

One of the most inspiring moments in my life came during graduate school. The phone rang, and I was awakened from a night of much-needed sleep. It was Brian. He called to let me know that presidential candidate Barack Obama was coming to our neighborhood that day on his campaign tour. It was seven o'clock in the morning, and I was not in the mood to be trolled. "Get the fuck outta here." I responded. "I'm dead serious," he responded. "He will be at Vernon Park at eleven o'clock, but they opening the gates at nine," he added. It was the *Change We Need Rally*. When I heard those details, I knew he wasn't bullshitting me. I jumped out my bed, took a quick shower, and left Allentown as soon as I could.

The plan was to I meet up with Brian on Chelten Avenue. I arrived around nine-thirty and met with Brian as planned. The place was already packed. There were hundreds of police officers, both uniformed and plain-clothes, and secret service everywhere. There were snipers posted in buildings, on rooftops, and in plain sight atop police trucks. I just wanted to make sure that I didn't make any moves or gestures that would be remotely considered as threatening. I didn't come down there to die.

It was the first and only time in my life that a presidential candidate came to my neighborhood. It wasn't a pretty location either; he was in the hood-hood. I respected that. For decades, other politicians delivered their speeches in universities, huge auditoriums, and in downtown city hall-like locations. I believed in his message and was inspired by his courage. His presence in a location where people who needed to be represented most matched his words.

For the first time in my life, it felt possible that a so-called black man had a legit shot at being president in America.

I didn't get to meet him personally, but I was inspired enough to believe that anything was possible. Through him, I saw a bigger picture for myself. I learned that I shouldn't set low reaching goals—that I should dream big instead. I'll never forget that day. It was Saturday, October 11, 2008. I knew I was witnessing history. I could feel it in my bones. I'm sure many others could as well. That's when I decided to vote for the first time in many years. On January 20, 2009, he was elected president of the United States.

GRADUATION 2009

I took that motivation and finished my master's program with a 3.2 GPA. I graduated nearly one year to the day from when I began the program. The graduation took place in Wilkes Barre, Pennsylvania, which was about three hours from Philadelphia. My father was too sick to attend. He was still recovering from the stroke he suffered years earlier. I didn't graduate alone though. My family was represented by my brother Wale, my niece Nevaeh, Brian, Nas, and his girlfriend at the time, Jennifer. They were all so proud. It was like they graduated too.

I was now the first person in my immediate family to graduate with an advanced degree. It was the proudest moment of my life. I reflected on my journey, and I knew I was beating the odds. Once again, I cried. I knew my mother would've loved this moment.

After graduation, I moved into my own apartment in Lansdale,

Pennsylvania to be closer to my family and friends. No more driving an hour and a half to hang out with them. It was time to reconnect with the people who had my back since day one.

FINDING ME

I reflected on the past few years. It had been a very tough road that I was forced to travel. But each step had brought me closer to new milestones both educationally and professionally. And I had gained confidence and experience in my career. Through that experience, I was able to touch lives, which helped me understand that I have value. That value confirmed that I had something more to offer to the world. I just needed to hone my skills and stay focused.

My heart was cleansed and relieved from five years of resentment when I was able to make amends with Shantel. Seeing her five years after the fact, helped me see how much I had grown personally; both of us could tell that I was a very different person. Being able to resist my urge to be sexual with her was a milestone; in the past, she was like kryptonite. I took it as a test that God put in front of me to see if I was still stupid.

Thankfully, I passed. All things considered; it was a good year. Never one to be naïve, I knew no matter how far I had traveled, there were still more opportunities for growth ahead and more challenges that I needed to overcome. The challenge that came next was one for which I was not prepared.

CHAPTER 12
SOUTHERN HOSPITALITY

Thanks to the reputation I earned working with TJ and completing my master's degree, I was able to get jobs as a mobile therapist. Th e purpose of my position was to help families connect with and understand the mental health challenges their children were facing. The clients I served had a wide range of clinical diagnosis; some were on the autism spectrum, and others had conduct disorders. The position was per diem just like my TSS position had been, but the new position paid twice as much, which meant I needed fewer cases to be financially comfortable. Everything was going well for me. I had a good-paying job, my own apartment, and a reliable car. The only thing I didn't have was love.

HUNGER FOR MORE

After several months of working as a mobile therapist and saving money, I decided to look into broadening my horizons. I wanted to move out of Pennsylvania and pursue my dream of living in California. I had lived in Pennsylvania for nearly 30 years, and I was tired of digging my car out of snow blizzards, shoveling paths, and driving on salted roads. I was ready to trade in the snow for the sun. It had always a goal of mine to make a life for myself in sunny Californ-ia.

My Aunt Marlene and my cousins Markus, Jonathan, Steven, and Victor lived in San Jose. They would be able to offer guidance and help me acclimate to a new environment. I figured that if I could gain employment anywhere in California, I would be able to build a reputation and eventually move to where I chose. I just needed to start somewhere. Taking a risk wasn't something that was foreign to me.

I began shopping my resume online to mental health agencies in California. After some persistence, I was able to land a job interview at Coalinga State Prison. Coalinga was near Fresno. I applied for a position as a mental health therapist working with convicted felons. I also had an appointment to take the fitness test for a position as a San Jose police officer. Both jobs were a considerable jump from working with children and families, but I was confident that I could take on the task.

UNTHINKABLE

Prior to taking the trip to California, I began talking to a beautiful Chilean woman on Facebook. Let's call her Pamela. She and I had a mutual friend on Facebook, Marty; he and I had attended Virginia State together. Pamela and Marty both happened to be living in the Atlanta area at the time. She knew Marty through his cousin, a woman with whom she worked.

I first noticed her as we both frequently weighed in on thought-provoking questions Marty would post on his timeline. He had a segment called *Marty Wonders*. Many people responded to the questions he posted. I used to read all the comments just to see people's opinions. Some of the comments were ridiculous, but others were well-thought-out, whether I agreed or disagreed with their logic. It happened to be a pastime that Pamela and I both shared.

After several months of reading the comments, I couldn't help but notice that she and I had the same points of view most of the time. The similarities in our perspectives led to us liking each other's comments and at times teaming up against others who disagreed. Being who I am, I also couldn't help but notice how beautiful she was.

Feeling that we had a connection and seemed to have the same interests, I decided to slide into her DMs to shoot my shot. The message read, "I don't know who you are, but I would like to." I guess she liked the message because she responded by introducing herself, and we began getting to know each other. Naturally, we exchanged phone numbers and began having late night conversations. Those conversations became a part of our daily routines, and they often lasted from the late night into the early morning.

Over the next several weeks, we covered a wide range of topics. I felt rather free talking with her. Our conversations grew from talking about our relationship statuses to our family backgrounds. We talked about what we thought of modern relationships, gender roles, and every other social topic. The conversations were refreshing to me because I was used to going straight into talking about sex. We eventually touched that topic, but it was not until a few weeks later. We kept each other interested with genuine curiosity about each other.

She told me that she had an eight-year-old son and asked if that was a concern for me. "Absolutely not," I responded. I told her I spent my life and career working with kids and wanted some of my own someday. That conversation led us to talk about deal breakers. I told her that I didn't date women who smoked— that it was a turnoff for me. "That's good because I don't smoke, but I drink occasionally," she responded. I told her that I didn't drink myself, but I didn't mind that she did as long as she wasn't constantly drunk.

I told her I had plans of moving to California to follow a childhood dream. "That's inspiring," she responded. "My brother and I are going to be visiting California in the next two weeks for a job interview and to visit our family there," I offered. She asked whether we were taking a direct flight or had any stops. I told her we were flying Delta Airlines and that we had one stop each way. Ironically, Atlanta was one of our stops on the way to California.

When she learned that, she wanted to meet me in-person because the airport is a public place. She wanted to make sure that I wasn't an "axe murderer," which is exactly what she said. I definitely wanted to see her as well, so we arranged a time and location inside the terminal to meet. Now, I wasn't just preparing for a job interview, I was getting ready to meet Pamela.

HARTSFIELD-JACKSON

The day came, and I was nervous. We only had a short amount of time to spend with each other because she was coming to see me on her lunch break, and I had a connecting flight to make. If you've ever been to

Hartsfield-Jackson, then you know it's one of the busiest airports in the country. I was concerned that it would be too difficult to find her and that we would miss each other. Fortunately, Pamela was very familiar with the airport, and she knew where I would arrive. We eventually met up near the concourse train.

When I saw her, she was even more beautiful in person than on her Facebook page. It was a pleasant surprise, but she had another for me. Pamela had a gift for me. She bought me a keychain from the Things Remembered store; she'd had it engraved with an inspiring message, "Always follow your dreams." I gave her a kiss and a hug, feeling her warm embrace for the first time.

We only had a small window of time to spend together before my plane arrived. Pamela wanted to make an impression, and she certainly made herself memorable. She stayed on my mind as I boarded the plane.

VACATION TO CALIFORNIA

Just as I promised, I called Pamela to let her know that Wale and I made it to California safely. Then, it was time to get on with the reason for my trip. I did well on my interview at Coalinga State Prison. After the interview, I was told that I would be placed on the hiring eligibility list. Since it was a government job, it could be years before my name was called. I knew that before I decided to apply, but I figured having my name in the pot was better than nothing.

A few days later, I took the physical test for the San Jose Police Department. I passed all the events of the fitness test rather easily since I had been training weeks before. Afterward, I hung out with my cousins while they gave me a tour of San Jose. While on the road, I couldn't help but wonder whether it was the right time for me to move to California. Don't get me wrong, I absolutely loved it. However, my mindset had shifted to wondering what I would miss out on if I passed Pamela up. I decided to explore a relationship with Pamela rather than following my passion; just as my mother had when she met my father.

LANSDALE

Pamela came to visit me at my apartment in Lansdale a couple weeks after I returned from California. It was very exciting because we couldn't wait to see each other and spend more time together. I took her to Chili's to get one of my favorite snacks, spinach artichoke dip. I couldn't believe she had never tried it before. Once she did, she loved it. Afterward, I gave Pamela a mini-tour of the area. I wanted to show her some of the nicest houses in the Philadelphia area.

When Pamela saw the houses, she agreed they were beautiful. "How much does houses like these cost?" she asked. "These houses start at around $500,000 and go up from there," I responded. Pamela proceeded to tell me that I could own the very same sized house in Atlanta for less than half the price. I was skeptical. We spent the rest of the ride talking about the pros and cons of living in both of our places of origin.

Later that night, we rented a movie that we never got around to watching. The moment that she and I had been anticipating was upon us. With due respect to her, she was experienced, and I liked that. She knew how to maneuver herself when she rode me. She started off by riding the tip gently sliding in and out. She continued until I was begging for her to give the rest of it some love.

When she did, I was ready. You know that eggplant emoji that people use today? That's how ready I was when I was finally allowed to thrust the full me into action. As soon as I felt her release, it was time for me to give her a time that she would never forget. I proceeded to let her know that my stroke game was real. When I felt she couldn't take anymore, that's when I released. Pamela and I spent the rest of the night releasing all the sexual tension between us.

Apparently, I wasn't the only one who enjoyed the sex. She told me she had a major Freudian slip when she talked to her friends how her trip to see me went. "That was the best spinach artichoke dick ever!" she proclaimed. I could not stop laughing. That slip confirmed that I did my damn thang to her. According to her, all her friends were in shock and began laughing too. She basically told on herself because they didn't know that we had sex. Pamela and I took turns visiting each other every two weeks thereafter.

HOUSE SHOPPING

Suddenly, I had a dilemma on my hands. I took Pamela's advice and began looking at houses online to see what the average price was. I could not believe that the houses were so cheap. Mansion-sized houses were going for less than $200,000, but the same house in Philadelphia would be in the $500,000 range. The taxes were also cheap at only a few hundred dollars per year.

After not hearing back from Coalinga or the San Jose Police Department for several months, I decided all signs pointed to Atlanta. Waiting the two years or more for my name to be called didn't sound appealing to me. I began looking for all kinds of jobs in the Atlanta area, but I had no luck. Most of the jobs I found required a licensed social worker, which I wasn't. I had never had too much difficulty getting jobs once I interviewed for them, so I wasn't worried.

A LEAP OF FAITH

After filling out countless applications but getting no responses, it was time for me to make a decision. I bet you probably think that I decided to stay in Philly and put things on hold with Pamela until the right opportunity presented itself. If you were thinking that, thank you. Unfortunately, the wrong head and my heart took control of the wheel. With those two navigating alone, there is no telling what the outcome would be.

Being the risk taker that I am, I decided to move to a place where I had no family, no friends, and no job. I had enough money saved to last me until I found a job. Informing my friends of my plan was pretty easy; Nas and Brian were both supportive. My father and Wale were not so sure. My father never really like the idea of me moving away from Philly, dating back to my choice to attend Virginia State University. Wale was skeptical for another reason.

Wale thought I was making a decision too hastily. And given that I had just returned from Allentown, he didn't want to be separated from me again. He was right on both counts, but it's not like big brothers go around seeking advice from their younger siblings. "What if something happens and you are not around?" Wale asked. These were the same kinds of questions or insinuations that were asked whenever I chose to branch out. I wasn't going to live my life in fear, so I didn't really give it too much thought.

ORDINARY LOVE SHIT—THE DRIVE

The day came, and I was all packed to go. Pamela flew up a day earlier to help me with the move. Before hitting the road, I decided to invite Wale, Brian, and Nas to have dinner with Pamela and me before we left. We all met at Chili's—the same one where I took Pamela when she visited earlier.

There was weird energy in the air. I was both excited and anxious about the move, and I think Pamela was in a similar space. Wale was constantly grilling Pamela with questions about her intentions. "Make sure you take care of my brother," he said. "Don't worry, I will," she replied. Knowing Wale, I don't think he was all the way sold, but he didn't make a big deal. Brian was quiet and observant as usual. Nas, on the other hand, was physically present but mentally elsewhere.

Nas had been having an argument with his son's mother prior to meeting us at Chili's. I won't go into further detail, but I will say it involved going through her phone call history and not being happy with what he saw. "What's wrong with you?" I asked. "Nothing man, nothing," he said. I had known Nas all my life, and I knew there was clearly something wrong. In fact, everybody did. His silence was deafening even as he did his best to be polite and engaged.

After dinner, it was time for us to hit the road. I gave pounds to my friends and gave Wale a hug. Pamela and I hopped on I-95 South and headed toward Atlanta, Georgia. During the drive, Pamela asked me what was going on with Nas. "He found something in his girlfriend's phone that he didn't like," I responded. "Why was he going through her phone in the first place?" She asked. That's when the doubt first entered my mind.

In my mind, the fact that there was something in her phone that Nas, her boyfriend, wouldn't approve of was the problem. For Pamela, the fact that he went through her phone was the problem. "So, it's ok that she was possibly doing something that she knew he wouldn't like?" I asked. "I'm not saying that, but he wouldn't be angry if he didn't go through her phone," she countered. I didn't understand that logic. We had a 12-hour ride ahead of us. After going back and forth about which came first the chicken or the egg, we decided to change the subject and focus on the future we saw for ourselves.

Even though we changed the subject, her perspective never left my mind. No matter how minute the impact of her comments was, it still showed a side of her that made me uncomfortable. Here I was traveling to her apartment with money saved but no job. The reality that Wale was trying to convey to me began to creep in. It made me more anxious than I already was.

By the time we got to Virginia, Pamela was tired and wanted to take a nap. She wrapped herself in a blanket and put her coat hood on her head. I was just as tired as she was, maybe more considering all the packing, and I was the one driving. I had never driven for more than five hours in one stretch, and it would be another seven hours until we reached our destination. I decided I would put on some music to keep me awake and engaged so I wouldn't fall asleep on the road. To my surprise, the music triggered her.

Pamela thought that I was turning on music to disturb her sleep. "Why you playing music all of a sudden?" She asked. "It's loud too," she added. I tried to offer my reasoning, but she wouldn't hear of it. "You never played music in the car with me before, so why now?" she continued. "I never played music in the car with you before because we were getting to know each other and had limited time to do so, and music would've cut the time even shorter," I explained. "Now, you are going to sleep, and I have a long drive ahead of me, what do you want me to do?" I asked. She knew I loved music because it was a huge part of our initial all-night conversations. I didn't understand her angle.

That's when it hit me. She was still salty about our disagreement about Nas's situation. For me, that conversation was over a few states ago. In her mind, I was being petty and trying to prevent her from sleeping. That was the source of her attitude and why she suddenly wanted to go to sleep. My point of view was totally different. I wasn't going to play monotone music to make myself even more sleepy, so I played it as I normally did. The latest back and forth was my first hint that she was a resentful person, a trait that never had an opportunity to present itself before. This whole ride got more and more petty as the wheels turned.

"Self-control is a strength. Calmness is mastery. You have to get to a point where your mood doesn't shift based on the insignificant actions of someone else. Do not allow others to control the direction of your life. Don't allow your emotions to overpower your intelligence."

—James Allen

CAPACITY

Over the course of the drive, I ignored that pettiness and tried to focus on the music. When she realized that I was no longer responding to the pettiness, she turned up the heat. Everything became a problem to her; it was too hot in the car; my arm was taking up the armrest; you name anything petty, and she was willing to poke at me for it. It was like she was testing me on purpose to see how I would react. After a while, it began to wear on me.

I could no longer take her antagonizing me, and that's when it happened. I called her a bitch and to keep it all the way real it was more than once over the course of the argument that ensued. Even then, I knew it was wrong, and I should've practiced more restraint. After the shocked look she gave me, an hour-long argument ensued. Eventually, cooler heads started to prevail. I took full responsibility and sincerely apologized to her, and she accepted. If she couldn't handle our differing points of view about Nas's situation without resentment, I knew I was never going to live down calling her a bitch.

Even though our journey, which ironically was the longest time we spent together at one time was tumultuous, I was looking to start anew.

ATLANTA

Pamela and I eventually arrived in the ATL. We didn't talk about the ride much. We focused on what was in front of us instead. Pamela and I unpacked my things and went out to eat with her friends for dinner the next night. We ate at a place called Taco Mac, which was weird because the place didn't sell tacos. It was like a diner slash sports bar. That's where we met up with her friends, Derrick and Rachel, who were also a couple.

It was nice meeting her friends and getting to see how they interacted.

We exchanged pleasantries as we waited for the waitress to approach us. When she arrived, they ordered a few beers with chips and salsa. I was really hungry, so I ordered a plate of shrimp and pasta. Pamela gave me a weird look but didn't say anything. When the check came, I reached for my wallet to pay for the meal. Pamela insisted that she would cover it as she wanted to take me out as I had done for her at Chili's. I allowed her to pay for the meal because I was not about to have a debate about male and female equality.

On the way home, Pamela constantly made jokes and comments about my meal choice. "We just came here to relax and have a few beers. We didn't go there to have dinner," she said. I didn't see anything wrong with my meal choice, but I was not willing to argue with her. "You know I don't drink, and I was hungry," I explained. "It's not a big deal; it just looked weird," she added. "To who?" I asked. "I'm sure Derrick and Rachel thought it was weird," she said. I doubted that they cared about what I ate at the restaurant. I just left the conversation alone.

Later that day, I noticed her smoking cigarettes, which is the exact opposite of what she said when I told her it was a turnoff to me. Now, you don't just start smoking cigarettes out of nowhere; it was obviously an addiction for her. I guess she thought that if we could get to a place of emotional connection, then her smoking would be less of an issue. To me, it was a bait and switch, but I tried to be open-minded. I didn't want to just cut her off as I had done to several other ladies years earlier. If I was going to evolve, then I had to do it all the way, including in tough moments. In hindsight, I should've left once I realized she lied to me about a deal breaker. If she lied about that, then anything else was fair game. Only time would tell if she would let me slide on anything that she thought I was dishonest about.

After a short weekend, it was time to get busy. When Pamela dropped her son off at school and went to work, I hit the Internet looking for jobs just about anywhere that had a listing. I put in around 10 to 12 applications per day. I couldn't wait to get a job so that I could contribute to rent and other bills. My long-term goal was to get my own apartment so that we could take things a bit slower.

Over the next several weeks, finding a job proved to be more challenging than I anticipated. In addition to filling out applications, I began to take a more old-school approach. I dressed business casual and began walking around downtown Atlanta to show myself physically, hoping to talk with some hiring managers. I had lukewarm results. Most of the time, I wasn't allowed to speak to hiring managers or anyone in human resources; instead, I was given an application. Other times, I was told the places were not hiring.

As a man, it was punishing to be living with a woman without being employed. It's not something that I felt comfortable with. I wanted to contribute, but the money I had saved was wearing thin. I decided that I would try to contribute in other ways to lighten the load on Pamela. When I finished filling out applications for the day, I would make sure her house was thoroughly cleaned. I made beds, picked up toys, vacuumed, washed dishes, and did other chores. I even began picking up her son from school when she needed me to; anything that I was able to do to help her, I did it.

Over time, my inability to find a job wore on us. She would constantly ask me questions about where I applied. Most of the time, I had applied everywhere she mentioned unless it was a place that I had never heard of. Then, I would take that information and apply there too. I even applied to fast food restaurants like McDonald's and KFC; I wasn't too proud. I gave her daily updates on the status of each application.

Whenever we had a disagreement of any kind, she would throw it in my face. "I need a boyfriend not a housekeeper," she'd say. What could I do in those moments? She was basically kicking me while I was down and invalidating all the efforts that I put in to help her. "When I met you, I just got my master's degree and had a job paying decent money," I told her. "Do you think that I did all of that to come down here and live for free?" She had no answer. How could she?

Just like the Nas argument during the move, I didn't understand her point of view, but she didn't care to understand mine. As a result, the pettiness continued, and the arguments became worse and worse. At this point, we could barely be in the same room with each other because the tension was so thick. Eventually, she admitted that she still hadn't gotten over me calling her a bitch months earlier. "I apologized for that, and you accepted," I reminded her. "I thought we moved on from that." It was clear that I had moved on from it, but she hadn't. Instead, she spent her time telling me how great she was and how her son's father wasn't shit as an example of how she had been treated by men. As I observed her pettiness and vindictive nature, I wasn't so sure about that story.

I remember talking to my friend Tabitha, a long-time pen pal from my Virginia State days. When things got crazy, I'd talk Tabitha's ear off for hours about my relationship issues. I couldn't trust my own judgement on how to take conversations or texts from Pamela. I wasn't too good with hints. You'd have to hit me with a brick sometimes to get me to understand. I wanted to understand things from a woman's perspective and she was always willing to help. I listened as she deciphered the female code-laced language Pamela used. I soaked up every drop until she offered her conclusion. "Really, I think you guys need a clean break," she said in a matter-of-fact tone. Intellectually, I knew it made all the sense in the world, but my obsession and ego wouldn't allow me to give up that easily.

One day, things came to a head. After another explosive argument, she asked me to leave. "I need you to leave. I can't think with you here," she said. She sounded like Regina King talking to Will Smith in *Enemy of the State*. It wasn't what I wanted, but things weren't going according to plan, so I didn't make a big fuss about it. I packed my things and got on my Kenny Rogers, *on the road again*, alone.

"If a man doesn't seek humility, humility will seek the man."

— Bill Duke

RETURN TO PHILLY

It was a long ride back to Philly. On the way, I thought about how I was going to reestablish my life when I arrived. I'd be lying if I acted like breaking up with Pamela didn't affect me. To keep it one hundred, it plagued my mind on and off throughout the ride. I thought about my missteps and wondered about the red flags that I missed.

When I got back to Philly, I stayed with Nas. Nas already knew about the turbulence in our relationship, but I gave him more than an earful anyway. He didn't mind much, besides he bent my ear whenever he had relationship problems. I told him Pamela was making judgments about him even though she didn't really know him and our arguments were based around my defense of him. "How is she gonna take a position on me when she don't even know what I found in her phone?" he asked. "She don't even know me," Nas added emphatically.

Nas was working as a delivery man for a dairy company. He drove huge refrigerated trucks. Not wanting to be alone and needing to vent, I decided to ride with Nas during his deliveries. Over the next couple days, I brought Nas up to speed on all the events that transpired leading to my departure. "She is selfish, and she hates men," Nas said. "Think about it. She's defending MY girlfriend who she never met; she has no idea about our history and doesn't care if she was cheating on me or not," Nas offered. "Well, that's ironic because she thinks you hate women," I responded.

I was fine during the day because I had Nas to bounce ideas off and talk about my relationship issues. He was real with me. "You think you moved down there with her too fast?" he asked. "Ask yourself this question: If the shoe was on the other foot and she moved to Philly, what would her friends and family say about you for kicking her out?" he asked. It was questions like that that brought perspective to our problems.

Nighttime was when I needed the most help; left alone, my depressed and obsessive mind began to devour me. It was as if depression came through like, "Yo, bruh, move over, and let me lay with you." I couldn't get Pamela off my mind. My mind was too obsessed with all the details. I couldn't get any sleep because I was dreaming about the mistakes I made and things I allowed. As a result, I was tossing and turning all night as I slept on Nas's floor. The heartbreak was overwhelming. It felt as if my heart was bleeding and would stop beating at any moment. I legit thought I was going to die.

The lyrics to Mayer Hawthorne's song "Strange Arrangement" kept playing in my head on repeat. Prior to Pamela, I never even heard of the dude. I got confusing subconscious messages as Drake's summer smash record "Best I Ever Had" played in my mind as well. When I woke, I resisted the urge to call her. "If you think you were at her mercy then, imagine if you called her," Nas said. He made a good point and validated what I was already thinking. During my waking hours, I did whatever I could to keep myself busy. Most importantly, I wasn't as active on social media as I had been in the past. I needed her to wonder what she had lost and have no clue as to what I was up to.

According to her, I must've been living a good life and comfortable. I didn't come crawling back, so naturally, she called me. Nas got a huge kick out of that. "There go ya wife calling! What you gonna do?" he teased. I took my time getting back to her after she left a voicemail. "Hey, it's me. I want to talk to you. Give me a call back when you can," her message said. I waited about six or seven hours before I returned her call. I couldn't let her, a Leo like myself, see me as desperate.

THE AT "L"

Now, this is where I should get the crying Jordan meme for stupidity. When I called her back, she apologized for overreacting and said that she wanted to work it out. "I want to take you out to dinner if you are willing to come back to ATL or are you over it?" she asked. I wish I could tell you that I was over it, but I wasn't. In fact, I was so in love it sounded like a good idea. I apologized again for calling her a bitch, and I told her that I was down for a do-over. A few days later, I was on the road again.

Halfway down to ATL, I received another call from Pamela. "I'm excited to see you. What time will you be here?" she asked. "I'll be there around 6:30 or 7:00 p.m.," I told her. It was a good feeling to hear that she was excited to see me again. It felt like a new beginning, one that I felt we both deserved. It took six more hours before I could see her again, and I played Toni Braxton songs for every minute.

When I arrived, I met Pamela and her son at a diner. We gave each other a hug and a kiss as we waited to order. "I missed you. I want to move past it all and start over," she said. I apologized to her in person and told her that it would never happen again. I told her that I loved her and that I didn't want us to fight any more. We were both on the same page. After a good meal, the three of us went home to watch a movie together. It was a peaceful night. The next morning, I resumed my routine of looking for jobs and filling out applications.

It wouldn't be too long before we were back on our bullshit. The pettiness returned as we got into arguments over the smallest things. Pamela seemed to have an attitude with me about everything, and her mood swings were sharp. "What's going on? How come you seem to be angry or unhappy all the time?" I asked. "I don't know; I still having trouble with it," she responded. "Trouble with what?" I asked. "You calling me a bitch," she responded. "How many times do I have to apologize for that?" I asked. "I can't go back in time and change it," I added. Still, she brought me up on charges because her ego got killed, and I held the smoking gun.

The more days that passed, the more things went downhill. We argued more frequently and more explosively. "I am not going to stay in a relationship with a person just because the sex is good," she said. I didn't understand where that comment came from especially since our arguments had nothing to do with that topic. It was good to know that she loved my pound game tho. In hindsight, that might be why she wanted me to return to ATL, I thought. After a few more arguments where we were both tossing insults, the petty level rose to new heights.

ORDINARY LOVE SHIT—EXACTING REVENGE

Pamela started taking her son to her mother's apartment so that he and I could no longer connect. The clinician in me thought she was reliving the problems she had with her son's father who wasn't in her life and did not provide for her. I wondered if what I was experiencing were her traumatic responses. So, I didn't respond or react when her petty thermometer increased to its boiling point.

I didn't respond when she would roam around the house giving me the silent treatment. I didn't respond when she would tell me that she was going out and wasn't coming back for the night. I knew all she was doing was either going over to Derrick and Rachel's or to her mother's apartment. When she would come into the house on the phone pretending to be flirting with a guy, I ignored it. I paid no mind to her when she started laying her outfits on the living room couch to insinuate that she had a date that night. I knew she was trying to bait me into arguments based on jealousy. My goal was to wait out the pettiness and not feed into it.

> *"I don't have to attend every argument I'm invited to."*
>
> — Unknown

Over time, it became more and more clear to me that she only wanted me to come back to ATL so that she could get her revenge on me. You see, when I was in Philly, she had no idea as to whether I suffered in any way. No information was offered on Facebook to confirm that I was having a rough time. To her, I was living the good life. Pamela's ego, anger, and resentment went so deep that she made it her goal to try to break me. She told me that I was "sick in the head" and I should "get help"; I just stood there listening to Harley Quinn assess me. I would tell ***her*** to do some soul searching, but it's hanging up in my closet with her skeleton. At this point, I'm with Tyrese: "What more do you want from meeee?" If you don't know what I'm referencing, shame on you.

When she realized that I was not going to be baited, she used her ace in the hole. She told me to leave. That's where I get the second crying Jordan meme for stupidity. How do you get kicked out twice by the same woman? I had very little money and still no job. It's like it was a victory to her when she got the chance to act like a dick to me. Pamela had the ultimate advantage and knew she could lean on that to hurt me. I moved my things out a few days later. My dumb ass should never have returned to ATL.

IVAN ALLEN JR BLVD

This was my new address. It was also the address of the Atlanta Mission for Men, a shelter. I didn't have enough money to make the drive all way back to Philly. This was the lowest point in my life. I never imagined that I would be living in a shelter. When I was doing the intake, I was in no mood for a lengthy conversation. It felt demeaning to have to prove to the director that I wasn't a crackhead. I showed him my master's degree and told him how I ended up there. I was probably more educated than he was, but somehow, I had managed to find myself homeless and at his mercy. Fortunately for him, he hadn't made the poor choices that I had; my self-esteem was nonexistent.

I gained admission to the shelter, but I had to wait a few days before I could get a bed. The rules stated that I had to have been living on the street for a few days to be technically homeless. I slept in my car surrounded by plastic bags of clothes, hangers, hats, and a TV in my backseat. I was staring at graduation tassels hanging from my rearview mirror wondering how I fell this far. Over the next few days, I was cramped and cold with only a blanket to hold me. l barely had any food to eat. Even if I had food, I was far too depressed to eat it.

Once I got my bed, I was relieved, but the whole experience was terrifying. I was in a room of about 15 to 20 bunk beds. The room smelled like rust and ass. The place was so dirty that I was afraid to take a shower. I thought I would catch an incurable disease. Maybe it was psychological, but at that point, everything was.

To make matters worse, the guy one bunk to my right was yelling violently and threatening someone only he could see. We had to follow a schedule while residing in the shelter. We had to leave the shelter by 7:00 a.m. and could not return until after 5:00 p.m. Then, dinner was served. I was so depressed that I couldn't eat for days. "If you want to commit suicide, pills are much easier," one resident said to me. He noticed that I wasn't going to dinner or eating. I wanted to tell him to go to hell, but we were already there.

About five days went by before I took my first bite of food, it was chicken with gravy and rice. By that time, I had lost nearly 20 pounds. To my surprise, the food in that shelter was actually good. Shout out to the cooks in there for getting busy. I only ate at dinner time and that was because my stomach was killing me. It took me over an hour to finish my meal, as I could barely open my mouth for a bite. I was still massively depressed, but I wasn't missing meals nearly as often.

Eventually, I got a job phone call from Devereux Residential Facility, a place where I had applied when I was at Pamela's. I went for the interview and somehow managed to get the job despite my depression. The job was to work with extremely emotionally disturbed teenagers. Once I notified the director of the shelter that I had a job, I was moved to a different part of the shelter. This side was less disgusting and filled with people who were getting back on their feet.

After working at Devereux for over a month, I saved enough money for a security deposit and first month's rent. I was able to get my own apartment.

I chose to live in the same complex where Pamela lived. It was the only area I was familiar with and besides that, the apartments were nice *and* cheap. Though we lived in the same large complex, our apartments were at least two blocks away from each other. I still had to stay in the shelter for another month before I could move in because the complex had to get the apartment ready.

> *"Rock bottom will teach you lessons that mountaintops never will."*
>
> —Unknown

THE NEW APARTMENT

Once I moved in, I took a shower for what seemed like five hours. Prior to that, I hadn't taken a thoroughly relaxing shower in months. I got to sleep in my own bed for the first time in what seemed like an eternity. Once again, I was putting my life back together little by little. I was independent for the first time in eight months. It felt good to be getting back to myself, being able to provide for myself.

Before I knew it, I had furniture, shower curtains, cable, and Internet. The job didn't pay that much, so I wasn't balling, but I was squeaking by. I still had my car note to pay which was several months past due. I was so late on the payments that I was getting threatening repossession calls daily. If the apartment complex hadn't been gated, they probably would've repossessed my car.

Out of nowhere, I got a message from Pamela. I told her that I got a full-time job and moved into my apartment. Knowing that I had bounced back must've pissed her off because she began demanding money from me. According to her logic, I owed her money for all the times she took me out to dinner. In reality, she offered to take me out to eat and made the decision to pay for dinner. Here she was again being petty not feeling like she was through with her revenge. It was like she was angry that I was no longer suffering as much as she thought I should be.

She tried to make me feel guilty by saying things like, "You are going to take money from a single mother." She didn't have any problems offering to take me to dinner when we were together. Now all of a sudden, I'm some asshole who took money from her. The texts kept coming. At this point, it was our means of communication, but there should not have been any at all. I didn't want to fight with her anymore; I was exhausted. To get rid of her, I told her that I would repay her for whatever she spent.

It was stupid, I know, but it was the only way I could bring a conclusion to what had been a disaster from the jump. Over the course of the next few months, I gave her whatever I could to resolve what she saw as debt. You think that stopped her from breaking my balls every chance she got? Nope. Whenever she found herself thinking of me, she sent me a mean message or a threat of some kind. I paid her threats no mind and eventually finished paying her off. Soon after, I got a new job.

A NEW GIG

Acting on a previous tip that I got from Pamela's friend Derrick, I applied for a job with the Department of Family and Children Services. The position was for classic social worker role, doing home visits and child abuse investigations. It was a higher paying job, and I needed the money. I was working in the most rural of rural areas in Georgia. I'm talking I have no teeth, I might fuck my sister, confederate flag on the back of my pickup truck while driving with no shirt rural. It was the scariest thing in the world for a city slicker like myself. At night, there were no streetlights or cement in most places, just dirt roads and ditches.

As an African man, it was not the place to be. Imagine going into these homes trying to teach these people how to keep their children or worse having to remove them. To make matters worse, the county that I worked in was completely unorganized. Things just seemed to happen on the fly with no planning whatsoever. There was no strategy around anything. My life was chaotic already. I didn't need a job that reminded of it. That's when I knew this job wasn't for me. I decided to start looking for other jobs.

I started putting out applications, and I got an interview at a place called Pathways, a mental health agency. The interview went well, and I was told I would be contacted for a second interview the next week. I felt relieved because I was going back to my roots, a position where I felt most comfortable. However, a curveball came out of nowhere so fast it would make Nolan Ryan jealous.

A few days before my second interview, I was at my desk in the county office entering notes into their intranet system from a case that I had been working a few nights before. The door opened and I was approached by the county director Judy and the investigations supervisor Jamie. Judy was a black woman in her late 30s or early 40s. Jamie was a pregnant Asian lady in her late 20s or early 30s with a bitchy attitude. She thought she was big shit because she had been promoted to her new position.

When they entered, I knew some bullshit was about to happen. "Do you still have that notebook I gave you?" Judy asked. "Yes, it's right here," I responded. I handed her the notebook while trying to figure out why it took two people to ask for it. "We are going to have to let you go, and we need the rest of the supplies," Judy said. "Please don't make a scene," Jamie added.

Georgia is an "at-will" state so they didn't even have to give me a reason for firing me. Judy seemed to take pleasure in firing me as she had a sly smile on her face the entire time. I remember thinking, "What made them think that I would cause a scene?" If I were going to cause a scene, what would a barely five-foot-two, 8-month pregnant woman do to stop it? The whole situation was ridiculous. I hated working there, so I wasn't angry that they were letting me go. I damn sure wasn't going to give them any satisfaction of seeing my rage over losing a job that I was looking to leave in the first place, and that's when it hit me.

Judy found out through the grapevine that I had been looking for a new job and that was the reason she decided to let me go. It was one of those you know your boyfriend is about to dump you, so you break up with him first situations. I thought it was corny and petty, but I still didn't care. I was waiting on a phone call for my second interview at Pathways. That phone call never came.

Apparently, it was the lady at Pathways who called Judy to let her know that I had interviewed a few days earlier. She wasn't calling to check my references either. I learned that through a friend I had made while working in the county building. She overheard Judy and Jamie talking about it a few days later. I had been set up, and now I am unemployed, again.

I applied for unemployment and while that was in process, I started applying for jobs again. This roller coaster life in Georgia was getting old, and fast. My money was running low, really low, and I had no source of income to replenish it. I managed to get a therapist position at a place called Covenant Youth Empowerment—a job that came in clutch for me. The downside was that they paid once per month, and I was hired at the end of a pay period. That meant I wouldn't be paid until the end of the coming month.

"Money is numbers and numbers never end. If it takes money to be happy, your search for happiness will never end."
—Robert Nesta Marley aka Bob Marley

Ever feel like the world owe you something?
Too naïve to see that the world owes you nothing
Lost lives, lost jobs, got you feeling hopeless
Living everyday blind, with no sign of focus
Never did a drug, but wondering where the coke is
Neighborhood full of violence, in your fam, you're ignored
Instead of admitting depression, convince yourself that you're bored
Watching your dreams rise and fall
Only fear is God, last night set it off
Scared to take your own life, whether gun or a knife
So you wished you didn't wake up
But the thought of leaving your brother makes you shake up
Don't know what to do, so you're confused with life
Can't trust no girl, it's hard to believe in a wife
Feels like the world is against you, nobody shows love
So you walk with a vendetta, attitude of a thug
You got three main hustles and none of them working

Can't get hired for a job, can't say that you're working
Life is short for a black man in lower class
The world is moving slow, but you need money fast
What good is a car without money for gas?
Still, you hold your head up as the hard times pass
You're life's a blind man driving and it's bound to crash
The world is running a race and you come in last
Don't know whether you want to live or die
Too confused or scared to decide
You're motivated to live, yet you're looking to die
You owe electric, phone, and rent, all delinquent
You live, lose, owe, and die in that sequence
You got a lot of problems and it's plain to see
If you could relate to this, then you must be me
In the mirror

Song: "*M.I.T.M.,*" **Artist:** *Me,* **Album:** *The Death of J. Storm* **Year:** *2003*

CHAPTER 13

LIVING WITH SHADOWS

Even after a twice-failed relationship with Pamela, becoming homeless, being fired from a job that I hated, and battling serious depression, I was still determined to make a life for myself in Atlanta. I felt that I could not give up on myself. I am an African man in America; I don't have that luxury. On top of that, I could not let Pamela get the satisfaction of seeing me fail. However, bigger problems were on the horizon. A few days later, I got the phone call that would completely shatter my life once again. This situation was one that I never dreamed could even be a possibility.

THE BLACK CLOUD

My father called me to tell me that my grandmother, his mother, had passed away. He told me that both he and Wale had returned home from a trip to the store when they discovered her. At this point, I was very shocked and uncertain how to feel.

"What happened?" I asked. "I think she might've fallen and hit her head," my father responded. I couldn't understand why a 90year-old woman would be left alone in a house full of construction tools and sharp objects, knowing she had dementia. Pairing this with my depression, life for me was going to shit, quickly.

My grandmother and I did not have a real relationship because she did not speak English, only Yoruba. She was already in her 90s and senile when

I met her for the first time. Regardless, she was my grandmother, and it hurt me deeply to hear about her death. I was already at rock bottom prior to hearing the news. And what made things worse was that I was unable to afford transportation to attend her memorial or her funeral. While I was experiencing depression and heartbreak, Wale was forced to handle all my grandmother's post-life matters. And then came the circus.

THE PHONE RINGS

About three to four days after her death, I got another phone call. This one was from Wale. He was calling to inform me that our father had been arrested. I was completely puzzled. "Arrested?! What for?" I asked. That's when the bomb was dropped: Wale informed me that our father was arrested for the murder of our grandmother, his own mother. There are no words that can describe my state of mind after hearing the news. I couldn't believe it. It didn't even sound real. "There must be some mistake," I thought. I was certain that the mix-up would be sorted out, and my father would be set free. After all, my father had never shown a propensity for violence, certainly not to the point of murder. I was trying to figure out how the police came up with their findings. I was feeling even more terrible because I had to learn everything over the phone. I was completely powerless to help with the situation while in Atlanta.

Meanwhile, Wale was left as the sole person to deal with the fallout. He had to be subjected to accusatory questions from the police, having all the neighbors in our business, and worse of all was being followed by reporters. Reporters were everywhere putting cameras in his face and invading his privacy. My father's house was on the news, and Wale had to be the one to navigate through all the tragedy and embarrassment. Again, I felt so powerless because I should have been there to be able to help him.

Naturally, Wale was highly stressed and enraged. He had every right to be. Wale was against me moving to Atlanta in the first place. Even though I had moved to Atlanta 10 months prior to my grandmother's death, Wale still felt that I was responsible for leaving him to deal with the freak show that was our family tragedy. It destroyed our relationship, at least from my point of view. He had no idea about what I was really dealing with in Atlanta; he thought I was "enjoying life" as he always said, while he was getting the worse end of the stick. I was feeling very guilty. I was unable to share with him what I was experiencing because he was constantly raging about me not being there for him during this tough time. Besides, how could I talk about what was going on for me when our grandmother's death was far more important? I was not willing to be that selfish.

THE AFTERMATH

I endured all of Wale's rage towards me and tried to take it in as a way to allow him to vent. I knew that he was speaking about me from an uninformed place. He thought I was purposely choosing not to return to Philadelphia to help him. He didn't know it was financially impossible for me to return at that moment. I had $12 to last me until my first paycheck from a job that paid once per month. On top of that, my car was on the verge of being repossessed. I was constantly getting calls and threats of legal action against me. I basically had to hide my car and quit answering their calls to avoid losing that too.

The more he called me, the more he raged at me. The usual sequence of the phone calls started with him calling me names and graduating to at one point threatening to kill me. "Don't let me see you because if I do, I'm gonna pop you," he said. He was always overly emotional; however, I took the threat seriously. I called my friends Brian and Nas to inform them of the threat. "If something ever happened to me, Wale did it," I warned. No matter how many times he would call, I answered every time. I knew he was calling just to tell me how much he hated me, but I never hesitated because I love him. I knew he was in real pain, and it was pain that I was powerless to heal.

I felt Wale's pain. From his point of view, he was the younger brother having to perform tasks that he was not ready for and should not have to do. Wale had to move to our mother's house alone because our father's house had been locked down and wrapped with caution tape. It was being treated as a crime scene. I couldn't imagine what this must have been doing to my little brother. His two oldest brothers should have been there to support him. Our grandmother should not have died. My father should not have been charged and arrested. I should have been living in Philly. Femi should not have been incarcerated. My mother should be alive. Life was just falling apart for all of us and seemingly forcing Wale to face it all alone while wearing 3-D glasses.

> "Brothers don't let each other wander in the dark alone"
>
> —Jolene Perry

THE GET-BACK

Meanwhile, I had to get my life together—and quick. I had just come from living in a shelter and from being employed to being unemployed with an apartment. I didn't have two things that matched. Kool-Aid, no sugar; ham, no burger; peanut butter, and no jelly. My life was just like Chris Tucker's famous line when he played Smokey in the movie *Friday*. If you haven't seen *Friday*, shame on you.

My plan was to drop everything and get back to Philly as soon as I got my first check. After I completed the first pay period for my job at Covenant Youth Empowerment in Atlanta, I quit my job. I let the folks at CYE know that I had a family emergency and needed to move back to Philly. I'm sure they thought I just came for a quick check, but I couldn't worry about that. I needed to help Wale and find out what was going on with my father.

Once I got my first check, I was on my way to Philly. My things were already packed and ready to go. I knew I was going to have a short-term place to stay at Nas's apartment. At the time, Nas was sharing an apartment with his then-girlfriend, Anna. It wasn't the most ideal situation for me, but beggars can't be choosers. Besides, I was thankful to have a place to stay at all.

When I arrived in Philly, I recruited my friend Brian to assist me with getting the rest of my things from Atlanta. That meant, I had to drive back to Atlanta and then back to Philly. That's 12 hours each way, 15 hours if you add in stopping for gas and food. Brian was more than happy to help. He knew what I was going through and the tragedy of my grandmother's death. I am grateful that I had those two to help me during one of the most difficult times in my life.

REPARATIONS

First thing I did when I finished my final trip from ATL was call Wale. I wanted to connect with him and see what he needed help with. He didn't answer any of my phone calls. A few weeks later, he sent me a massively long text expressing how angry he was with me. As usual, it was filled with curse words, name-calling, and hateful innuendo. I told him that I came back to Philly as soon as I could to help him, but he was not interested in receiving the very help that he requested.

The way Wale saw it was I wanted to live anywhere but home. His point of view was to stay close to family. He had feelings of abandonment dating back to when I left to attend Virginia State University. He took my absences personally. He thought I was trying to get away from him when I went to college and to ATL. He felt I messed up the tradition of being one of the elders who could reach back to teach him. He was concerned with how he was going to learn what he needed to survive.

Wale didn't know how to deal with the funeral plans, picking out a casket, and cremation. When our mother passed away, Femi and I were involved in the planning. It was his turn, and he wasn't ready. Why should he have been? By the time, I came back to Philly, Wale had dealt with everything, so he didn't need my help. When I came home from ATL, he saw me like a dad who came around once the child was 18 years old and tried to be a father.

None of what he thought was accurate; in fact, it couldn't have been further from the truth. However, when Wale makes up his mind, there is no convincing him otherwise. At this point, I extended my hand to help when I was in a position to, and he resisted. I did not have time to play cat and mouse with him or explain the same things I had said to him many times before. Either he wanted my help, or he didn't, that was my mentality.

Meanwhile, I had to get my life together. I needed a place to say, so I called Nas. He looked out and told me that I could stay with him until I get on my feet. He knew my work ethic and that it wouldn't be long until things came together for me. I didn't take his kindness for granted. Even though I was still massively depressed, I still had to get on my grind.

While living at Nas's apartment, I wanted to make sure I wasn't overstaying my welcome. Even though I did not have a job right away, I still didn't play around like a deadbeat although I felt like one. When Nas got up for work at the Rosenberger's Dairy Delivery company, I woke up too and went with him every day on all of his routes.

> *"Experience is the best teacher and I'm it's favorite student"*
>
> —Adekunle Ige

DOCTOR NAS

The rides I took with Nas were very eye-opening. It was kinda like therapy. All I did was talk about my failed relationship with Pamela. Nas would do his best to give me a new perspective. "I think you are obsessed," he offered. "Yo, if she really cared about you, would she have let you be homeless?" he asked. "I think she called you back down there because she didn't feel that she got you back enough," he added. "And my dumb ass thought she wanted to reconcile," I said. I still never ran from the fact that I screwed things up. I am the one who spazzed on her, even if I thought she was baiting me.

In true Nas fashion, he thought the best way for me to get past Pamela was to go out there and get at someone else. To be honest, I wasn't in the mood. When I wasn't with Nas at work or applying for jobs, I distracted myself by watching old episodes of *In Treatment* on HBO. I wanted to move on, but I knew I was in no place to. At night, I tossed and turned for hours with heartbreak. At the time, I didn't know whether it was because I was stupid enough to return to ATL or because I lost Pamela.

On top of all that, I was still emotionally ripped apart because of the murder of my grandmother, the incarceration of my father, and the broken relationship with Wale. I needed an outlet, something that would help me get my mind where it needed to be. I needed something I could refocus on and move on. Think about it, here I am a man with a master's degree, unemployed and homeless, sleeping on my best friend's floor and having my family destroyed. I was sinking so far into depression that trying to smile was painful, laughing was foreign, and hardly anything brought me joy. I knew this depression would eat me alive sooner or later. With everything going on, I didn't want to end up in a mental hospital or having a psychotic break as I'd seen with my mother.

TAKING LS

All my overachieving with ladies did not come without some losses that I was forced to accept and wished I could get back. I decided to take Nas's suggestion and put it into action. Towards my last two weeks in ATL, I had been talking to a beautiful Italian woman; let's call her Sofia. I graduated from Lock Haven University with her. Our conversations were through Facebook. Sofia knew that I was coming back home to Philly, which was close enough to her because she was living in West Chester, about a 40-minute drive away.

Our conversations started out with mild check-ins about where we were in life and discussing our peers. Eventually, the conversations became sexual. I was with every minute of it. Over the course of that conversation, I learned what she preferred sexually and that she hadn't had a boyfriend in a long time. Sofia invited me over to have dinner and watch the Phillies game.

Given that it had been a while since I left the house, I was more than happy to oblige. When I arrived, Sofia looked and smelled great as she gave me the warmest hug. It was the first hug I had in about eight months. I arrived just in time for her to make one of my favorite meals, shrimp fettuccine alfredo. She poured me a glass of red wine, which should've been white wine because of the dish she was serving, but I wasn't going to let something like that get in the way.

We began having small talk about how great it was to see each other again for the first time in about five years. Then, the conversation moved on to the Phillies baseball game. After we finished our meals, Sofia went to the bathroom and then into her room. She was in there for about five minutes or better. The old me would've taken that opportunity to shoot my shot so I could shoot my shot. See what I did there? But I didn't. For once in my life, I'm trying to be on my best behavior. I paid it no mind.

When Sofia came back to the living room, we continued to watch the game. After it was over, we exchanged pleasantries and I gave her a hug. "Let me know that you got home safe," she said. I told her that I would. I sent her a text when I got home telling her that I made it safely and that I had a good time with her. She didn't respond to the text. No matter, I went to bed.

A few days passed and I still hadn't heard from her. So, I decided to send her a text. "Hey Sofia, how is your day going?" it read. She didn't answer that text either. Another day or two went by, and I got a massive message from her. In her message, she wrote about not wanting to be in a relationship and that I was expecting too much from her. I didn't understand the message at all; I was confused. I never said that I wanted to be in a relationship with her or that I had any expectations for her. I was thrown all the way off. I didn't respond to her text. I felt it was unwarranted anger.

Nas laughed when I told him how I found a way to fuck this up too. "Yo, you drawin," he said as he laughed some more. I told him that I was so confused by her response to me and her expectations. At that moment, I felt like the ladies that I used to smash and forget. "I think the problem is, I don't have that much dating experience," I said. "I know. You tripping. She wanted you to smash her back off," Nas said. "Why is she mad that I didn't though?" I responded. "If I had smashed her and never talked to her again, I'd be the jerk, right?" I asked. "Yo, fuck her feelings. Why do you care what she wants?" Nas responded. "I think the problem is that you care too much about what she would've thought." he added. "What would you do if a chick made you think you was going to smash and then she didn't let you?" he asked. I laughed with him, but I was still mentally lost and confused trying to replay the night back to see what I missed.

I never took her as the kind of person for a one-night stand, so that wasn't the energy I brought. In my mind, going over there just to smash would be offensive to her. I thought more highly of her, and I wanted to be respectful. For whatever reason, I couldn't think straight; I couldn't be me. If I were in my normal state of mind, I would've gone over there specifically to fuck the shit out of her and not think about tomorrow. If anything came of it after, so be it; otherwise, it is what it is. Instead, I was second-guessing everything. Even my second thoughts had second thoughts. I could've at least had sex with her, but in the end, I left without even friendship from her. Either way, I took an L.

GETTING OUT MORE

One of the things that helped me move on from my obsession with Pamela was supporting my friend Nas at his semi-pro football games. It was humbling to reintegrate with my friends and return to the community that raised me. It felt safe and stable for the first time in over a year. I won't pretend that I was over my depression, but it felt great to be genuinely happy about something.

Nas played for several semi-pro football teams in Philly. Every weekend was an event that I was more than happy to attend. I never missed a game. Whether Nas and I were traveling around Philly for the games or traveling out of state, the games were tense and fun. I enjoyed the social interaction and the warm embrace from people I went to high school with or hadn't seen in years. The most fun was watching Nas win the championship and being there to celebrate with him.

One day while traveling on the team bus to a football game in Washington, DC, I received a phone call from Pamela. It had been a few months since I heard that ringtone. Nas knew the ringtone from the first time I came back to Philly. Instantly, Nas had all the jokes. "Uh Oh, what you gonna do?" Nas teased. "Your booboo is calling," he continued. I did my best to downplay the call. "Nothing. She probably wants some more revenge," I responded. Curiosity plagued my mind as the phone rang, but I needed to resist. I was trying to move through my depression and get to happiness. I decided not to take the phone call and let it go to voicemail.

Nas thought I didn't want to take the phone call because both he and his fiancé, Anna, were teasing me. "Don't mind me, go ahead and talk to her," he teased. I could deal with the trolling, but I knew talking to her would do more harm than good. I checked the voicemail, and even hearing her voice was cringeworthy to me. "Hey, it's me," Pamela said. It was not in an Adele hello from the other side voice either. It sounded as if she was bored or depressed. "There is a fire at Overlook apartments on your side of the complex, and you need to get out," she added.

I didn't know what to make of her affect. I mean, if I cared enough to call someone to let them know that there was a fire in their building, there would be more of a sense of urgency in my voice. Nas thought it was her ploy to reconnect with me. I wasn't quite sure. One thing that is apparent is that she was unaware that I had moved back to Philly months ago. Also, by her saying "Overlook" instead of in the complex or something similar let me know she had also moved prior to the call.

To figure out whether this was an angle she was using, I decided to google my old apartment complex in Duluth, Georgia. Sure enough, a fire was reported on the local news. I told Nas the fire was legit and asked what he thought upon hearing the voicemail. "I dunno; she still cared enough to call you," he responded. "Don't start obsessing again though; learn from before," he added. I knew he was right; I needed to leave it alone for my own sanity. I couldn't handle the Sofia situation right, so talking to Pamela would've definitely turned me into The Joker. I decided to not to return the call or text back.

"I pressed 7 and took the phone from my ears."

—Joe Budden

HAPPY BIRTHDAY

Still massively depressed about the apparent murder of my grandmother and the lack of relationship with my brother, I had no plans to celebrate my 30th birthday. I could barely bring myself to smile let alone enjoy the day. To quote Joe Budden, "I was on my On Demand in the house shit." That's when I received a phone call that I didn't see coming. It was Wale.

Given the type of communication that had transpired since my grandmother's murder, I was less than excited to get the call. I was fully expecting him to take the opportunity to start an argument and finish telling me how much he hates me. Cynical, I know, but it was the only pattern I could count on given the state of my life at the time. Thankfully, I was wrong.

"Yo, Happy Birthday, man," he said. "Thanks," I responded hesitantly. "What you doing today?" he asked. "Nothing, I'm just chilling watching a movie," I told him. "Why are you turning 30 years old in the house alone?" he asked. "What am I going to do? I don't have extra money," I said. That's when he invited me to go meet him on South Street near downtown Philly.

It was about an hour's drive from Hatfield where I was living. I decided to take the drive. It would be the first time I'd seen him in nearly a year.

I met Wale at Fat Tuesday's, a bar and grill that serves liquor on South Street. When I arrived, he gave me a firm handshake while looking into my eyes like a laser beam. It was damn-near the way Michael Corleone looked at Fredo in *Godfather*, part two. "I'm about to meet up with this chick I'm trying to smash," he said. "She's with a few of her friends," he added. Great, I thought sarcastically. I was in no mood to be partying or hanging out with ladies.

We caught up to the ladies at a dive bar a few blocks down from Fat Tuesday's. Wale approached the girl he came to see while I played the wall near the entrance. When he returned, he had a hurricane drink he bought me. It was an orange juice based alcoholic drink. "You know I don't drink," I told him. "Man, this your 30th birthday, and you are depressed. You need to lighten up," he responded. He was right. I took the drink began to sip. I looked up and that's when I noticed a beautiful Latina glancing over at me with a smile every so often.

Let's call her Eva. She was in the group of women that Wale planned on meeting up with. You know how in Martin Lawrence's stand-up show, *Run-teldat*, he talked about instantly sobering up when the cops asked him where he bought his weed? That's exactly what happened to me when I noticed her looking over at me. It was like my depression went on vacation instantly, and my cool came back.

Eventually, the group of women walked over, and our two groups merged. Wale introduced me to the woman he came to see. "This is my brother Kunle, and today is his birthday," he added. "Happy Birthday," they said in unison. "How old are you turning?" Eva asked. "Today is my 30th," I answered. "Wow, that's a milestone," Eva asserted. "What are you planning on doing for your birthday?" she asked. "I came down here just to chill with my brother," I told her. "Well, since it's your birthday, we have to make it great," she added. We began bar hopping and getting to know each other.

After a few more drinks and shots they bought me, we were all lit. When the bars became too hot, we hit the streets just to cool off in the midnight breeze and continued talking. During the conversation, I learned that she was a talented makeup artist. Eva asked me about my name and the meaning.

I told her that I'm Nigerian and that my name means that I'm a King. She told me that she was French, Puerto Rican, and Black. She looked every bit of that combination. She was so bad to me, that I had an erection since I met her. Jamie Foxx said, "blame it on the alcohol," so I will.

EVA

The most important thing I learned about Eva that night was that she lived in Hatfield. She didn't just *live* in Hatfield. No, it got more tempting than that. She lived in Hatfield Village Apartments, the exact same apartment complex as I did. In fact, her building was about two buildings away from mine. When I told her that I lived there too, she didn't believe me until I showed her my ID. Afterward, we exchanged numbers. To me, it was a divine moment. I mean, what are the chances that I would be in South Philly and meet someone that lives in my apartment complex in Hatfield? Philly is huge; the chances had to be astronomical. I should've played the lottery that night, but I was already winning.

A few weeks and a few visits later, I invited her over on the late night. She told me she had a boyfriend and that they were on the outs. I didn't care either way. This was about redemption. It was not going to be a Sofia moment; I wasn't taking no Ls. It's going down! When she got there, I could see in her eyes that she wanted what I wanted.

Eva and I started having uncontrollable sex, and it was passionate. We both came into it trying to escape reality—her boyfriend problems and my personal issues. I explored every inch of her well-toned and great smelling body. The perfume she wore could've made Jack's Beanstalk grow. She jumped on top of me and began riding me like she was trying to let me know of her skill. She was wet and creamy, and I was hard enough to cut diamonds. The pleasure was immense. I grabbed her and lifted her off me in a bench press motion and tossed her onto the bed. It was my turn to show her the beast she awoken. I pounded her as if my life depended on it, and to me, it felt as if it did. I could hear her growl and moan in ecstasy.

Just when she thought it was over, I flipped her in the overkill position. It was time to strong dick her from the back. With every pump, I could feel my erection getting harder and harder. Her nipples were so hard they felt completely solid. After she orgasmed the second time, I still wasn't through. I wanted to snatch her soul and rid us both of our burdens. When I came, it was like releasing all the depression at once, even if only for the moment. It was like an out of body experience. Afterward, we laid naked together taking deep breaths, glistening in sweat, and seeing stars. And then I jumped back on. IT'S. NOT. OVER.

HOME SWEET HOME

Shortly after, Nas and his fiancé moved from the apartment where we all lived. He began renting a townhouse around the corner. Because Nas moved early from his lease, he would've either had to pay an early termination fee or keep the apartment. It's a dilemma we've all faced before. We had a solution.

I recently returned to my former jobs as a therapeutic support staff (TSS) and a mobile therapist (MT). I was getting back on my feet the way I was used to before the Atlanta disaster. Nas decided to let me sublet the apartment without the management's knowledge, of course, to complete the lease. I was more than happy to oblige. I couldn't assume the lease outright, because I still owed money to my apartment in Duluth, which I was also making payments on. I was thankful to have my own place, again. Also, Nas and his fiancé had their privacy back it was a win-win.

Working as a TSS and MT was good for starters or as second sources of income, but not as a primary gig. The referrals were drying up, and I was down to three to four clients. It was certainly not enough to survive on. I needed a better full-time job, and quick. I hit up Janelle, Nas's former roommate and mutual friend, and asked her if she knew of any places hiring for full-time work. She told me that I could get full-time work at Nutrisystem working as a weight loss counselor in Fort Washington, Pennsylvania. She had been working there on and off seasonally over Christmas for some extra money.

I must admit, I was averse to working at Nutrisystem. "What do I know about dieting and weight loss?" I asked. "Don't worry; they will train you, and it's not as difficult as it sounds," she assured me. "It's a call center," she added. Either way, I had to take a chance and apply for the job. Fortunately,

I got the job due to my experience working in call centers and counseling people. The position was a temporary to permanent position, but it was full-time and consistent.

Over time, I completed the lease from Nas's apartment that I was subletting and got my own place in the same building. I was able to pay my car note, which meant I no longer had to hide it and get threatened by the lenders. My refrigerator was full, and I was able to begin paying past due amounts on bills. After the impotence of being homeless, this was like a life orgasm.

SHARON

While working at Nutrisystem, I met my friend Sharon, a redhead woman of Irish and Czech ancestry from Northeast Philly. We met during training. Sharon was hired as a permanent employee. We connected through making inappropriate jokes and laughing at the many weird people at work. I thought Sharon was cool because she enjoyed dark and controversial humor like I did. I enjoyed coming to work because Sharon and I always had stories to tell about whatever happened while the other was off, like the time when a guy was fired on my shift.

Full disclosure, I don't know all the details regarding this guy's termination. In fact, I didn't know the guy at all because he worked in a totally different department on the other side of the building. All I know is out of nowhere as I walked to the vending machine I heard, "What? Fuck y'all. This some fucking bullshit," he said. This was followed by, "Fuck you, and Fuck you, and Fuck this white bitch," as this angry brother pointed his finger in his supervisor's face. I felt for the guy. I knew the situation was unfortunate, but the scene he was making was classic.

When he was done cursing everyone out loudly as the rest of the building looked on, he stormed his way towards the door. When he got to the exit, he pushed the door like he was Warren Sapp trying to get to the quarterback. Boom! His intent was to burst his way out of the building. Unfortunately, the door was the fire exit and it had a mechanism that needed to be pressed and held for the door to open. Naturally, the force he used on the door forced him backward. I was so fucking weak. I hadn't laughed that hard in a very long time.

At the call center, they had their way about firing people. They would come to an employee mid-shift, call them to a meeting, and dismiss them on the spot. The terminations were not usually because of poor performance or tardiness, it was mostly about trimming down the temps. The way it was designed, everyone on the floor knew what was happening to the person. The person never got to come back to their desk to get their things. A few minutes later, the director, this boiled-egg-shaped woman, would go the victim's desk with a box while laughing as she collected the remaining items. Sharon and I witnessed this scenario over and over.

I thought it was sick that this woman enjoyed firing people. One day, she fired at least seven people in a row. It was disgusting seeing the pleasure on this woman's face as lives were ruined. She was a Dr. Robotnik-looking woman, who smelled like pork fat. I know I laughed at the guy who caused a scene, but it was the scene that was funny. I would never laugh at a person's life being turned upside down. I've already been through it, several times over.

After she finished firing everybody one day, the most gratifying thing happened. The higher-ups called her to a meeting and fired her. She knew exactly what was happening as she teared up on her way to the meeting. It was mob style. They let her do all the dirty work, which she enjoyed, before they whacked her. Minutes later, a team came with boxes to collect the items she had left over. Rumor had it that she had been working at Nutrisystem for several years. I guess she thought she was safe. Sharon and I both laughed for weeks about the instant karma she received.

"Sin is the thin line between love and hatred."

—Black Thought

A NEW PATH

I knew that my days at Nutrisystem were numbered because I was a seasonal temp. I had been looking for meaningful employment in the social work or psychology field since I started at Nutrisystem. I wasn't having much luck; I must've put in over a hundred applications without anyone getting back to me. As my tentative end-date was approaching, it became stressful. I was not willing to be unemployed or homeless ever again.

One day, Sharon asked me an important question. "You have a master's degree in social work, right?" she asked. "Yes," I responded. "Have you ever looked at PATH as a place to work?" "No, I never heard of the company before," I responded. "It's a mental health place over on Castor Avenue," she said. "They have a website, and they are always hiring," she added. I decided to give it a look.

PATH was the acronym for People Acting To Help. They served all sorts of mental health clientele. I decided to apply for the alternative education program therapist position. It was a school-based therapist position for middle school students who have been expelled from other schools. Given that I had the experience with youth who exhibit challenging behaviors, I figured it was the right opportunity.

I remember my interview like it was yesterday. There I sat in Philadelphia Learning Academy South waiting for my turn to be interviewed. I looked around the room at all the pictures they had of successful people from Philadelphia and other successful African people. I thought about the impact they had on the world and my intentions when I decided to do this work. I began hearing the answers to all the questions I was about to be asked.

Finally, I was called in to meet the program director and sit in a group interview. Like any other interview, I was asked about my experience and strengths. Instead of giving the traditional and generic answers, I began to deliver all the knowledge that I got from those pictures I had been staring at prior to being called into the interview. It was like Keyser Söze in the movie, *The Usual Suspects*. I told them about TJ, the five-year-old client that his school thought wouldn't make it through first grade. I also told them how I worked with him until he no longer needed me and was doing well in first grade. After that story, the program director began shedding tears; that's when I knew I had the job.

"Success never goes on sale. You must pay the full price."

—Unknown

CHAPTER 14
RISKING IT ALL

GIVING BACK

My new job as an alternative education therapist came with many perks. For starters, I worked inside a middle school and had a school schedule, which meant that I got summers off and had the opportunity to work during the summer for twice the pay. Another perk was working with an amazing staff of therapists. All of us came from different backgrounds but shared the same passion. That brings me to the most important perk, which was giving back to my community.

Because I grew up in North Philly, I knew about the disadvantages and pressures these young middle schoolers faced daily. At the time, I was 30 years old. I wasn't too young or too old to connect with the students effectively; I was in the right age range. That meant I was familiar with all the things they saw as popular including hip-hop music, Air Jordan sneakers, and video games. I enjoyed the looks on their faces when I would finish verses from their favorite songs or occasionally show up at school wearing the sneakers they wore.

Another perk that came with my job at PATH was working alongside the same principal and vice principal that I had in high school. It was a trip going from being a class clown and almost high school dropout to their colleague. It was another example of growth in my life and journey. It added authenticity and credibility to their assemblies and family nights when parents showed up. I became a testimonial to the messages they were trying to spread to the youth and families.

"You can be anything in the world you want to be," Mr. Pelzer, my former vice principal, told parents and the student body. "All you have to do is listen to the instructions given by your teachers and be willing to do the work," he added. "We have a live example sitting amongst us that came up from the same neighborhoods and same schools as many of you," he proclaimed. "Mr. Ige, would you stand up please?" he asked.

As I stood and looked around the room, I noticed all the lives that could be touched and the hope that many of the youth and families needed. "Tell them. Tell them what schools you attended and who your administration was," Mr. Pelzer asked as Mr. Cage, my former principal looked on. "I went to Edward T. Steel Elementary, Elizabeth Gillespie Middle School, and Simon Gratz High School," I said proudly. "Those schools are all in the neighborhoods where many of you and your family members live and attended," Mr. Cage added. "Tell them who was in your administration in high school," Mr. Pelzer requested. "Mr. Pelzer was my vice principal, and Mr. Cage was the principal at Simon Gratz High School," I responded. The students and families clapped.

It was nice to be in a position of credibility and be able to give back to my community. It showed that I wasn't some guy who was born in the suburbs with a big fat silver spoon in my mouth. The students and their supporting loved ones knew that I was one of them, a kid from the struggle who had beat many odds and returned to give hope and support to them. Most importantly, I never forgot where I came from.

BOWLING

Now that I had a meaningful job that gave me a new sense of identity and stability, I needed a place to exercise my competitive nature. Since I no longer played basketball competitively other than shooting around here and there, I wondered what my new challenge would be. I remember watching Nas and his fiancé going to the bowling alley and playing in leagues. Nas was all geared out. He had his own bowling ball, a bowling glove, bowling shoes, and a bowling bag. I used to laugh and tease him that he was taking it way too seriously and tell him that he had too much time on his hands. To me, bowling was an old white man's sport and a pastime that people played in the background of little kids' birthday parties.

Nas often tried to school me about how challenging the sport was and how technically the game is played, but to me, it wasn't that serious. Nas was really good at bowling. I watched as he threw strikes in bunches as he hooked the bowling ball into what I learned was the pocket. I didn't understand how he was able to make the ball react the way he wanted it to, so I often asked him about details of the game.

Nas taught me about oil patterns and how they play a part in how the ball reacts. He taught me about the different kinds of bowling balls and their weight. When he realized that my questions were getting increasingly more in-depth, he realized my interest in the game was growing, so he reminded me of my initial reaction to the game. "You thought I had too much time on my hands," he said jokingly. We both laughed at my change of heart. Through those conversations, I learned about how and when he knew to make adjustments during the game. I became a student of the game. I continued to attend Nas's games to support them and observe the culture of bowling.

When their league was over, all of us would go to the bowling alley to practice and socialize. Nas had been playing for years and I knew I was far behind his skill level because I was a beginner. So, when I practiced, I took it to the extreme. I would play 40 or 50 games in a row daily just working on my release and finish techniques. When my hands got cut from playing so much, I got bowlers' tape, covered the wound and continued playing. I worked on my approach to the lane and my pre-roll routines. When I wasn't practicing, I was studying the great Norm Duke arguably the greatest bowler of all time. I studied Norm Duke with the same intensity that I studied Michael Jordan in basketball. I even watched the PBA Tour on ESPN every weekend. Before I knew it, I was a full-blown try-hard.

When July came around, I joined the summer league with Nas and his fiancé, Anna. By the time I joined the league, I had been bowling for only a month and a half. I bought my own bowling ball, bowling bag, other items. I went from knowing nothing about bowling to averaging 168 points per game. We ultimately won the championship in that league, beating the team that Nas's team lost to in the winter league. My confidence in bowling grew immensely, and I continued to work on my game.

In another league, I caught fire and knocked down eleven strikes in a row. On the next roll, I would be going for an achievement not many people reach. I remember rolling that final ball down the lane with my heart pounding out of my chest. As the ball left my right hand, I stared at it as if my eyes were guiding it. "You better go all the way and get them all," I remember thinking. When that ball smashed through those pins, I clenched my fist like Jordan in the finals and screamed! It was my first 300-point game, a perfect game!

When I turned away from the lanes, the entire bowling alley had been watching my final roll to see if I was going to complete the perfect game. When I took my headphones from my ears, I could hear them erupting with excitement. Everyone was hugging me and congratulating me. The feeling was overwhelming, and I was just trying to soak it all in. It was extra special because my best friend Nas was there to witness that epic game and share the moment.

RUDE AWAKENING

My life was getting back together again. The only thing I needed to feel complete was to reconnect with my brother and try to hash out the issues between us. I really wanted to let him know all the details about my life in Atlanta and support him as best I could for what he had been dealing with in Philly. We had not really had a sit-down; I mean, we barely spoke outside of him constantly insulting me. I figured since we had a good time hanging out on my 30th birthday that it would be a good time to resolve our issues, and I should try to reconnect with him.

Little did I know that I would be faced with a new challenge— the challenge of being alone. I received a phone call from Wale telling me that he had already packed his things and was moving to California to live with my cousin Markus. He talked about wanting to get away from Philly and have a new experience.

Wale always complained that he never had the chance to live anywhere but Philly. "I'm a grown ass man that never been anywhere," he'd claim angrily. "You been all over the fucking country, and I ain't never go nowhere. My dumb ass always stayed home with Daddy, trying to make sure he was ok," he'd say angrily. It was an argument and perspective that I'd heard many times over the years.

In the past, I always encouraged Wale to branch out and move to experience more of what the world had to offer. I wanted Wale to graduate from high school and attend Virginia State with me. "Daddy made his choice when he came from Nigeria to plant his flag in Philly," I'd tell him. "That doesn't mean you have to spend the rest of your life in Philly," I continued. "Daddy will be all right; that's what we have cell phones and cars for. We could always visit him or vice versa," I would add. That wasn't a popular response for him. He felt because he was the baby, he should stay home. Wale was now beginning to understand what I had been trying to teach him over the years about the importance of traveling and experiencing more out of life.

Wale's decision blew me away because I was hoping to mend our relationship, but I had to support him and keep the same energy that I had in the past about him branching out. I told him not to worry about our father and the affairs of his property, that I would take over. "You faced so much stress in the past several months on top of losing childhood friends to street violence," I told him. "Maybe this is a message from God for you to finally break free," I continued. I told him to let me know when he got to San Jose safely. About a week later, he let me know he made it, and he seemed happy. I was happy for him.

Over the next several weeks, Wale was homesick. He would call me telling me about what was going on in the hood, in Philly. When it wasn't about people we knew getting murdered or arrested, he complained about how different California was from Philly. In those conversations, he was always angry and stressed, the exact opposite of the reason I wanted him to go to California. "Wale, you left Philadelphia physically, but you are refusing to leave it mentally. That's why you are not enjoying your new journey," I told him. "You spend more time trying to find out what's going on in Philly than you do exploring your new environment," I continued. "Of course, California is different from Pennsylvania, but that's the reason you moved there, for a change," I reminded him.

My plan to have a face-to-face sit-down with Wale had a monkey wrench thrown into by his decision to move to California, but it was probably for the better. Maybe getting out of his routine and daily stressors would help tame his anger, and one day we could have a civil conversation, I thought. It would be a win-win. Without Wale, I ended up spending Thanksgiving with Nas and his family, which was fitting since Nas was damn-near my brother, and his mother looked at me as another son.

TAKING OVER

Taking care of my father's financial affairs and properties proved to be a difficult and stressful task. I began to understand more about what Wale had been facing while I was in Atlanta. It was very challenging living in one location and trying to manage a property that I knew nothing about. I didn't know what deals had been made by my father to keep his house from foreclosure or what he owed on the house. Remember, to my father, everything was one big secret, and here I was being thrust into the job of deciphering it, like Wale had been before me.

The house was very old and needed more repairs than I could ever afford. There were only two reasons to try to save his house, and neither of them made much sense to me, but I was trying anyway. One reason was for sentimental value. I mean, this was the house where I spent a large portion of my life. The other reason was on the outside chance that my father would be found not guilty for some reason and released early, which was highly unlikely in such a high profile case. I wrestled with what to do and how to do it. Meanwhile, I was trying to keep my life together and pay my bills.

My routine became impossible to maintain. I wasn't willing to exit my apartment lease early to live at my father's house that could be taken away from me at any moment, leaving me homeless. I decided I would wake up in the morning and try to spend time on my father's block and in the house so that people would not treat it as abandoned. Then, I would go to work and stop by after work. Sometimes, I spent nights in the house so people could think I lived there still. I even spent the weekends in the house and on the porch like I used to.

When Jay-Z famously said. "The Streets is Watching," he couldn't have been more right. Philly is a place where everybody is watching your moves and routines; it's an instinct for survival. It's not an easy place to fool people. It wasn't long before the vultures in the neighborhood that used to break into my father's house when we were kids saw an opportunity.

Now every time I went to my father's house, I'd notice something was off. A table had been moved or the back door was open. One day after work, I came home to my father's house and saw the front door was wide open and the living room was turned upside down as if I was a major coke dealer that the feds got the drop on. I wasn't sure whether someone was still in the house or whether this had happened recently, so I called the police to assist with securing the property.

When the police arrived, they refused to enter the property. That's how badly the living room had been destroyed. There were clothes all over the place, furniture upside down and broken, and power tools everywhere. I don't know what the burglars were looking for, but they damn-near turned the house upside down trying to find it. The police, who were there to uphold their motto to protect and serve, were afraid to enter my father's house because they said it was unsafe. Would I have called the police if the place was safe? Think about that.

On top of all that, I had to deal with the neighbors constantly asking questions that were none of their business regarding my father's case. When I wouldn't answer their questions, they had other plans for us. The evil neighbors began calling city licensing on us because the grass was not cut and stupid shit like that when they knew our situation. In Philly, it doesn't have to be wintertime for people to be cold.

TRYING TO HOLD IT TOGETHER

The stress of trying to dig myself out of a financial hole and stabilize my life plus taking care of my father's affairs was daunting, to say the least. It began affecting my daily functioning. At first, I was having trouble sleeping. I would stay up late at night pacing in the house trying to strategize and worrying about impending doom. I wasn't sure that I would be able to take another life-changing event.

I was constantly thinking about how my family life got completely destroyed. Never in a million years did I think that I would have to travel to

State Road in Philly to see my father in jail. In the midst of trying to keep his affairs in order, I was visiting him in meeting rooms where he couldn't touch me, and people had to supervise us. The man who raised me was in an orange jumpsuit and had been diagnosed with psychosis, while I was there to put money on his books.

My father was completely unkempt. His breath coming through his yellow teeth was foul smelling. His normally trimmed fingernails were now long and yellow like the crypt keeper, he could barely walk without assistance, and when we talked it was like he had very little idea who I was. When he spoke to me, he would tell me all kinds of illogical stories. "Last night, the swat team came into my cell and shot up everybody on the tier," he said. "Everybody is dead, and they threatened to kill me next," he continued. I wasn't used to seeing my father, a very intelligent and proud African, look so lost and meek. Adding in the fact that he murdered his own mother in a psychotic rage was a lot to bear. To be honest, it fucked me up.

One night after I finally went to sleep, I was awakened with extremely intense stomach pain. I don't know what being pregnant and having contractions is like, but the pain I was experiencing is what I imagined it was like. With Wale living in California and me living alone, I decided to drive myself to the nearest hospital. Because I did not have insurance, I had to wait for what seemed like an eternity to be seen. Once I was evaluated by the doctor, I learned that I had a stress-related ulcer. The pain was so intense that they treated it with Dilaudid, an extremely strong pain medication. It was so powerful, that once a drop from the IV landed in the saline, instantly my stomach stopped hurting. As strong as that medicine was, it did nothing for my daily stressors and worries, which caused the ulcer in the first place.

THE RIGHT MISTAKE

After taking a toll on my body, the stress began to take a toll on my mind. I began forgetting things at work and missing deadlines. One day, I was approached by my supervisor at work about a treatment plan that I was supposed to get signed by a parent and it was passed the deadline. She said she wanted it within the next 10 minutes, which was impossible for me. I knew that I would be in big trouble if I didn't get it signed because she had warned me a few times. At that moment, I decided to sign the parent's name myself and hand it to her. My goal was to stall her out until I could get it officially signed later that day. I did not want to lose my job on top of everything else I was dealing with. I knew it was wrong, but I did it anyway, something I would never have done in my right mind.

My supervisor asked for the chart so that she could audit and make sure everything was on the up and up. A few minutes later, "Come here, Adekunle," she called sternly. When I entered her office, she was holding the treatment plan. How come this signature does not look like the signatures on the previous plans?" she asked. "I signed it," I responded. I didn't lie to her. I did not have the energy for the charade or anything else for that matter. I was mentally and physically beat.

After admitting to signing the plan myself, I began crying. She thought it was about me being caught, but it was actually about what I had been carrying all this time. "What made you sign it? I know you are much better than that," she asked. I told her what had been going on in my personal life and what lead to my decision. "Oh, Adekunle, I wish you had said something before," she responded. "I didn't because I was embarrassed about my family situation," I explained. "I was worried that all the mistakes I've been making would cost me my job, so I made a bad decision," I continued. "I have to report this, Adekunle," she informed me. "I am not sure what is going to happen, but I know there is a no tolerance policy for fraud," she added.

When we got to the main headquarters to meet with the founder, I told my side of the story both verbally and in written form. I expressed regret for making an unethical decision and pleaded for any discipline other than losing my job. I could barely write my statement because tears were dropping all over the paper. I had the support of my program director; she loved me like a son. I was very sad to have disappointed her.

I submitted my written statement. My program director fought for my job. She spoke about all the good things I brought to the young people and the bonds I created with the most challenging students. She discussed the difference I was making in creating new ways to connect with the students. However, she was unsuccessful in saving my job. The founder of the company overruled her. There it was; I was terminated for the second time in my life, at least this time it was my fault. I was devastated, but I understood it was what I deserved for my actions.

> "All the adversity I've had in my life, all my troubles and obstacles, have strengthened me... You may not realize it when it happens, but a kick in the teeth may be the best thing in the world for you."
>
> —Walt Disney

ON MY GRIND

Once again, I was faced with another life-changing event. The one thing that I was trying not to be was unemployed, and that's exactly where I found myself. My depression was telling me that he was back to reclaim me, but I could not let him win. I remember taking a couple of dollars and playing the lottery thinking that with all this bad, something good was bound to happen. I was banking on the law of averages. Unfortunately, like most of America, I did not win, but it was good to have something to look forward to even if only for a week.

I was looking for a positive sign anywhere in the world. I figured I'd continue to use the cable I'd paid for earlier in the month before it was cut off to watch the NFL. The Patriots, my favorite team, were in the Superbowl. A win from them would've given me something to feel positive about. Unfortunately, that did not happen. Thanks, Wes Welker and Mario Manningham.

This time, I was not going to allow myself to go back into a depressive hole. I decided that there was nothing left for me in Philly and that I was going to join my brother in California, the place I always wanted to live since I was a little boy. It was not going to be an easy task, but I came up with a plan.

Instead of feeling sorry for myself and letting go, I decided to treat every day as a workday. My new routine was to wake up, take a shower, and eat breakfast. Then, I would go online applying for jobs in the San Francisco Bay Area from 9:00 a.m. to 5:00 p.m. Monday through Friday. I stuck to the schedule daily, even giving myself a half hour for lunch before returning to the grind. I used my cousin's San Jose address on each application. I wanted to make sure that I would be considered for each job fairly. On the weekends, I'd research jobs that I was going to apply for in the coming week to get a head start.

After about four days of grinding, I began getting phone calls from potential employers. One company gave me an interview over the phone. To prepare for that phone interview, I put on a suit and had my portfolio ready as if the interview on in person. That's how serious I took the interview. It went very well, and I was offered an interview on Skype. That one went well also. The next step was to meet the staff in person for a final interview. We scheduled the interview for a few days after I was scheduled to arrive in San Jose. I was excited about getting the prospect of moving to California and being employed.

The next day, I received a call from another place called Bay Area Youth Center. I did a phone interview and felt pretty good about my chances of obtaining employment with them as well. The job sounded very similar to my previous position at PATH, with the exception of working in a school. BAYC specialized in working with former foster youth through therapy. Finally, I had options of potential employers. It felt great because my plan was working, and life finally seemed to be moving in my favor.

The interviewer, Marsha Vaughn, was from New York City and had moved to California 12 years earlier. She was familiar with moving across the country. She gave me advice about the drive. "When I moved to California, it was around the same time of year," she said. "When you take the drive make sure you take it slow because believe me, you never saw snow like this before," she offered. I listened to her advice, but I thought to myself there was just a blizzard here in Philly, I'm familiar with snow. She must've been living in California too long, I thought.

The next week, I began packing my things preparing for the move. I informed my apartment complex that I would be moving out and arranged to repay the early termination fee. I called my friend Brian and let him know of my plans. I would've called Nas to help, but at the time, we were having one of our periodic arguments and separations that brothers usually go through. Brian helped me load as many items as I could fit into a U-Haul trailer that I planned to pull with my 2003 Honda Accord Coupe.

> *"In the mind, in the heart, I was always home. I always imagined, really, going back home."*
>
> —Miriam Makeba

PURSUIT OF HAPPINESS

A few days before taking the road, I calculated the amount of money I had left from my final check from PATH and my early tax refund, which wasn't going to arrive by direct deposit for another day or so. Based on the dates of my job interviews, I had no choice but to take the risk and hope that tax refund made it on time and didn't leave me stranded in the middle of the country. I only had about $1,100 to my name, and I was about to drive across the country. With that amount of money, I knew I could not take the scenic route to California. In fact, I knew I would have to make the trip in three days. I only had enough money to afford two hotel stays.

If I was going to make this trip, everything had to be precise. I used Google Maps to plot out where I was going to stop and at which hotels I would stay. I chose hotels that had complimentary breakfast so I wouldn't spend extra money on food. My goal was to drive from Hatfield, Pennsylvania to a hotel in Newton, Iowa, which was little over a 15-hour drive. After getting a few hours of sleep in Iowa, then it was another 15-hour drive to Salt Lake City, Utah. San Jose, CA, my destination, was about a 12-hour drive from Salt Lake City. If all went according to plan, I'd have just enough money to make it safely.

The prospect of making a drive across the country in three days would be daunting for most people. I imagine some of you are thinking that it would be a suicide mission, but I was confident. I knew that I could make the trip. When I moved from Atlanta back to Philly, I had to do two trips, which meant I had to take the 12-hour trip three times in three days. I looked at it as practice for the big game, and *this* was the big game.

The day finally came, and I was ready. Brian helped me pack my last few items. I drove him home afterward, and then it was "go-time." I put the address of the hotel in Iowa into my windshield-mounted GPS and hit the road in my 2003 Honda Accord Coupe. I took interstate 80 because it was basically a straight-line route. It felt so freeing to be traveling towards my lifelong dream, California. For most of the drive, I put the car into cruise control to conserve gas. I brought plenty of CDs, yes people CDs, to keep me company for the ride. Jay-Z, Nas, the Lox, and several other artists provided the soundtrack for my journey similar to my journey to Virginia State University.

THE ROAD AHEAD

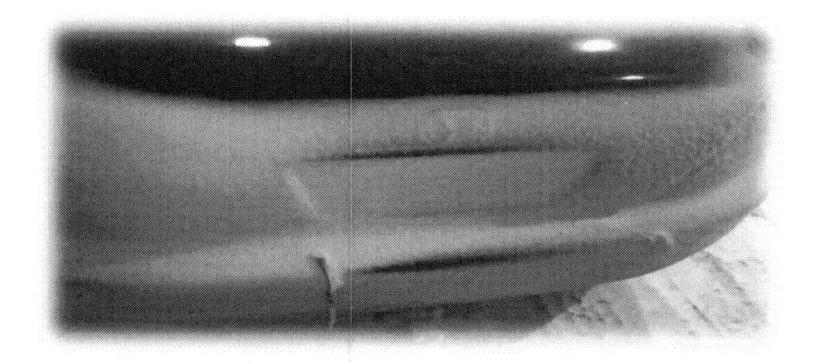

The biggest challenge I had faced to this point was driving a car that did not have heat and had severely worn tires during a blizzard in Philadelphia. There I was wearing a peacoat and gloves as I drove in my car packed to the roof and pulling a UHaul trailer. The weather wasn't getting any friendlier either as I traveled through Ohio, Indiana, and coldest of all Chicago, stopping for gas as needed. I could feel my bones shaking and my lungs hardening as each breath was visible like in the movie *Sixth Sense*.

Fortunately, I made it to Iowa and into the heat of the hotel safely. I needed food, a warm bed, and a hot bath. I got food and a warm bed, but I settled for a shower instead of a bath. I did not have the time to chill, I was on a tight schedule. After a night spent in Iowa, I woke up around 5:00 a.m. to continue my drive towards Salt Lake City. I was cruising through the cornfields of Nebraska straddling the borderline of Colorado as I headed towards the northern part of the Rockies. It was amazing to see the huge mountain range with the iconic snow caps at the peak. It felt like I was in a movie.

Everything was going smoothly until I hit Wyoming. Wyoming was a totally different beast, and that's where I was reminded of Marsha's words of wisdom. For starters, it was noticeably colder than any of the states I'd traveled through. In fact, the temperature decreased at least 15 to 20 degrees. To make matters worse, I was caught in an active blizzard that lasted as I drove across the entire state. Marsha was correct when she said, I'd never saw snow like this. It was literally impossible to see more than two feet in front of my car.

You think that's bad? Well, it got worse. There was no plowing on interstate 80. Can you imagine that? The largest and most traveled highway in the state was left with no care. The road was completely covered in about 18 inches of snow and a very thick layer of black ice supporting it. Given the weather conditions and considering my nearly bald tires, I decided to drive very slow as did most travelers on the road.

The flow of traffic was about 50 miles per hour, while I was doing about 35 miles per hour on a highway with a 70-mile-per hour speed limit. My strategy was to follow directly behind 18 wheeler trucks to gain grips on the road. It worked pretty well for about 15 miles with the exception of the occasional huge sheet of snow that would slide off the top of the big rigs.

I knew following the trucks was risky, but it was my best chance to make it to my destination safely—that is, until I watched two 18-wheelers slide on the black ice and off the road before colliding with each other. The collision was about five feet in front of my car and one truck nearly flipped over. Luckily, a police officer was on the road a few cars behind. That was one of the few times, I was happy to see them. I prayed that both the truck drivers were safe.

As for me, I wasn't even close to safe. The road presented more challenges the farther I drove. After another 15 to 20 miles of basically skating on ice, I finally saw a plow truck coming in my rearview mirror. It felt like my prayers were answered. Finally, someone was going to clear a path so I could make it to my next stop safely. It was a godsend. Since we were driving so slowly on I-80, I was able to flag him down. "Thank God for you, brother. How far are you going to be plowing?" I asked. "I'll be plowing for the next 10 miles," he responded. That was fantastic news, but there were another 370 miles of the blizzard and black ice that I needed to avoid before exiting the state. Something was better than nothing. I decided to follow the plow truck for the next 10 miles because it was my safest bet. After that, like most of my life, I was on my own again.

I drove for about another hour or so before my gas light came on. Unlike today's vehicles, I had no idea how many miles I had before my tank would be on empty. I began looking for gas station signs along I-80, but I was traveling through very small towns. Therefore, all the gas stations were closed. I began to get very nervous. I decided to call the police to see if they were available to bring gas or at least let me know of the nearest gas station that was open for business.

Fortunately, I was able to get ahold of the state troopers. Unfortunately, the dispatcher let me know that they were 75 miles away, and it would take at least an hour and a half to two hours to get to me. The answer to my second question got the same answer. Wouldn't you know it? I was also 75 miles from the nearest open gas station and over 100 miles to the next hotel as well. The dispatcher gave me the address of the nearest gas station that was open for business. It was far too cold to sit and wait the possible two hours for the police to show up, especially in a car that had no heat and was running low on gas to boot. It was too risky to continue driving while hoping my Honda could make it. So I didn't hope; I prayed as I continued driving. It was a risk that I had no choice but to take.

By the grace of God, I was able to make it just in time to the gas station. It was nothing short of a miracle. While I was pumping my gas, the dispatcher called me back to let me know that the state trooper was on his way. It would've taken him at least another hour and a half from that phone call to get to me, which would've been nearly four hours of waiting in the freezing cold. I made the right choice. I let the dispatcher know that I made to the gas station safely.

I felt more secure once I got a full tank of gas, but I still had to deal with the increasing haziness and the snow that continued to fall. Even though I made it to the gas station, there was still the matter of the hotel that I needed since the weather conditions were getting worse. I had to change my plans on the fly because there was no way I was going to make it to Salt Lake City, Utah in the worsening conditions. Unfortunately, I was in a town where the population was so low that the hotels closed around 8:00 p.m. I had to continue driving until I found the nearest town with an open hotel. It was over 100 miles away and fatigue was setting in. Fortunately, I made it to Rawlins, Wyoming, which had a population of just under 10,000 people. Most importantly, they had a hotel that was open and that's where I stopped to stay the night.

The next morning, my car wouldn't start. After some investigating in the biting cold, I learned that the cable connected to my starter was frozen stiff and detached from its base. It was too early in the morning for mechanic shops to be open and even if they were, I didn't have enough money to pay for any repairs. Luckily after messing around with the cord, I was able to get a spark by attaching the cable briefly and starting the car. I used electric tape to patch the cord to the starter and hit the road headed for San Jose. The distance I had to travel was three hours longer due to staying in a hotel earlier than I had planned, but I was determined.

The issue with my starter was an ongoing saga throughout the rest of the trip. Every time I stopped for gas or to use the restroom, I ran the risk of my car not starting. The tape I had used to patch my starter had frozen and come off during the drive. Sometimes, my car would start with no problem or with a little finagling; other times, it took nearly an hour to get it started.

The most mind-blowing part of my journey was reaching Nevada. The weather went from several degrees below zero, blizzards, and black ice to 80 degrees with bone dry roads instantaneously. I had never seen anything like it—I felt like I had traveled to another part of the world in a time machine. It was like going from late December to early August or from the Colorado Rockies to the Nevada desert instantly. There were no more black clouds following me with freezing rain and snow, just pure sun. I had literally weathered the storm.

I took off my gloves and peacoat because I was in the desert, and my hands were already thawed and sweating. I popped in Jay-Z's *The Blueprint* album and continued cruising on the now safe roads. I cruised through Nevada while eyeing Reno from the freeway. Before I knew it, I was at the California border getting an agriculture check.

If you never had an agriculture check before, don't feel bad, neither had I before this trip. I was used to stopping for tolls along the way, but this was a different stop. "Sir, I have to search your car and ask you to open your trailer," the attendant instructed. The attendant wanted to search my car and trailer to make sure I wasn't smuggling animals or maybe even drugs into the state.

Once the guy looked into my car and saw how packed it was, he was satisfied. "My trailer is even more packed. I'm moving from Philadelphia, PA," I informed him. After opening my trailer less than a third of the way, he looked in and realized if he opened it fully, everything would fall out. It was my final test on the journey, and I passed. I made it through the high elevation and foggy mists of Lake Tahoe as I mastered the winding roads. It would be another five hours before I finally made it to San Jose.

As I continued to my destination, I couldn't help but reflect. I thought about all the risks I had to take to make it to my goal. The car with no heat and worn tires, the blizzard and black ice, almost getting into a car accident with two 18-wheelers, nearly being stranded without gas or heat, and my starter problems. It was like the devil was trying to prevent me from escaping, but each time God found a way for me. The journey was similar to my life flashing before my eyes. It was a physical metaphor that represented how my entire life had been, in real time.

> *"Forget former things, don't well in the past. For I am doing a new thing. I am making a way. I will even make a roadway in the wilderness, and rivers in the desert."*
>
> —Isaiah 43:19

Long story short: If God brings you to it, he will bring you through it.

SAN JOSE

Finally, after all I had been through, I made it to San Jose safely. It was past midnight. I parked my car and was met by Wale, who I had phoned earlier letting him know of my arrival. I thought he was going to show me to my cousin Markus's apartment. I was tired from the drive but somewhat energized by the experience, call it a second wind. Wale had other plans. "Get in the car. I'm taking you out to celebrate," he said. I didn't want to say no to a positive interaction with Wale and on top of that, I didn't have to drive.

We hit a bar where we met up with my cousin Markus and his roommate Seve. After having a few drinks and check-ins, we went to get a burrito from La Victoria's. Side note, if you ever visit San Jose, be sure to get a burrito from La Victoria's and get the orange sauce, just trust me on this one. California was a new world for me. Up until this point, I thought Taco Bell and eventually Chipotle was real Mexican food. The food and drinks were great, but I didn't want to celebrate for too long. I was on a mission. That mission was to secure a job.

GETTING STARTED

It was a blessing to have my cousin Markus and his roommate Seve welcome me into their home. They allowed me to live with them until I got a job and my own place. Though I was thankful for their hospitality, I didn't want to overstay my welcome. I did my best to stay out of the way and not be a burden. If I learned anything at all from the Atlanta debacle, it was to keep my fate in my own hands.

I was living with my cousin Markus in a crowded two-bedroom apartment that included his roommate Seve and Wale; my goal was to get on my feet as soon as possible. I slept on the floor while living off ramen noodles and food from Wienerschnitzel, a fast-food hot dog place. I needed to conserve money because I had no money coming in. I only had 30 days before I'd have to pay a full month's rent for the items from the trailer that I put in storage. I had two job interviews coming up and that gave me hope.

THE INTERVIEWS

I spent my free time studying both the agencies that had invited me for interviews. The next few days were spent reviewing their websites, reading reviews, and testimonials. I tried to learn as much as I could because I refused to come home without a job. Making a successful life for myself in California had been a lifelong goal, so I wanted to gain any advantage that brought me closer to making it a reality.

Finally, the day came for my third interview with the company that I skyped with while I was still in Pennsylvania. The night before, my cousin Jonathan, Markus's brother, gave me a haircut. When I entered the interview, I noticed there was a very hostile vibe coming from the program director and staff. It felt less like an interview and more like an interrogation. Even asking me about my strengths sounded hostile. "What do you think you are good at?" the interviewer asked in a condescending tone. "So, you never worked with a homeless population before?" she asked in a surprised tone. I was just surprised that she hadn't read my resume before I crossed the country.

The condescension continued throughout the interview, even going as far as to criticize my resume. I stayed professional and answered each question honestly. I wasn't going to allow their energy to become my energy. When I left the interview, I thought I had no chance of landing the job. After experiencing their energy, I didn't want to work there either way. I knew it wouldn't be a good fit for me. However, I needed a job, and beggars can't be choosers. I had one more potential employer to interview with, and I was hoping for the best.

NOW OR NEVER

A week later, I had my first in-person interview with Bay Area Youth Center (BAYC). The interview was very warm and welcoming. Like any interview, there were tough questions to answer and scenarios to navigate, but I felt comfortable, and the environment felt serene. It was the exact opposite of the experience I had with the other agency interview. I knew it was the place I wanted to work. I left the interview feeling hopeful. I guess the feeling was mutual because I was invited to a third informal interview a few days later.

The Thursday before my third interview with BAYC, I received an email, which was an offer letter from the first agency where I had interviewed. It was great to have a job offer, but I dreaded having to work for that program director. If I were to describe the feeling of getting that offer, I'd have to quote the great battle rapper Hollow Da Don, "I'm not excited." I prayed that night asking God to make sure I didn't have to work for her.

My final interview with BAYC was on Friday. It was informal as advertised. This time, I got to sit with some of the youth that I would be serving.

Their job was to give a final say on whether they thought I would be a good addition to the agency. Once I got their approval, I received an offer letter a few minutes later. To add icing to the cake, the offer was more than $4,000 higher than the one I had received from the other agency the day before. My prayers were answered, and I couldn't have been happier.

When I accepted the job, Marsha, my new supervisor, smiled. "Have a good weekend," she told me. I couldn't help but smile. I felt so relieved. I left the building feeling like I had wings, and I was ready to soar the clear blue skies.

Just for some added comedy, my car failed to start after getting the job at BAYC. Marsha saw me trying to fix the car and offered to help as she exited the building. I told her I could handle it and that she already helped enough. "It happens all the time since the drive," I told her. "You were right about the snow," I added. We both laughed. Eventually, I got my car started and went home to share the good news with Wale and Markus. As for my car, I ended up getting a new starter installed by a mechanic about a month later.

"Life is a long journey, with problems to solve, lessons to learn, but most of all experiences to enjoy."

—Unknown

CHAPTER 15
MATTERS OF THE HEART

Life in California was coming together the way I was hoping for. A year later, I had a new car, a BMW 545i, and an apartment with food in the refrigerator. I was no longer sleeping on my cousin's floor and surviving off ramen noodles. The fresh start allowed me to do some soul searching about other changes that I wanted to make in my life. I wanted to change my perspectives around relationships and take more accountability for my outlook and roles I played in previous relationships. I decided that when I got involved with another person, I would be more of a gentleman and less of the savage I'd been in the past.

MYA

I met Mya on an online dating site. I was drawn to her because unlike Pamela, she seemed to be a really happy person. For me to have a fresh start, I needed that energy. After talking for a while on the phone, we decided to meet in person to get to know each other. She was from Concord, and I lived in San Jose at the time which was an hour away. We decided to meet in downtown Oakland by the library because it was a midway point for us.

The date was organic as we walked, talked, and of course, passed each other's eyeball tests. From then on, everything was traditional. I took her on dates over the next several weeks to the movies, restaurants, sporting events, and every now and then, we took trips to Santa Cruz Beach. Other times, we chilled at my apartment talking. Does anybody know what's missing here? Give up? Sex. I wasn't sweating it. I realized that sex didn't matter as much to me as it had in the past. What really matters is the bond and connection between a man and a woman. Plus, I was trying to be on my best behavior.

Normally, I would've gotten into the bed with her and let my lust take over. Lord knows I wanted to. I decided that if I wanted to get different results, then it would require me changing in my approach. I was in full gentleman mode. I never brought up the issue of sex or initiated. I literally and figuratively thought outside the box, mine and hers. Mya was the only one I was seeing or spending time with. I was appreciating the companionship without the drama.

One night, after coming home from the beach, I guess Mya was in a mood. It was a mood that I knew anywhere. We started kissing as I felt her body and all of its responses to me. She reached out and grabbed me by my penis through my grey sweatpants to pull me closer. Before I knew it, we were both naked and I could see her beautiful body. She never dressed overstated, so I was very pleasantly surprised. We were both at the highest levels of excitement, so much so we almost went there without a condom. After a quick trip to the gas station for some magnums, we enjoyed a sensual night of lovemaking.

ONE STEP FORWARD, TWO STEPS

It was the first time for us, but it wasn't the last. The next few months were full of dates and occasional sex. Fast forward about a month, and I was getting ready for my 31st birthday—the first since I moved to California. The previous year, I spent my birthday with my brother and Eva who turned out to be someone else's girl. This year, I wanted to spend the day with a woman that might be my own.

Mya and I had planned to spend the day together weeks earlier. I didn't know whether she was planning something special for it or not. Either way, I didn't care. As long as I got to spend time with her, I was good. "What time are we meeting up?" I asked. "I'll be down there later on this afternoon, maybe around 1:00 p.m.," she replied enthusiastically. I used the time I had to get my hair cut and grab a nice outfit, so I could be fresh on my birthday.

I texted Mya around 1:45 p.m. because I hadn't heard from her. I wanted to know if she was ok or if she was just running late. "I'm running late," she responded. I wasn't tripping. I just waited while I took calls and responded to people on Facebook who wished me a happy birthday. A few more hours passed, and then it was a quarter to five. I decided to give her a call. "Are you still coming through?" I asked. "I'm not going to be able to make it. I'm hanging out with my friend," she said. The friend she was referring to was a female friend she introduced me to a few weeks back. Regardless of whom she was referring to, I wasn't happy about being ditched on my birthday. There was no prior argument or issue. In fact, up until this point, we hadn't ever argued.

"Why would you do this on my birthday after we planned to hang out?" I asked angrily. "I'm sorry, but I wanted to hang out with my friend. I haven't seen her in a while," she responded. "We hardly get to spend time with each other because of our work schedules," she continued. I couldn't believe that she was trying to make me feel like an asshole for *her* ditching *me* on *my* birthday. "You really going to choose to do this on my birthday?" I asked. She stayed on the phone speechless. I hung up the phone on her. I was done.

I felt personally insulted. Instead of having a good day, I was at home wondering why she didn't want to spend that time with me. Even though we were not yet boyfriend and girlfriend, it still hurt that she didn't think it was worth seeing me that day. This is a woman who constantly talked about wanting to be in a relationship with me and about us taking gradual steps to get there. Now, before some of you ladies out there start taking up for her, let's think about it. Be honest with yourself. If a man you'd been seeing for months had done this to you, how would you feel? To quote the great Jay-Z, "If you can't feel that, your whole perspective is wack."

Indirectly, I had to hold myself partly responsible. My relationship history wasn't squeaky clean, and I had made plenty mistakes over the years. When I was being a savage, I took advantage of people. Now, that I was "Mr. Nice Guy," I was being taken advantage of—the irony. Though I never did anything wrong to Mya, it could've been the direct karma for my treatment of Carla and Shantel just as easily. I got a taste of my own medicine, and I was the one who ended up sick. So, the disappointment and the loneliness I was left with, I had to eat it.

GETTING BACK TO ME

Those feelings of being taken advantage of and overlooked reminded me of my childhood. Over the next few months, life changed for me. Now, instead of living in an apartment space with roommates in San Jose. I moved to a one-bedroom apartment in East Oakland. I spent my time grinding the on-call schedule at work for extra money. My coworkers dreaded working on-call because they always had something going on for the weekends, and on-call would get in the way. I decided not only would I do my own on-call, but I would do theirs as well. That extra $430 per week was worth it to me.

My goal was to change as many things in my life as I could, both internally and externally. I was no longer rocking my traditional goatee; I grew a full beard with a Caesar haircut and waves. I focused on the foster youth that I was working for and trying to help them improve their independent living skills. Some of them were applying to colleges, going to the military, or working. I found peace in helping youth grow and believe in themselves. I loved seeing the youth make strides towards their life goals.

As I watched the brave youths I served work hard to transcend their circumstances, I started thinking about my own life. I thought about all the mistakes I had made over the years in college, past relationships, and the challenges I had to overcome. I thought about the changes that I could make in my life to improve as a person. The youths that I was inspiring were now inspiring me. I appreciated what I called, the circle of hope.

> *"No man, for a considerable period, can wear one face to himself and another to the multitude, without finally getting bewildered as to which may be true."*
>
> —Nathaniel Hawthorne, *The Scarlet Letter*

ROUND TWO

You know that moment when you know you are moving in the right direction and then the devil comes in to fuck all of that up? If you said yes, then, this is one of those moments for me. If you said no, fuck you and your perfect life, love you.

Around the beginning of November and out of the blue, I got a text message. "Hey, it's me, Mya. I was just thinking about you. How are you doing?" the text read. Now, the old me would've said, "You mean after being ditched on my birthday and having you pop up out of nowhere pretending you give a fuck? I'm doing all right, considering." The new me was on that new year-new me bullshit even though it was still the same year.

Another text came through before I could respond. "I want to apologize for how everything went down, and I wanted to know if you were willing to give me a call." This is one of those once-in-a-million times where women apologize to a man for wrongdoing in a relationship. They usually just offer you something to eat or ask, "Are you still mad?" Fellas, you ever experienced a sincere apology? If so, play the lottery using the numbers of her birthdate, and I want a 30 percent cut of our winnings.

Instead of responding on impulse, I decided to wait a day or two to respond. I thought through the last situation and how disrespected I felt. I thought about all the mistakes that I had made in past relations with ladies with whom I had connections. I'm far from perfect, and so is she, I thought.

Though I feel it was savage for her to do me like that on my birthday, I must acknowledge our imperfections.

I hit up my bro, Nas. I told him that Mya randomly hit me with a text. After teasing me about her hitting me up, he asked the same question I had been pondering. "So, what you gonna do?" he asked. "I don't know. What you think?" Nas knew why I stopped talking to her.

"Well, like I told you before. I don't think she was hanging out with her girlfriend. I think she was hanging out with another dude she liked better and that's why she played you," Nas said. "I think she only came back now because for whatever reason her and that guy are not on good terms. Otherwise, it wouldn't have taken so long for her to apologize," he added. Whether she was or wasn't hanging out with another guy wasn't the problem for me. I mean, we were seeing each other, but she wasn't technically my girlfriend. I was just pissed about being ditched on my birthday.

I thought about Nas's take. I wanted to break the cycle of madness in my life. I decided to give her a fair second chance, something I never gave and never received from anyone. A day later, I responded to her. I told her that I accepted her apology and that I was willing to give her a call. Once I did, we talked for a few minutes about things we were up to since we last spoke. After the small talk, she invited me to dinner at a restaurant. "This is new," I thought. What could I lose by going to dinner with her? I decided to take her up on the offer.

Since I was now living in East Oakland, she met me at my apartment so we could drive together. When I saw her, she was still beautiful and seemed happy to see me. She approached me and gave me a hug. "What's all this?" she asked while rubbing her hands on my cheeks. She had never seen me with a beard. "What do you think?" I asked. "I like it. It looks good on you," she replied cheerfully. "Thanks," I responded. It was cold out, so we got in the car soon after.

We drove to a nice Italian restaurant. We ate pasta while furthering our conversation about updates in our lives since we last saw each other, other than the fact I had a new beard. She talked about wanting to make up for lost time and apologized for disappointing me. I didn't dwell on it; I just enjoyed the moment and the dinner. When the night was over, we drove back to my place.

When we arrived, she got out of the car and asked, "Is it ok if I kiss you?" Part of me was hesitant, and the other part wanted the night to end on a good note. I decided to let her kiss me, just a quick peck. Afterward, she got in her car and went home.

Over the next three weeks, we began hanging out with each other and were slowly getting back to our normal routine. We went out to dinner, to the movies, and to see the Warriors play at Oracle Arena. She even took me to meet her parents on Christmas day. Everything was on the up and up, but I was skeptical. I had seen this movie before, and I was wiser this time around.

Soon after, the flaking and rescheduling started up again. I started to not hear from her for days, and sometimes a week would pass with no contact. It started to feel like what Nas said was true. Maybe she was using me, the gentleman as a cushion or fallback guy until she could find the guy she was really looking for. When we went to the movies one day, she was distant from me for most of the time, but she paid the most attention to a random guy in the parking lot who was spewing the most ignorant shit he could say at the time. Maybe that's the sort of guy she *really* wants, and the gentleman that I was with her was what she thought she *should* want. Either way, it didn't seem like she was who I wanted to waste time on anymore.

One day, I just said, "fuck it." Do I want to spend any more time with a woman who isn't sold on me after all this time? How many times will I allow her to play me like a sucka? Maybe she sees me as "too nice" or not genuine. I thought all of those things before I arrived at my conclusion. I remember thinking to myself, "She'd appreciate me better if she knew who I was before". In the words of Beyoncé, "She must don't know about me." I'm way more savage than she's ever seen from me. In an attempt to turn over a new leaf, I found a rattlesnake.

I didn't want to talk to her ever again, so I wrote her a letter expressing how I felt. Mya was stringing me along, and I wasn't going to take it and try to jump rope. "I'm not wasting my time anymore. I'm moving on with my life," was the message. To be honest, I don't remember what I wrote word for word, but I'm sure my savage came out in that letter. I decided that I would return the Christmas present she bought for me and anything associated with her so she would know that this time was final. I put it all in a box, took it to her apartment, and put it on her back patio.

A few days later, she texted me. She must've discovered the box I left because she started answering questions that I don't remember asking. "I was going to call you and let you know why I was being distant," she wrote. I never responded because I didn't care. It didn't matter to me anymore. When I think about why I stopped fucking with her the last time and add it to this time, I realized I was wasting my energy. I treated her with more respect than she had earned, never again though.

I FINALLY FOUND YOU

I spent the next several months getting myself together, so I don't carry the baggage of Mya with me. By the time March arrived, I was ready to try again, but this time with someone actually worth spending time with. I decided to go on Match.com to see who was out there. There were quite a few interesting profiles to read—everyone saying this was "their first time" and how they were "testing the waters" blah-blah-blah. There was one woman, however, who caught my eye. Her name was Nelly.

Nelly is a five-foot-three beautiful Latina of Salvadoran heritage. What attracted me to her was her beautiful smile. Anyone who has ever done online dating knows that it's a mixed bag. You see things like "I only fuck with this type of person" or "If you are not this kind of person, then get the fuck off my profile." Those kinds of passages say a lot about the person and it's not the best impression to give. To me, it reads baggage, and I had plenty of my own already. That's another reason why Nelly's profile stood out to me; she had a very simple, yet humble profile. She wasn't damn-near naked, inciting my lust. Instead, she was insightful and silly enough to put up pictures of her making crazy faces with her friends. Her face wasn't caked up with makeup; she was comfortable with being her. She incited my curiosity.

Through our online conversations, we talked about all sorts of things. I learned that she liked to work out and she did belly dancing as a hobby. Nelly told me she loved the headline from my profile. The headline read "What if *Mr. Right* were a lefty?" She thought it was clever. Nelly liked the fact that my profile wasn't filled with me talking about my penis size and the car I drive, ya know—all the bullshit that people do that has nothing to do with whether we would actually like each other in real life.

I wanted to know more about her, so I asked her out on a coffee date. I had enough dinner dates that were a complete waste of time and money. Over the years, I paid for too many dinners for people that I never spoke to again. After dealing with Mya, I was so over the fuck shit. "I love coffee," Nelly responded while accepting the invite. I wasn't too familiar with the area given that I lived in Oakland, so Nelly picked the location. Just like that, our date was set for a few days later, and we met up at Starbucks in Walnut Creek.

When I entered, I saw that Nelly was already waiting in line while staring at the menu. As I approached her from behind, I noticed that she was nicely shaped and had long curly hair. I tapped her on the shoulder. "Are you Nelly?" I asked. When she turned around, her hair swung around seemingly in slow-motion like in one of those cheesy romantic movies. "Yes," she responded with her beautiful smile.

I could tell by the way she looked at me that she was feeling ya boy. I was fresh. I had a crisp haircut, a nice button-up shirt, and a nice pair of jeans. Look, I'm a Leo; I had to talk my shit somewhere in here. Nelly told me that she really liked my smile. "If she only knew the price I had to pay to be able to smile," I thought. I thanked her for the compliment, nonetheless. I was definitely feeling her. Nelly wore a nice cardigan-like sweater with a tank top underneath, some very flattering jeans, and some heels. I love a woman with a nice heel-game. Nelly was even more beautiful in person. I didn't want to get caught staring, so we ordered and I paid for both drinks.

> "Nothing is more beautiful than the smile that has struggled through the tears."
>
> —Demi Lovato

UNEXPECTED VISITOR

During my first date with Nelly and in mid-conversation, I saw a woman approach from my rear while walking past me to the right. I saw the woman from the corner of my eye, and I thought I was seeing things. The woman looked a lot like Mya. In fact, I knew it was her. "Oh shit," I thought as Nelly continued talking about her job. The woman walked straight as she headed for the bathroom she eventually entered. The room went silent, and all I could hear was the opening guitar solo from Cream's song "Sunshine of Your Love." If you are cinema-savvy, you know it as the song that played when Jimmy decided to whack his crew in Goodfellas. That scene was the same mood I was in.

What was I going to do if it was Mya? I had to think quick. The tension was so thick my anxiety levels must've shown up on the Richter scale. It was like the final scene from *The Sopranos*. Would she come out the restroom and then all of a sudden everything would go black for me? If she did, I knew I'd be whacked. All I needed was Journey's song "Don't Stop Believing" to play in the background, and the scene would be complete. Meanwhile, Nelly was oblivious to the situation I was damn near having a panic attack over.

After a few minutes, the woman exited the bathroom and walked towards us. There was no doubt left to be had, it was definitely Mya. I was stunned. I thought about Nas because this is the kind of situation that would happen to him. "Hey, how are you?" she said. With my heart pounding as if I had just finished running for my life, I stood up quickly and gave her a hug. Even though I was disgusted at the sight of her, I had to stay even keeled like a mob boss who planned to whack their associate. "I'm doing well. How about you?" I responded. I didn't give a fuck how she was doing. I just wanted her to go away before my date thought too much about her.

Mya happened to be in the shopping center and saw me enter the Starbucks alone. She probably thought she'd step in on some "what a coincidence" shit and connect with me for round three. I wondered how salty she was to see me on a date with a beautiful woman who looked very interested in me. To me, it was so fitting for her to see who she'd lost and another woman ready to reap the benefits of her blunder. I can't lie; I got a kick out of it.

Before I knew it, I was giving her the hint to leave. "It was nice seeing you," I told her. When she left, Nelly and I continued our date without missing a beat. I really liked that Nelly didn't start tripping. No "Who is that bitch?" or "Where you know her from?" Her lack of reaction was refreshing. In fact, Nelly never mentioned it at all. It was weeks later before I told her who the woman was and even then, she handled it with class.

"Never apologize for how much love you have to give, just feel sorry for those who didn't want any of it."

—Tupac Shakur

THE SHOW MUST GO ON

After a near-death experience and a wonderful time with Nelly, it was time for our date to conclude. I gave Nelly a hug and was ready to get into my car. "Hey, you want to have dinner?" Nelly asked. "Sure, I could eat," I answered in my best Antwone Fisher voice. By the way, if you haven't seen or heard any song, show, or movie that I referenced, then you have some homework to do. I will be grading papers, and there may be a quiz.

We got into Nelly's car as she drove to a nice Italian restaurant called *Il Fornaio* in Walnut Creek. We ate and talked more about ourselves and what we wanted in a relationship. It felt good to talk to someone who was genuinely interested in what I had to say. Mid-conversation, my phone rang. I forgot that I was on-call for my job, so I had to go solve a minor dispute between a couple of youths I served.

When I came back, Nelly asked why I had two phones. Normally, I would be thinking "You don't even know me to be asking me that. You are not my girl." But I liked Nelly, and I didn't want her to think I was a drug dealer or into some other sort of shady shit, so I told her. "I don't want the youths I serve to have my personal cell phone number because then, I'd be on-call even when I'm not," I explained. It made for good conversation and allowed me to go into depth about other aspects of my job.

The waitress came by with the check, and now it was time to test her. Some of y'all not going to agree, but fuck it; it is what it is. I purposely didn't reach for my wallet. I was looking for two things. I wanted to see how much she liked me and whether she was willing to pay for the meal that she invited me to. This way, if she and I didn't work out, it would be on her dime, not mine for once. I had more than enough money to pay for the meals. It was only like $60. I paid for many meals over the years.

Nelly hesitated briefly and then paid for the meals gracefully. She didn't seem to care, and that was a major plus for me. Based on history, I wondered whether she would throw it in my face somewhere down the line. I got good vibes from her. I felt patient and calm around her, and for the first time in months, I felt like myself.

We went for a walk after dinner to continue talking to each other. It was a nice night to take a stroll. The weather was just right for a night on the town as we watched couples gaze at the stars. Nelly had on a low-cut dark pink tank top underneath her jacket which was unzipped. I'm not even gonna hold y'all— that's "not going to lie to you" in Philly slang—I was looking down her shirt. I might be a reformed man, but every now and then, I get a visit from the devil. She never noticed, and I never made it obvious; besides I was still genuinely interested in what she had to say.

After the walk, Nelly drove me back to the Starbucks where I had left my car. It was a great night, and I wanted to seize the moment. I let her know that I had a great time with her and wanted to see her again. I gave her a hug and a kiss before getting into my car to replay the night in my mind on my way home. From that day forward, we were inseparable.

"I finally realized I was never asking for too much, I was just asking the wrong person."

—Unknown

WELCOME TO MY HOUSE (FLO-RIDA VOICE)

A few days later, I received a text from Nelly. It was an evening after work, and I was watching TV in my T-shirt and sweats as routine. The text read, "What are you doing?" "Nothing, just chilling and watching TV," I responded. She told me that she enjoyed our date and wanted to spend more time with me. "Why don't you invite me over?" she asked. Me being the man that I am, of course, I invited her over.

The goal was to watch the movie *Crash*. We laid on the couch together and started watching the movie as planned. That's when the devil tapped me on the shoulder. "Yo bruh, you better not take this L," he said. Even a broken clock is right two times a day, I thought. So, I made my move. On this one,

I won't get into too much detail. It will become clear why later on. For now, just know that it was the first time we made love together.

MURDER WAS THE CASE

Three years had passed since I heard any solid updates about my father's case. Finally, I got a call from my father's public defender advising me of the court date. "Are you able to make it?" he asked. I told him that I would be present. I just needed to make sure that the date would be solid and not pushed back another year like the last one. "It won't be pushed back this time. I already spoke to the judge to inform her that you would be flying out from California," he assured me. That's all I needed to purchase my plane ticket and be on my way.

Advised by his lawyer, my father took a prearranged plea deal because there was far too much evidence against him. He also had a savage female prosecutor who had no intentions of letting him off, and for good reason. If it were up to her, he would've gotten the death penalty. It was a capital murder case, so she was looking for a life sentence. It was surreal.

On my flight to Philly, I thought about the irony that my father didn't drive downtown for me when I got arrested for stealing, but here I am flying across the country to attend his sentencing for murder. There were so many mixed emotions running through my mind. My father who had clearly suffered from psychotic episodes was far from the man I knew growing up was now being sentenced for murder.

When I arrived at the courtroom, it was just like on TV. The reporters who originally covered the crime were present for the sentencing. I sat on the right side of the room behind the defendant, my father, and his lawyer. The prosecutor, a black woman, sat on the left side of the room. I didn't know what I was in for or what to expect. The prosecutor was ice grilling me as if I was a part of the crime. The judge, a white woman, entered and proceedings were under way.

The plea was already entered, but the fiasco was just starting. The prosecutor argued for my father to get the maximum sentence of life in prison because the victim, my grandmother, paid the ultimate price, her life. It was a strong and reasonable argument. The public defender argued for a more lenient sentence because of the mental health issues that preceded the attacks. I watched in disgust as the prosecutor described what my father had done to my grandmother.

After the back-and-forth bickering between the lawyers, it was my turn to speak to the judge as a character witness. The prosecutor objected and didn't want me to speak fearing prejudice. "You honor, I am not only here for my father, but I am here for my grandmother as well. She was my grandmother, so I am a victim myself," I offered. "My younger brother is attending Berkeley City College in California. I am a Master of Social Work and a public servant like yourself. Those two things would be impossible without the guidance and the teachings from my father," I continued.

I told the judge that my father was not the monster that his actions showed. "Your Honor, I am more hurt than the prosecutor could ever be because *my* grandmother was murdered, *not* hers. My life is being torn apart here. My father is going to jail, and my relationship with my younger brother is destroyed. I am asking that you give a sentence that would allow us to heal as a family. I am asking for leniency," I continued.

The judge deliberated for a while, taking all arguments into account. "All rise," the bailiff instructed. Bracing for the worst-case scenario, I stood up to hear the sentence. "Mr. Adegbola Ige, you have pled guilty to the murder of your mother, Ester Ayodele Ige. You are sentenced to a mandatory eight years in the prison, which considers the three years you already served while awaiting trial and eight years of parole for a total of 16 years," the judge rendered. There you have it. With good behavior, he would be coming home in five years, 2018.

The prosecutor was pissed, but I didn't care. It was the best outcome that I could've hoped for. The judge gave my father the minimum sentence allowed by law, especially for such a high profile case. My father would be in his early 70s when he would be eligible for parole. I was so full of conflicting emotions that I forgot to thank the judge. I came back into the courtroom just before she could return to her chambers. "Hey judge, thank you," I said. "You're welcome. Continue doing the good work that you do," she instructed.

After admitting to beating his own mother, my grandmother, to death over time with weapons like belts and a cane, my father was now a convicted murderer. It's hard to feel good about any of this because my grandmother lost her life to her son, and my family was in shambles. On the flip side, he could've and probably should've gotten life in prison; think about that.

WHAT THE FUCK?

I received a phone call from Nas. He called just to shoot the shit, and I was more than happy to oblige. Nas had been asking me over the years to watch the HBO hit series *The Wire*. We always suggested shows for each other to watch. I suggested *The Sopranos* for him, so I told him that I would watch *The Wire* if he would watch *The Sopranos*.

To give more context, the main reason I wanted Nas to watch *The Sopranos* is that I saw so many similarities between him and the main character, Tony Soprano. Over the years, I explained the similarities I saw and pointed out episodes that fit real-life challenges Nas was having. Nas was always hesitant to watch the show. He wanted to hear about the show but was not interested in seeing it. I guess hearing about it makes it renounceable, but seeing it makes it real. Sometimes, people break mirrors because mirrors break hearts.

Fast forward to the current conversation, I remembered to let Nas know that I finished watching *The Wire*. "What you think?" he asked. I told him that I didn't really like the first few seasons; I thought they were boring, but the last few were cool. Apparently, that set him off. "You always talk shit about the shows I watch. You never were there for me," he continued. I was baffled because even though we've had arguments in the past, it was never at this level.

Before I could respond, his rant continued. "You don't even know that I tried to watch *The Sopranos* and didn't like it. I didn't tell you because I wasn't trying to throw it in your face," he continued. He was so angry he was just screaming at me. "I don't understand why you are taking my not liking *The Wire* so personally. It's not like you were a writer, director, or producer of the show," I responded. Had he told me that he tried to watch *The Sopranos* and he didn't like it, I wouldn't have cared. I didn't create the show.

It couldn't have been about the TV shows, I thought. It just sounded too personal. I didn't get the chance to finish my thoughts before he cut me off and continued yelling at me. Nas was screaming so loudly that I could barely understand what was being said. I was so confused; we always critiqued music, movies, and women together. Soon after, he hung up on me, which was even more puzzling. I didn't call back for obvious reasons.

In the nearly 20 years I had known him, I had never heard him like that. Forget the TV shows, I couldn't believe that he said I was never there for him. What he was accusing me of was unfair and untrue. I went to every one of his football games even when they were out of state. I sat with him when he cried about the conflict between him and his son's mother. Every time he needed to vent about things going on in his life, I was there. I would call him up just to hang out with him while he was at work even when I had a job of my own. I just couldn't understand why he had so much rage.

Nas called me back a few weeks later, but I didn't answer. I was still highly offended and shocked that he would talk to me that way; we were family. What was I going to say to him? I would never have done anything close to that to him; I had too much respect for him. He called again a few days later, but I still wasn't ready to speak to him.

THE TWENTY-SECOND OF JUNE

While going to the fridge, I noticed my phone ringing. In case you haven't noticed already, the phone ringing in my life is usually a sign of doom, and this time would be no different. It was Rasool, Nas's older brother and by extension, basically one of mine. I hadn't spoken to "Big Sool," as I called him, in a while. When I answered the phone, it all started to make sense.

"Wassup, Big Sool?" I asked. "K, I have some bad news for you," he responded. "Nas passed away," he continued. When he said that, I damn near dropped the phone. My heart was beating like it was going to burst out of my chest. I could barely breathe enough to respond to him. "Wh-what?" I responded. "He passed away on June 22nd." Instantly, I began crying uncontrollably. "What the fuck happened?" I asked him. "He was shot in his apartment," he responded. When he said that, I couldn't believe it. "His fiancé was in the house, and the police are still trying to figure out if she shot him or if it was suicide," he added. I was in pure shock. None of it felt real. "Why would she shoot him?" "Why would he commit suicide?" I asked. I didn't understand.

"When is his funeral?" I asked. "We already had his funeral a few days ago," he responded. "How come nobody called me?" I asked. "It was a small gathering. We only had direct family there," he responded. "We are having his memorial on July 10th. I know you are in Cali, but are you able to come?" he asked. "Yes, I'll be there," I promised. Do you remember the comparisons of Nas to Tony Soprano that I eluded to? The irony is, Nas passed away literally three days after James Gandolfini, the legendary actor that played Tony Soprano.

"Walking with a friend in the dark is better than walking alone in the light."

—Hellen Keller

MEMORIAL

By the time I flew to Philly for the memorial, it was established that Nas's cause of death was suicide. Having to bury your best friend, console his mother, or speak at his memorial are things you should never have to do ever. I had to do it twice. Nas had such an impact on my life that I couldn't believe that he was gone. I mean, we went to every school together from elementary through college. He was my first apartment roommate. I was wrecked. I knew my pain was nothing in comparison to what his family must've been going through.

When I got to the church, I saw Janelle, Nas's former roommate and our friend, in the church with her husband. Brian and I sat a few rows behind them. It still didn't feel real to me. The church was full of people who loved him, from family members and people we went to high school with to his semi-pro football teammates. However, the church felt lonely and cold. It wasn't until I saw Nas's picture on the podium that it really hit me. I started crying uncontrollably as I sat on the church bench. I could barely lift my head from my arms.

I spoke at his memorial about the kind of man he was, the father he was, and the friend he was. I wanted people to know how much he inspired and motivated me throughout my life. Seeing his mother cry as I listed many of the memories I had shared with her son really broke me up. I gave her a hug, but what could I say to her to put her at ease? She had to bury her son, something that should never happen. My heart was broken for her.

Afterward, I finally met his fiancé that he met after I moved to California. She told me that he had been struggling with his mental health and other challenges. "When he was calling you, it was to apologize," she informed me. "Other times, I told him to talk to you because of the way he talked about you; I knew only you could calm him down," she continued. Those words were both soothing and saddening. The words were soothing for obvious reasons. However, I was sad because he really needed me in those moments, and I was too busy being hurt over how he treated me.

I didn't want that last call to be our final conversation. I started blaming myself. "I can't believe I didn't see it," I remember thinking. Nas's rant towards me had nothing to do with me. He was crying out for help, and I was too emotionally involved to hear it properly. Maybe I could've prevented his death, I thought. I was always able to talk him down from anger in the past. Not answering his phone call is something that I'll regret for the rest of my life. The skeletons in my closet were starting to have bunk beds. His fiancé told me what happened in Nas's final moments. For the sake of his family's privacy, I won't go into detail. I'll just say, I had no idea he was struggling that much with his demons.

I went to his mother's house after the memorial to have dinner with his family. Nas's mother said, "I know you wish you could've saved him, but there is nothing you could've done." "He knew you loved him and that's all that matters," she continued. I knew those words were genuine and true. They landed on my heart because they came from his mother, his strong mother. I came over to comfort her, and here she was comforting her extended son.

My world had changed forever, again. Nas never left my side. I still hear him when I'm making decisions and when I talk to people who knew him. I still ask myself what Nas would say or think in any given situation. Nas, if you can hear me, just know that I love you brother and I'll never forget you. I hope you and Lex are chilling together once again.

THE CIRCLE OF LIFE

Almost a year and a half later, Nelly came out of the bathroom with a positive pregnancy test as I sat in the living room. She gave me a kiss as she showed me. "We are pregnant," she said. It was the best news that I could've gotten. Nelly and I had already passed the "I love you" stage in our relationship. I wanted to make sure that my baby would be born in a two-parent home full of love. My woman deserved more than to be a baby mother, no shade to those who are. I needed her to be my wife, a married mother. That's when I decided to marry the woman that I always wanted.

My cousin Jonathan and his wife Megan own a jewelry store called Forever Diamonds in San Jose. I decided to pay them a visit and tell them what I had been planning. When I told her I was going to ask Nelly to marry me, Megan responded, "I knew you weren't the type to have a baby mama." I confirmed, "That's never been my style." Both Jonathan and Megan helped me pick out, customize, and size a beautiful ring for Nelly. I even got the ring box that lit up when opened to give the diamonds a brilliant shine.

On the day of the proposal, I had to be sneaky as I drove to San Jose to pick up the ring that I had selected a week earlier and get back to Nelly before she was any wiser. She noticed that I was running late, which is something that I never do, but she wasn't tripping. Nelly knew that I traveled to see clients for my job, so she understood. I called her sounding stressed and angry about traffic to throw her off what I had in store for her.

When I arrived at the Starbucks, where we first met, I asked her what she wanted to order. As soon as she turned to the counter to look at the menu, I tapped her on the shoulder just like the day I met her. As she turned around to look at me, I got down on one knee and opened the ring box. My heartbeat sounded like buffalo stampeding through the plains of Africa. "Nelly, I love you. Will you marry me?" She said, "Yes!" I stood up and gave her a kiss and a hug as the baristas clapped and congratulated us. We didn't get any free coffee though; we got dinner elsewhere instead.

THE WEDDING

The day of the wedding, Nelly and I went to the courthouse in Martinez to apply for our marriage certificate. It was cold and raining. We were stressing wondering if anyone would show due to the weather as the time for our vows grew closer. We were letting other couples get married ahead of us to give people more time to show. Eventually, people showed up one by one and then group by group. It was a relief for us. We were about to take the biggest step in our lives, and we wanted the most important people in them to be present.

Nelly looked stunning in her white wedding dress. She was even more beautiful than she was the day I met her. Of course, I was bossed out in my white tuxedo, black bowtie, and black vest with white pants. Although my mother wasn't able to attend the wedding physically, I am sure she was present spiritually. My father couldn't attend because he was in jail, but God always has a way. The pastor who married us was a Nigerian woman, so my roots were in the house of the Lord.

My brother Wale, my Aunt Marlene, and her sons came, so my mother was represented. My bros Corey and Zimbabwe came with their wives to support our union; it was beautiful. Most of Nelly's family members were present at our wedding. Nelly and I got married on Christmas Eve 2015 while she was eight months pregnant with our baby boy.

We didn't know at the time, but Nelly's cousins made reservations and paid for everyone to have dinner at a restaurant called Jacks in Pleasant Hill. When we arrived, the restaurant owner learned that the dinner was for newlyweds, and he gave us the entire second floor for free. That's God's work. Many of the guests stayed for dinner as we ate, laughed, and enjoyed the moment. It was raining really hard outside, but none of us cared. What started out looking like a rained out baseball game, turned into one of the best days of my life. It was yet another metaphor for my life's journey.

FATHERHOOD

Prince Gabriel Mateo Ige was born on February 13, 2016, weighing in at seven pounds and five ounces. His first name Prince represents that he is the son of his ancestors, African Kings. Gabriel means God is my strength, and

Mateo means a gift of God. All those names accurately describe his importance to the world he came to inhabit. There are two times in a person's life when their life flashes before their eyes, when a person has a near-death experience and when their first child is born. The entire journey of my life, all the setbacks and all the progress led up to this moment.

My wife Nelly risked her life to bring our baby boy into this world because she loved us that much. "You did it, baby," I told her after he arrived safely. I gave her a kiss and told her that I loved her. Prince was born in a room full of family and people who loved him. I am now a father, and it is my job to make sure that he never feels the emptiness and longing for love that I felt in my life. It's my job to make sure he knows that he has the love and support of a tight-knit family, and I'm up to the task. There is no greater feeling in the world.

Every time something great happens in my life, I think about the people that I lost and the journey. I think about the fact that my son will never meet his grandmother who would've given him tons of love. I think about how he never will meet his uncles, Lex and Nas. However, when I look at him, I can see my mother's face. He looks more like her than he does me. I guess this is God's way of giving me the best of both; I'll take it.

When I finally got to hold him in my hands for the first time, I called to him. "Hey Prince, it's me, Daddy," I told him. He and I locked eyes as soon as he heard my voice. He recognized my voice since I had spent so much time talking to him while he was still in the womb. I gave him a hug with a tear running down my face as I kissed him on the forehead. Now, I thought, "This, this moment right here, is the greatest moment of my life."

"It is easier to build strong children than to repair broken men."

—Frederick Douglass

ARE YOU IN THAT MOOD YET?

If you think God doesn't have a sense of humor check this out. Six months after Prince was born, which happened to be a week before my 35th birthday, Nelly and I decided to take him out for a stroll in downtown Pleasant Hill,

California. As we exited the car and put my little man in the stroller, we began walking towards the main strip of stores. You will never guess who we saw approaching from the left to cross our path. Give up? It was Mya. That's right, the same Mya that ditched me on my birthday a few years earlier, and when I gave her a second chance, she essentially did the same thing.

The irony at that moment was unreal. For those of you keeping score, not only was she present for my first date with Nelly, but now, she was present to see us married and pushing our son in a stroller. The look on her face when she noticed us was priceless. It's like God was trolling her, and she looked pissed. She went from happily walking her dog to damn-near dragging the dog up the street. I could tell she'd gained a lot of weight. Nelly didn't recognize her, but the pettiness in me pointed her out.

She tried to hurry past us so that she wouldn't be forced to acknowledge us. It was pure hilarity to me. It gave me satisfaction to see her realize what she missed out on. It was the definition of the old meme, "this could be us, but you playing." I gave her a second chance, and she gave her ass to kiss. Well, there I was walking with a new salad to toss, and she was tight. Life is a cycle. As the world keeps spinning, what goes around comes around. This time I got the last laugh, and I was The Joker with it. The bottom line is, she fucked me real good, but karma fucked her better.

"If you want to know how rich you are, find out how many things you have that money cannot buy."

—Unknown

CHAPTER 16
IDENTITY

WHO I WAS

Over the course of my life, I've witnessed my mother struggling to balance parenting three hard-headed boys while she battled extreme mental health challenges. I saw her being wrestled to the ground, handcuffed, and carried to the police van as she struggled to free herself from what must've been a terrifying experience for her. I've witnessed my father struggle financially as we had our heat cut off and had to use kerosene heaters and eat peanut butter sandwiches as he tried to make ends meet. I've seen my brother sell drugs, get shot, and eventually imprisoned. I've seen people get shot, stabbed, and murdered. I've been caught in the middle of too many shootouts to name with bullets whizzing by my head. I found my best friend dead on the couch and had another friend who took his own life. I've lived through having my grandmother murdered by my father and seeing my family dynamic ripped apart as a result.

The scariest part about it all is that it wasn't until I started writing this book that I realized I had been traumatized all my life. After a while, I had become so desensitized to the events in my life that it was only recently that I noticed. Over the years, many of my actions were selfish and used as internal armor. I had to protect myself from all the traumatic events I experienced, and the helplessness I felt. I spent so much time trying to right perceived wrongs in my life and overcompensate for opportunities that I felt were unavailable to me. I began living with a chip on my shoulder, and I was going to get even at all costs. I had to show people and live the life that I wanted, but in many cases, I was trying to live a life that probably wasn't meant for me.

Reflecting on my life, I spent a large portion of it being a lost soul who wanted to be found and loved. I lived life out of desperation, ego, and dreams. Basketball was a passion and a dream that prevented me from selling drugs and becoming a regular in the prison system the way my brother had. He and I experienced the same trauma, but I was blessed to have an outlet. I kept experiencing disappointments when it came to the sport that I dedicated my life to. I thought I was going to the NBA and that success would alleviate the pain. Looking back on it, maybe God put basketball in my life to save it.

LOVE AND CONNECTION

The world can be a cold place when you feel hollow inside. That's the way I felt when I approached the world. I had no time to be empathetic; I only had time for me especially, when I considered the way I was treated throughout grade school and high school and how badly I was teased about my African culture and made to feel like I didn't belong. The irony is, those same people today are rocking Dashikis, posting Pro-African quotes on Facebook, and saying *Wakanda* forever; go figure. I can't blame them too much though; they had been lied to and miseducated to feel inferior just like I was.

> *"It's easier to fool people than to convince them they were fooled."*
>
> —Mark Twain

When it came to the ladies I met along the way, I was a savage. Though that term is commonly used today as something cool, there was nothing cool about the way I behaved. When I think of someone like Carla who came into my life with the purest intentions, the total disregard I had makes me sick. It's not that I wish I had stayed with her; I knew I didn't deserve her from the outset, but I was too selfish to let her go. Instead, I kept her around and gave her pain that she didn't deserve. That's who I was back then.

Booker T. Washington once said, "There are two ways to use strength, pushing others down or lifting others up." Early on, I wasn't using my strength to elevate people in my life. Instead, I pulled some of them down into the depths of insecurity and low self-esteem, the very same places I was trying to escape. I was always trying to knock something down sexually. It turned out that I knocked everything down, including relationship opportunities, some of the women's self-esteem, and my self-respect.

To me, love was like a drug. It meant that I was seen and cared for, that someone made decisions based on how I would be impacted. Once I got a good enough hit, I was willing to do almost anything to maintain that high. Over the course of my life, the dream of being emotionally fulfilled and completely stable was both a gift and a curse. I wanted it so badly, but I didn't know how to give it to myself. Every time my life was in order, in came a new woman. I was looking for stability in all areas of my life, but love was always the missing piece. To be honest, fixing the wreckage of my life became as routine as Tom Brady playing in the Superbowl. It was getting and maintaining a healthy relationship that was challenging for me. Each time, I risked everything for what I thought was going to be the long-lasting love I always sought.

In the process of trying find that love, I ended up hurting people who meant me no harm. In fact, I inadvertently hurt people who wanted the best for me, people who really cared about me. I think of Carla and Shantel who were put into my life to give me hope and to show me that love was possible. Unfortunately for them, I was in no place to fully appreciate what they had to offer. I spent a large portion of my life beating myself up for my wrongdoings and feeling remorse.

> *"If you don't heal what hurt you, you will bleed on people who didn't cut you."*
>
> —Unknown

WHERE SHOULD I GO?

Many times in my life, I was coasting like a car in neutral. I think about what life was like after my mother's death. After seeing her struggle with her mental health and all those years of going in and out of the hospital, I felt myself detaching. Losing my mother was so shattering to my soul that I no longer cared about anything. I wasn't worried about progression or regression. I really didn't give a fuck. I just went wherever my impromptu decisions took me. If that meant finding a chick to smash to feel something other than pain, that's what I did. Sometimes those decisions took me to places of pleasure, and sometimes those decisions brought about pain and suffering.

Most times, they took me nowhere at all, and that was when I faced depression. In moments of depression, I wondered whether I had anything to offer to the world or whether I was just taking up space. When Lex passed, I felt that same confusion and doubt. It felt like everything with which I had a strong connection was being stripped from me. For every time I was able to show resilience, it was like I was kicked down the ladder again. I often wondered whether I should try harder or quit trying at all. After each tragedy, it felt like I was in a whole new world. It felt like a world where the rules had changed, and my sense of where I fit in the new paradigm became more confusing.

Imagine taking your family dog, driving him to another city, and leaving him there in the middle of the street as you drove home. The cruelty that it would take to do that to the dog is the way I felt about some of the cards I was dealt and the odds I had to overcome. Imagine the confusion and disconnect the dog would feel after being in an unfamiliar place where many things are happening at once; that is exactly how I felt for many years. After a while, having to find my way became more comfortable than knowing my way.

"Life isn't about finding yourself. It's about creating yourself."

—George Bernard Shaw

WHAT I LEARNED

Sometimes trials and tribulations are necessary for growth. In my case, I was always hesitant to sort through the challenges in my life. I was always in survival mode. There is a scene in the Sopranos that features dialogue between

Tony Soprano and his therapist, Dr. Melfi. Their dialogue helps to capture the struggle and enlightenment of coming to grips with our past.

> *Tony Soprano once referred to the process of therapy as "like taking a shit." His therapist, Dr. Melfi, replied, "I prefer to think of it more like childbirth." "Whatever happened to Gary Cooper?" Tony asked. "The strong silent type," he added. "He wasn't in touch with his feelings. He just did what he had to do," he continued. "Once they got him in touch with his feelings, it was dysfunction this and dysfunction that," he argued.*

Both Tony and Dr. Melfi had very different takes on the process of sitting in vulnerability. Early on, I was with Tony. Who the fuck wants to sit and talk to someone about the worst things that ever happened to them, especially the things that took years to forget? Who wants to relive the most emotionally trying and traumatizing experiences again? If something gives you nightmares, are you eager to recollect them? However, the more I grew and the more I learned, my perspective shifted more towards Dr. Melfi's view. Sometimes we must embrace the ugly and painful process to achieve something beautiful.

Dr. Melfi's analogy to childbirth really hit home for me in another way. I must admit, it took me many years to realize the beauty in my struggle. Each time I was knocked down, I got back up. Each time there was a tragedy, I survived. Each time I faced insurmountable odds, I prevailed. For every problem or negative situation that I caused, I learned and executed a solution strategy that ultimately helped me survive. Most importantly, each setback birthed a new and improved me. My evolution was not perfect; I was and still am flawed, but with each incarnation, I improved in some way. Learning, improving, and progression are what life is about, and none of it is possible without failure. Failure taught me more about life and myself than any success ever could.

At this point, I realized that I had been doing it all wrong. Worrying about how unseen and unloved I felt by others created an environment in which I lived life without a mirror and, therefore, not seeing myself, which is worse. I had to realize that I have unique qualities that I was blessed with. Instead of suppressing them, I needed to embrace the fact that I am different with the same energy that I expected of others. I needed to realize that I am not my mistakes, nor am I the composite of the traumatic experiences that plagued my life.

I needed to free myself of feeling like a victim and take more responsibility for my role in some of the outcomes in my life, both positive and negative. Reflecting on my life reminded me that I am resilient, and I can break the cycle if I devote enough focus into creating a new outcome. In those moments when I wanted to die, I had to realize that the will it takes to live is the same will it takes to be great. Once I realized my strength, I began learning how to love myself instead of looking for love in everyone else.

"Never be a prisoner of your past. It was just a lesson, not a life sentence."

—Unknown

LOVING ME, ALL OF ME

In grade school, so much of what people had to say and their opinions impacted how I viewed myself. If you think about it, I allowed people to shame me for being me. That shame turned into a psychology and an ideology that was destructive to myself and others, which includes the ladies I met along the way. My self-esteem was so low that I couldn't be solo, back then. I had to re-learn that I come from great people.

Ever since then, I've been exercising my innate ability to be strong-willed. I realize that I don't give a fuck what people think. For example; if I think a movie or a song is wack, I don't give a shit if you disagree. That opinion is mine; muthafucka it belongs to me. I don't care if you see me as a "hater" or a "negative" person; that's your opinion, and you are entitled to that. The same goes if I like something that you don't.

"Everyone appreciates your honesty, until you're honest with them, then you're an asshole."

—George Carlin

I have learned over the course of my life: It's ok to be me, and it's who I should be. I learned that my opinion is just as valid as anyone else's. I don't have to like what's popular. I don't have to be a part of the "cool table"; besides, why try to fit in when I'm a standout?

The great poet and writer, Nikki Giovanni, said, "Once you know who you are, you don't have to worry anymore." Truer words have never been spoken. When I began to own and stand in the shoes of being an unapologetic, confident, and proud African, my soul felt secure and protected. It was like my ancestors said, "Ogbaa, Okare." or "Yes, well done," in English. If you are not directly connected to your lineage, it's difficult to explain how complete the feeling is. It is a sense of pride that no other event or situation can fulfill and a high that I will chase for the rest of my life.

In hindsight, I know that a lot of my anger and subsequent behavior was rooted in the trauma that I experienced over the course of my life. The trauma became personal and internal. Whether consciously or subconsciously, I was making people feel the pain that I lived with daily. The saying "hurt people hurt people" is accurate, and it plagues people who do not understand or haven't taken the time to process their trauma. I was one of many examples.

I am proud of who I am and even more proud of my ability to display resilience. I am willing to die for who I am and what I have to offer the world. I will never allow anyone to make me feel ashamed or less-than ever again. I also must keep that same energy and make sure that I am not making anyone else experience the trauma that I endured.

All the pain and tragedy that I have caused and endured humbled me. Bill Duke once said, "You are no better than anybody else, but nobody is better than you." That's a powerful message that keeps me motivated and grounded at the same time. I know a bunch of fake niggas who get one-up and think they are poppin. They smile at me like Method Man in Beanie Sigel's *Feel it in the Air* video. I know those same people think they have me pegged and doubt my ambition, but I just smile and nod. I realize they are where I was, so I don't judge. I just pray that they outgrow it sooner than I did.

"You deserve to be loved without having to hide parts of yourself"

—Unknown

THERE IS NO LUCK, ONLY GOD

I'm not the most religious man in the world, but even I know there is no way that I would've made it through my life without God protecting me. Looking back, I can see there were ongoing and repetitive themes that were all part of a plan well beyond my comprehension. Each situation forced me to access internal resources including strength and reflection, which ultimately lead to resilience. Each time I successfully passed a test, it built stronger character, and then another test was placed before me.

I didn't understand the mechanics of my life in real time; therefore, I spent my earlier years in survival mode. In some cases, I behaved that way because of what I saw as my life's shortcomings, such as my mother's mental health issues and ultimately losing her. Losing my two best friends Alex and Nasir were other examples of what I saw as unfair life experiences.

The devil defeated me so many times in my life, but God always put another quarter in the game. I had to get the devil out of me and start seeing the God in me and that meant, I had to start living for other people more than I lived for myself. I know that sounds counterintuitive, but I had lived my life only being concerned about my needs and how I felt cheated by life. In reality, I cheated myself in many of those cases with poor decision after poor decision based only on emotion need. Yes, I've had many tragedies in my life and other unfortunate events, but I still had a working brain and heart albeit a broken one, but a working one.

The desire to become a better version of myself, which I had hindered for years, drove me to make some life promises. I decided that I was going to live to make my mother proud of me and live to make Alex and Nas happy that we had been friends during their brief time on this earth. I wanted to make sure that my grandparents were happy to be my ancestors. Most of all, I wanted to live to be a better example of a man for my son.

Now, I have dedicated my life to lifting others up by giving the youth I serve the support and recognition I wish I had growing up—support and recognition these amazing youth so desperately deserve. My goals are to help change the lives of the young men and women who grew up in pain whether physically, mentally, or emotionally. I no longer live my life for me. Instead, I live for my wife, my son, the youth and families I served, and the next generations of greatness.

They say too much of anything will hurt you. In my life, I learned that too much optimism is dangerous because it leaves so much space for disappointment and pain. At the same time, too much pessimism is equally dangerous because it eliminates opportunities for happiness. I am a realist. In my opinion, it's the perfect balance between optimism and pessimism. *Merriam Webster* describes a realist as "Representing a person or thing in a way that is accurate and true to life." This definition could not be a more accurate representation of my aura.

Viewing the world from a realist perspective feels innate to me and has taught me that I am prepared for any gift or challenge that I encounter. I know that there are great opportunities in this world, and milestones will be reached if I can stay focused. If an opportunity is great enough, it will be accompanied by high risk and a potentially damaging sacrifice. In the past, I've described myself as an emotional chameleon, which is a metaphor that I live by.

For so many years, I walked with a black cloud of unfortunate circumstances, ignorance, and tragedies. That black cloud followed me from elementary school throughout my early adulthood. Despite the lightning and cold rain, I had to find ways to cope and make something from nothing, as my African ancestors had done thousands of years before me. The decisions I made over the years were not always rooted in the wisdom of my ancestors, but in the ignorance of propaganda and a system made to destroy me. Unlike my earlier years, I can't see myself as a victim because I accepted ignorance because it was easier than taking responsibility. If I had more self-esteem earlier in my life, I could've gone against the grain just as easily. The path I chose was a fun ride and ultimately landed me in places where I dreamed to be, but it wasn't without consequence.

Instead of wallowing in my misfortunes and the seemingly unfair challenges I had to face, I learned to stay grounded and present. The past is informative, but it is also gone. The future is the ability to see your efforts create a better journey, but the future is impossible without today. In this life, you need all three phases, but today is always the most important. It's where reflection is processed and evaluated. It is also where the future is strategized. The time is now, and I'm ready.

REMORSE AND COMPASSION

As grew older and more reflective, I began to think more about the people I've disappointed and the people that I hurt knowingly or unknowingly, some which I discussed earlier. I think about Wale and finding a way to be more considerate of his feelings and taking some of his advice for once. I always looked as him as my little brother, which he is, but I forgot that we are only three years apart. Sometimes, I forget to see that he is a grown man now, and I need to respect that more.

I think of Shantel and how poorly I treated her. One of the greatest and most freeing moments of my life was being honest with her and both of us getting closure. I think of Carla and the way I avoided loving her to protect her and myself from being hurt. I think about how I was not honest with her and that I was too selfish to let her go in the hopes that I would snap out of my funk. Instead of protecting her, I hurt her and that's something that I carried with me from 2004 until around 2010 when I wrote her on Facebook.

I told Carla that I did not want a response from her, but I felt she deserved to know why I acted so irresponsibly. I fessed up to everything I had done, including the situations with Amanda. I told her that I knew when I met her that she deserved more and that I was not in a place to give her what she deserved. I thanked her for trying her best to love me, even though I fought against it. By the time I wrote her, she was already married and had a child, exactly what she deserved. I told her that I was happy for her and was glad that she was happy. Carla never replied, and

I'm sure it was for a thousand reasons, all of them just. However, she did read my very lengthy explanation and honest apology, and that is all I asked. I regret not answering the phone when Nas called after the blowup. I wonder if he'd be here today if I had. I regret not understanding until later that he was in crisis and that the rage he showed was not personal; I just happened to be the outlet in that moment. Even as a trained therapist, I could not separate my emotions from the situation enough to hear that there were deeper issues going on for him. I guess that's why we were taught that it is impossible to be a therapist in our personal lives; we are too attached. I miss that brother like crazy.

One of the things you might notice, even in my early years, is the absence of drug and alcohol use. I saw plenty of negative examples of intoxication from the people I associated with. Inebriations usually got them arrested or killed, which contributed to my lack of interest. I did not want to sell drugs like the people who lived in my neighborhood. I did not want to spend my life looking over my shoulder for the police and stickup kids. I definitely did not want to get shot like Femi did.

I didn't begin drinking alcohol socially until I was 30 years old. I grew up in a place where being impaired in any fashion could be a one-way ticket to the grave. I had to be on my game at all times. Besides, basketball took up most of my free time anyway. I knew that I could never make it to the NBA if I were getting drunk all the time. I never wanted to be one of "the drunk guys" that we used to laugh at while we were on the porch. Back then, I thought the drunk guys were funny, but now I have compassion for them because I know nothing about their personal life struggles or what pain they were hiding from.

To this day, I have trouble accepting affirmations and positive feedback for a few reasons. I've grown used to people being critical of me for who I am or who they think I am. I can still hear those kids in third grade calling me Kunta and saying that my family lived in huts, rode elephants, and ate people. I still hear the many years of people making fun of my name and the clothes that I wore while calling me an African booty scratcher. As strange as it sounds, I learned to take insults better than I take compliments.

I always had a problem relating to the outside world because I had a problem relating to myself. So, every compliment feels like a verse to a song, and I'm always waiting for the punchline— you know, the backhanded comment that seems to come afterward. I know it's troubling to be this cynical, but it's a security system that was built into my psyche over the years. The cynicism has decreased as my self-esteem increased over the years, but it's still a work in progress.

> "History, despite its wrenching pain, cannot be unlived, but if faced with courage, need not be lived again."
>
> —Maya Angelou

WHO I AM...

I can see why it's fair to say that I am everything that I was; however, people change. That change comes about either through life lessons, reflections, or personal growth. The universe made sure that I received all three, for which I am thankful. I could never be a husband or a father with the way I thought and behaved in past relationships. I could never be a positive example to the youth and students I have served over the years, providing wisdom for them to avoid the same kinds of mistakes I made in the past. Without my own personal growth, I could never be an effective therapist for clients who needed help dealing with trauma, tragedy, and internal struggles.

I have held many identities over the years, and some remain. I was a class clown and almost high school dropout, but I am also a college and graduate school alum. I have been a bad friend, a good friend, a bad brother, and a good brother. I've also been a bad son and a good son. I've been a bad boyfriend, but today, I am a responsible husband and father. I've been hired to and fired from jobs. I've been hopeful, hopeless, sheltered, and homeless. I've literally experienced my life go from the peak of becoming the first person in my family to graduate from college to hitting rock bottom, but in true Ige fashion I fought back to regain my destiny to succeed. All these identities and the associated experiences have shaped the man I've become.

Even in the worst moments of my life, I remained a critical thinker, and the same is true today. The difference is I've grown from impulsive to preventative and from imaginary to proactive. I learned to think further ahead about each decision that I make, whether it be as simple as a purchase or as complex as a career move. I've been through a lot, and I don't want it to have all been for nothing. I have a greater responsibility to myself, my wife, and my son. I make sure that everything I'm doing will have a positive impact on people, especially on my son.

"Will you be a wounded hurter or a wounded healer?"

—Dr. Cornell West

STATE OF THE FAMILY

Though many things have changed dramatically in my life, somethings are still a work in progress, even after nearly a decade. Wale and I still have a rocky relationship that is combative at times, but it's better than it was when I returned from ATL nine years ago. Conversations are now longer and more productive. We even hangout once in a while and laugh at childhood memories while eating Eba or Iyan (pounded yam) with chicken stew, two staple foods in Nigerian culture. We talk about the miscommunication and misunderstandings of each other's experiences through the traumatic events in our lives. It took a long time to get here and there is still a long way to go, but we are making progress.

Femi was released from jail almost two and a half years ago, and he has passed his probation. Congratulations to him. I am proud of him for that even though he and I have yet to have any meaningful dialogue. For whatever reason, he chooses not to talk to Wale and me. He faces challenges of his own, and I still love him and wish the best for him. Last I heard, he has his own apartment in Philly and a job doing well for himself. I hope to reconnect with him some day.

My father has been released from the penitentiary and has moved with me in California. He served his time in prison with good behavior. I didn't want him to be homeless when he got out. In Nigerian culture, we take care of our parents. Since my grandmother's murder, I still struggle with the identities of either being a good son to my father or a good grandson to her. It's still difficult to come to terms with it all.

On the other hand, it's imperative that my son, Prince, has a relationship with my father, especially, since he will never have the chance to have one with my mother, even though he bears a striking resemblance to her. I guess my point is, that there are still problems, but the difference in my life now versus my past is that I don't have problems, my problems have me to deal with. I took the power away from negative and unfortunate situations and accessed the strength in myself.

> *"The world breaks everyone, and afterward, some are strong at the broken places."*
>
> —Ernest Hemingway

PRESENT DAY

Today, I am a proud African man who loves his culture. I love everything from Nigerian food, dance, and clothing. I love my name. I love that I know who I am and enjoy representing where I come from. By the way, my first trip out of the country will be to see Nigeria, my homeland, in person rather than in pictures and on websites. Traveling to see my family's origin is the last infinity stone I need to complete my gauntlet of fulfilment. Yes, I just made a Thanos reference.

I'm no longer a player who avoids love and deep connection, nor am I a broken man who seeks love to feel complete. I don't need to have sex with every beautiful woman I see, even though I still live with lust. Instead, I am a husband with a beautiful wife and a handsome son. I come home every night, and I love it. I get to be me, all of me, without fear of judgment which is the greatest comfort in the world. I live in California, which was one of my childhood dreams. I still go back to Philly as often as I can because I love the city that raised me, and it's always good to remember where you came from.

My life experiences have become my superpower. It's the basis for the work I do and the wisdom I want to pass on to my son and the youth I serve. I tell them, "If I was able to change after all the things I've caused and the craziness I've faced in my life, then I have complete confidence that you can too. I know you see me as this responsible adult, but when I look at you, I see me. We are not that different, I am you, just in the future." I realize how important it is for kids to feel loved and supported, and I make sure my son gets that all day every day.

Currently, I work with middle school scholars dealing with trauma that leads to poor school performance and behavioral problems. I wasn't kidding when I told those scholars, "I am them." It's a blessing to be a positive and consistent influence on their lives during the toughest and most confusing times for them. I get to provide the very support I needed when I was their age from not only an informed, but experienced position, which is satisfying.

These days it's the little things that bring me joy, like when I saw my son take his first steps or hearing him learn new words. "Hi, Daddy!" he says enthusiastically when he wants my attention. "I love you, Daddy!" he says randomly. When I come home from work and he sees me and runs to the door smiling to give me a hug, those are the moments I live for. The same goes for all the youth that I work with. They have dealt with trauma, and I love being one of the people in their lives to let them know that someone cares and understands.

When I get to hug my wife and feel unconditional love, it makes me feel like my journey was worth it. When I look into her eyes, I can see that she wants the best for me and to be by my side. I'm glad she got to know the man that I have become instead of the man that I was. Otherwise, I would've missed out on one of the great ones as Calogero from *A Bronx Tale* famously said. You only get three, and I've already forfeited two. I've made many mistakes over the course of my life, some ill-advised and others planned, but marrying Nelly is something I definitely did right.

These times of joy cause me to reflect on my life and ponder the unknown. An example of this is happening right now. As I am writing this, I am sitting in the bathroom hearing my wife play with my son and listening to her correct him when he pushes boundaries, as three-year-olds do. I want to intervene, but I can't. The door is closed, and I can't see them. I wonder if this is what death feels like. I'm surrounded by all white tile in this room, but I can still hear what's going on in the world, and these sounds make me happy. I know that if something were to happen to me, my son will be well taken care of and he will know I love him with everything I have. Sometimes I sit quietly and recall my mother calling me, "Kuunnleee!" I can still hear her voice; sometimes it's so loud it feels like she is still here.

When I think about how far I've come, I am more appreciative of where I am today. I remember not having medical insurance, but now I'm double covered, like Julio Jones on third down. Unlike my early years, I approach everything in my life with complete integrity. I want to make sure the interactions I have with people are pleasant and impactful, even if that means having an unpopular opinion that offers a different perspective. I never was a person who says what people want to hear. The most important difference between the old me and the new me is that I know who I am, and I am proud of it. I make sure in every situation that I am representing myself and my culture to the fullest of my ability, even if it turns some people away. Authenticity is more valuable than being accepted by sacrificing who I am.

I've heard every critique and made many more personal judgments on myself than anyone could ever know. I tell myself every day that I am my best weapon and my worst enemy. It's up to me to decide what energy I bring into a situation and the impact I wish to have. I know I am flawed, but I also know that every minute of every day, I have a choice to make that will either better or worsen my life. I do my best to make sure to avoid the latter.

The information I presented in this book is accurate and evidence of my evolution. So, before you put on your robe and approach the bench, before you lift that gavel, consider all the evidence before you. When the verdict is in and you are ready to judge, just know that I'm ready; I've got my court clothes on. I am a man who lived, loved, and lost. I am a man who provoked smiles and heartbreak. I am a man who was judged and was also judgmental. Through all the phases in my life, I learned and progressed. I am finally comfortable with both my experience and who I have become. Love me or hate me, but now you know the real me: I am no longer a lost soul. This is who I am. This is my Identity.

> *"If life is a journey, we all know by heart, then life must be love. That means pride and ego are all the detours we take out of fear."*
>
> —Adekunle Ige

ACKNOWLEDGMENTS

To all the people who supported me in my life's journey:
First and foremost, I have to thank God for giving me life and resilience. Second, there is no way that I would've been able to travel the terrain of life and bounce back so many times without the love and allowance of my mother, Jewel Ige. Thank you for giving me life and inspiration. To my father, Adegbola Ige, thanks for being a hard worker and an example to follow for most of my life. To Andrea "Peach" Boardley, Aunt Janet, Aunt Tina, Uncle Morris, Uncle Wayne, and Nevaeh Ige for being the best niece I could ever ask for, and her mother, Kesha Carter. To the rest of my family, y'all know damn well there are too many of y'all, and I don't want to forget anyone; I want y'all to know that I love y'all. To my brothers Adewale Ige and Adetokunbo Ige thank you for weathering the storm and being there to challenge me when I needed it; To Henry Oyewole, Jerald Bedell (aka Face), James McGee and their family, Kunle and the Ogedengbes, and Esau Carter. To Ms. Mary Walker and Ms. Funmilayo Whitaker for considering me like a son. I want to send a big thank you to all of you!

To Brian Farmer for 20 years' worth of inside jokes on top of inside jokes and for always having my back, pause. To Stewart Enos for all the laughs, real conversations, and being like a brother to me. To Coach Bill Ellerbee for looking out for me and taking a chance. To Jerritt "Beat" Davis for being my North Carolina brother, and to Lakeeva Lawrence for being one of the best friends I ever had and for buying Toni Braxton's *The Heat* album for me. I still play it, by the way. To Tabitha Drago for being my pen pal of nearly 20 years and always being there to hear out the drama in my life.

Shout out to Janetta Kennedy for too many reasons to name. We had our moments, but you know I love you, sis. I'll always have a special place for you. Sharooooon!!! To Sharon McMillan for helping me fight my depression through inappropriate comedy and helping me get back on track in my professional career. To my beautiful wife Nelly and my handsome son Prince for being the reasons I want to be a better man every day, the reasons why my heart beats, and the reasons why my whole life's journey was worth it.

To the agencies that hired me and the agencies that fired me, I deserved both. Shantel for showing me that I had the capacity to love and for being a part of this process. Thank you, Carla, for everything you ever did for me even though I was too broken to appreciate it in real time. Shout out to Amanda, thanks for looking out for me in my time of need. Thanks to Dr. Dwayne Marshall for being a mentor and saving me from the police. Thank you to Pamela and Mya for teaching me very important lessons in my life.

To Tupac Shakur (RIP), The Notorius B.I.G. (RIP), Jay-Z, State Property, Ice Cube, Major Figgas, NaS, The Lox, Joe Budden, King Sunny Ade, Miles Davis (RIP), Sade, Anita Baker, Toni Braxton, and so many other amazing artists for making songs that got me through so many tough times in my life. To Michael Jordan for helping me hone my competitive nature and being fundamentally sound in basketball, and to Mike Tyson for knocking people the fuck out.

To my community and the schools that educated me:
To the neighborhoods that raised me, whether right or wrong; my identity could not be without the environments that helped develop it. Shout out to Nicetown, The Hollow, Germantown, all of Philadelphia, Edward T. Steel School, Gillespie Middle School, Simon Gratz High School, and all the staff and faculty that had major impacts on my life.

Big shout out to Virginia State University for being the best school I ever attended. Thank you, Lock Haven University for training me in social work and thanks to all the people I met along the way. Thanks to Marywood University for helping me take my career further.

To those who helped me put together my first book:
Special thanks to Dr. Nunnally for teaching me the structure of writing; without your foundation, none of this would be possible. To my cover artist

Antonio R. Mcilwaine @armofcasso on Instagram thank you for being dope! To Querida Lugo, I love you for a million reasons and thank you for linking me with such a great artist. To my formatter Corey Lewis, thank you for being so accommodating and easy to work with! Big shout out to Marlon Wayans for hitting me back on Twitter and suggesting creative writing and scriptwriting books to research. Thank you, Shante Spears, for interviewing me for your blog and helping me promote this book.

To those that didn't live to see this moment:
My grandparents Esther Ayodele Ige, Merion Hudson, and Lavenia Armstrong (RIP). To my mother, Jewel Ige, thank you for saving me from myself and other dangers in the world. Thank you for being my motivation and inspiration. Until the day I see you again, I still miss you, 19 years and counting (RIP). Aunt Keji for always helping me through tough times in my life and for that Jollof rice; it's still the best (RIP). Also, I'm married now so you can stop wondering if I have a girlfriend; rest easy. To Nasir "Nas" Lewis for always being there for me and being my brother forever; I miss you battle buddy (RIP). To Alex "Lex" Oyewole for being my Nigerian brother from another mother; I miss you homie (RIP). Rest in peace Gary Hall, Alonzo Guy, Omar Reddy, Lil Ruckie, Dante "Dizzack" Benson, Spittage, Michael Blackshear, Peter Coimbre, Lance "A.L." Boykin, Pork, George, Terrance, and Ashley.

> "I zone further/past other grounds that I touched/It ain't over/ because of a chick, Gary got bussed/With my grandparents passing/Pork killed, crime of passion/T. killed, bike crashing/Pete killed, car accident/Ashley from asthma/George went out blasting/ Blackshear from hammers/A.L. died rapping/I carried Lex in a box/can't forget mom's passing/with all this as motivation/picture me not lasting."
>
> —Adekunle Ige aka Jonny Storm, "If I had to…"

Finally, to those who doubted me:
Thank you.

FROM PERSONAL IDENTITY INTO COMMUNITY

And now you know my story—the good, the bad, and the ugly. In this book, you have walked with me on my relentless journey to become who I am today—someone who has discovered and believes in his real **identity**.

Perhaps, you are on a similar quest. If so, I'd love to start a conversation on the topic of **identity**. I welcome the opportunity to answer questions about my story, discuss related current topics, and connect with my readers.

To join in and share your thoughts, reach out to me on social media:
Twitter and Instagram: @IdentityTheBook

Made in the USA
Lexington, KY
28 November 2019